THORSONS

ORGANIC
CONSUMER GUIDE

THORSONS

ORGANIC

CONSUMER GUIDE

Food you can trust

EDITED BY DAVID MABEY & ALAN & JACKIE GEAR

Foreword by HRH The Prince of Wales

THORSONS PUBLISHING GROUP

First published in 1990

British Library Cataloguing in Publication Data

Mabey, David
Thorsons organic consumer guide.
1. Natural food
I. Title II. Gear, Alan III. Gear, Jackie
641.3

ISBN 0 7225 2247 9

Published by Thorsons Publishers Limited, Wellingborough, Northamptonshire NN8 2RQ, England

Printed in Great Britain by Mackays of Chatham, Kent

1 3 5 7 9 10 8 6 4 2

CONTENTS

ACKNOWLEDGEMENTS

We would like to thank the following people, who acted as contributing editors on several sections of this book. Their knowledge and help was invaluable:

Working with the Land
Richard Young, Deputy Director of British Organic Farmers

Counting the Cost
Dr Nic Lampkin, Lecturer in Agricultural Economics and Development Director of the Aberystwyth Centre for Organic Husbandry and Agroecology, University College of Wales

Repairing the Damage
Richard Mabey, writer. Served on the Nature Conservancy Council 1982–86; currently a director of the environmental group Common Ground

Reading the Signs
Francis Blake, Symbol Manager of the Soil Association

The Organic Drinker
Jerry Lockspeiser, Director of Vinceremos Wines
Roger Protz, journalist and former editor of the *Good Beer Guide* (CAMRA).
An enormous number of people contributed in other ways. We would like to thank Alison Johnson, formerly of Scarista House; Glen Broughton, Director of the wholesaling company

Bloomsgorse/Agricola; Donald Cooper of Congelow Produce; Lawrence Woodward of Elm Farm Research Centre for a good deal of background information and papers; Ann Coghill of the Free-Range Egg Association; Richard Guy of The Real Meat Company, plus the hundreds of growers, suppliers, shop owners and restaurateurs who provided information about their activities.

Alan and Jackie Gear would also like to thank everyone at HDRA for coping while the book was being written and especially to Steve Gifford who helped with the proofreading.

Finally we would like to thank Kate Allen and her colleagues at Thorsons for their enthusiasm and hard work in producing the book with such speed and efficiency.

FOREWORD

I was delighted to be invited to contribute a Foreword to this most important and thoroughly useful book, because I believe that the many advantages of the organic approach to agriculture and horticulture need to be emphasized in this practical and unemotional way.

There is nothing revolutionary, or even particularly new, about organic growing, but nor is it a retrograde, unprofitable, or unrealistic pastime for people who would be happier living in the past. On the contrary, there are real advantages in growing crops and rearing animals in ways which are healthier and less destructive of the natural environment than applying large quantities of chemicals, in a way in which almost certainly cannot be sustained, and with no knowledge of the long-term effects on ourselves or the land.

Organizations like the Henry Doubleday Research Association, of which I am proud to be Patron, are now investigating traditional and more sympathetic methods in a scientific way, and showing what can be done by those who are prepared to look beyond the convenience of the sprayer and the fertilizer sack. Increasing numbers of farmers, growers and gardeners are now adopting the organic approach and proving that it is possible to produce food of the highest quality. I hope that this book may encourage others to do so. All the evidence suggests that they will find a ready market from an increasing number of consumers who are prepared to pay a premium for food that has been produced as safely and naturally as possible, and without damaging our environment.

HDRA

The Henry Doubleday Research Association (HDRA) is an independent registered charity concerned with all aspects of organic growing, though specializing in organic gardening. It is based at the National Centre for Organic Gardening near Coventry. Part of the Centre is laid out as a series of demonstration gardens – Ryton Gardens, open to the public all year round. The remainder comprises research trials into growing methods that do not harm the environment.

The HDRA publishes a range of books and booklets and a quarterly magazine which is sent to each of its 16,000 members. HDRA staff present *All Muck & Magic?* – the television series made by HTV West for Channel 4. During the last few years the Association has expanded its work into the developing world where a programme of research into trees that withstand desert conditions is underway.

If you would like to join the HDRA or wish to receive a copy of its 100-page organic gardening catalogue, please write to HDRA, The National Centre for Organic Gardening, Ryton-on-Dunsmore, Coventry CV8 3LG.

INTRODUCTION

Anyone with an apple tree in their garden knows that the fruit from it is unlikely to resemble apples sold in the shops. Home-grown fruit are all different sizes; some will be much larger than others, some will be misshapen. Quite a few will have marks on the surface, others will be colonized by maggots. If the crop is good enough, some can be put away for the winter. But once in store, some are bound to rot.

So, how is it possible for commercial growers to produce the near-perfect product found in the shops? The answer: by waging permanent chemical warfare in the orchard. The only way to ensure freedom from pests and diseases is to keep up a constant barrage of pesticide sprays. It is not a question of waiting for a particular problem to occur and then dealing with it. Today's strategy – known as 'insurance spraying' – is to spray whether the problem is there or not. In a typical orchard, spraying machinery will be at work dosing crops with chemicals at weekly intervals from March until the end of September; and this is to combat just one fungal disease. Different chemicals are used to treat insect pests such as greenfly and caterpillars. Weeds are also looked on as an enemy. Because they grow at the base of the trees, they compete for water and nutrients. So they are killed with herbicides. The yellow-brown strips of dead and dying vegetation that are a feature of commercial orchards are eloquent testimony to this scorched earth policy. If conditions for fruit pollination have been good, lots of small apples will begin to develop. This process can be helped along by spraying with a chemical that increases the fruit set and assists young trees beginning to crop for the first time. However, if all these young apples are allowed to grow to maturity, they will be far too small for the market. 'Fortunately', there is a chemical thinner which, when sprayed on the fruit, forces some of them to drop off the tree, allowing those that remain to grow bigger. This used to be done by hand, but chemicals are quicker.

Every year, the tree produces new shoots and branches. These must be controlled, usually by a mixture of pruning and by using a chemical growth retardent. In order to speed up ripening – so that the apples can be delivered early to market – the trees get another spray with a chemical that enhances their colour. But, if by the time of picking the apples are still a bit small, there is a hormone that can be sprayed on which prevents them from naturally falling off the tree. Finally, as they are picked and taken into store they are plunged into a bath of fungicide as a precaution against rotting. All in all, in its short life from blossom to greengrocer's shelf, an apple can expect to be dosed up to forty times with any one of up to a hundred chemical products.

IS IT SAFE TO EAT?

You might say, so what? All pesticides have to be Government safety-tested before they can be used. Any that fail the long and complicated testing procedure are rejected: those that pass are safe. The pesticide industry says so, the Government agrees, and the farmers go along with it. Why worry?

In the wake of recent food scares – salmonella, listeria, additives and much more – consumers *are* worried. They are beginning to ask questions. Is our food really safe to eat? Should we be considering different farming methods? And if, as consumers, we demand changes in agriculture, what price will we have to pay?

One reason for concern is that many of the pesticides still in use today were first developed back in the 1960s, or earlier, when testing procedures were a lot less stringent. A case in point is the growth regulating chemical called daminozide. Sold under the trade name of Alar, it was, until 1989, widely used by apple growers. However, a question mark had been hanging over Alar since the beginning of the 1980s. The

American Environmental Protection Agency (EPA) first proposed to ban it in 1985, because of the risk of cancer from eating apples contaminated with it. In 1989, the exact nature of this risk was put into hard figures by the US Natural Resources Defense Council (NRDC), an independent research body. It forecast that over their lifetimes around 5,500 American children would get cancer, despite the fact that levels of Alar found in apples were well below the legally allowed limit.

This news was dismissed by UK Government experts who insisted that the use of Alar did not pose a threat to the health of British children. Not everyone was convinced. The actress Pamela Stephenson, who went on to form Parents for Safe Food, commissioned her own tests of UK apples and apple juice. Though she chose only a small sample of products, the results were alarming. Levels of Alar found in the juice and in the apples themselves were double those found in American fruit. When these figures were shown to the NRDC, they concluded that 'if a child consumed a glass of apple juice a day with Alar at the levels found by Parents for Safe Food from birth through to age five, the estimated cancer risk could be as high as 1,000 cases for every million children exposed.' On the basis of new information received, it is understood that the EPA is now considering reducing the maximum level of Alar permitted in fruit by a factor of fifty. In October 1989, Uniroyal, the manufacturers of Alar, withdrew this product from the market.

Alar may have gone, but growers still have a lot of suspect chemicals in their armoury. The crop-thinning compound called carbaryl, sold under the trade names of Thinsec, Murvin and Sevin, is another product with a less than squeaky clean record. Published scientific research papers indicate possible cancer and birth defect risks associated with its use. Other orchard chemicals, such as captan, mancozeb, lindane and zineb, all have serious question marks against their safety. Indeed at the time of writing it seems likely that a whole class of fungicides, including zineb, will be the next to be banned.

PESTICIDES – THE RISKS
More than 2,500 pesticide products are available for agricultural use in the UK. Many, like Alar, are systemic in

their action. They are absorbed into the fruit or vegetable and can't be washed off. Independent experts have suggested that up to 40 per cent of all pesticide compounds may give rise to potential health problems.

According to a World Health Organization report published in 1989, one million people a year are unintentionally poisoned by pesticides. Even this may underestimate the scale of the problem, because as many as 3 million cases may go unreported. However, it is much harder to gauge the full long-term effects of eating food contaminated with minute traces of these poisons.

Consider how long it has taken to establish a link between cigarette smoking and lung cancer. Millions of pounds worth of research over many years have still failed to come up with all the answers. But with cigarette smoking, doctors can at least ask specific questions, such as: 'How many cigarettes do you smoke each day? When did you start? Do you smoke low or high tar brands?' With pesticides it is more difficult. A doctor could hardly ask: 'When did you start eating potatoes contaminated with tecnazene?' Or: 'In 1985, did you happen to eat watermelons containing high levels of the insecticide aldicarb?' When it comes to low-dose pesticide poisoning, many of the symptoms – nausea, headaches, depression, asthma, diarrhoea – are common to other illnesses. Doctors are unlikely to pin the blame on chemical sprays.

The pesticide industry is quick to dismiss any suggestion that its products might be unsafe. Whilst the existence of residues in food is irrefutable, manufacturers nevertheless claim that these are so tiny as to be completely harmless. Consider, however, homoeopathic medicine. It relies for its effect on ingredients diluted to levels far weaker than those of any pesticide residue. The fact that a chemical may be present in minute concentrations does not automatically guarantee that it is incapable of producing adverse effects.

BEWARE OF MEAT

When Edwina Currie blew the whistle on salmonella in egg production, the general public suddenly learned the truth about the battery system, and the conditions under which most chickens live out their lives. Though the debate centred on whether or not eggs were fit to eat, the more serious problem of salmonella-infected hens sold for meat didn't really come to light. The broiler industry must have breathed a collective sigh of relief when, a few weeks later, the spotlight shifted to listeria-contaminated soft cheeses and cook-chill foods. Though the Government subsequently introduced regulations covering the testing of salmonella in laying flocks, nothing has been done about eradicating salmonella from table birds. Official policy appears to be 'keep quiet and hope nobody notices'. This, despite an estimated 60 per cent of all chicken carcasses being infected.

One reason why the Government is loath to act may be that the way poultry is reared virtually ensures that diseases like salmonella are endemic. Only a root and branch reform of the whole industry will suffice. This is too radical a solution for the mandarins at Agriculture House. Much easier instead to set up a bureau and advise the public on how to cook an egg or defrost a frozen chicken.

Today's chicken producers believe that mass production is everything. An obsession with cheap food has brought to the farmyard the principles of an economy of scale that apply in a car factory. It makes good commercial sense to keep tens of thousands of birds cooped together in one shed. Food and water can be delivered automatically and labour almost eliminated. The snag is that in such overcrowded conditions diseases spread from bird to bird almost like a plague, and stress from these conditions tends to weaken the birds' natural defence mechanisms. Often the only way that diseases can be kept under control is by feeding the entire flock a continuous diet of antibiotics throughout their lives.

The same economic principles apply to breeding as well as rearing. Nowadays, few farmers raise their own chicks. Just a handful of hatcheries produce all of the chicks for the entire industry. These pullet production lines are the first link in a chain of infection. From here, salmonella-infected birds are dispersed to farms all over the country. But the most worrying development of late is that the antibiotics are no longer working. Some of the more recent strains of disease have developed resistance. Unless new drugs can be developed, these diseases will become untreatable.

Poultry are not the only animals to suffer from overcrowded conditions leading to stress and disease. Similar methods are employed in rearing pigs. Once again, the solution is treatment with drugs. Sulphadimidine is one of the more frequently used compounds. Though farmers are supposed to discontinue treatment several days before slaughter to give time for any traces of the drug to disappear, this frequently fails to work in practice. It is estimated that up to one carcass in twenty contains sulphadimidine residues at levels greater than the official maximum. In 1989, the American authorities announced that they were considering banning sulphadimidine because of the possibility of a link with cancer of the thyroid.

The other main reason for the spread of disease is the feeding of contaminated rations. In the drive to maximize output, either by increasing the number of eggs laid by a hen, or by speeding up the process from birth to slaughter, farmers have come to rely on concentrated feedstuffs which are rich in cheap protein. It wasn't long before someone came up with the idea of putting animal offal, a waste product, into animal feed. When salmonella-infected dead hens are processed by methods which don't entirely get rid of the bacteria, and are then fed back to chickens, the result is infection. That is the root cause of today's problems.

Similarly, cattle that have eaten the brains and spinal cords of sheep infected with the brain disease 'scrapie', start to develop bovine spongiform encephalopathy (BSE), or 'mad cow disease'. BSE didn't exist before 1985. Now there are on average 600 new cases a month and more than 8,000 cows have already been destroyed. Though the feeding of offal has since been banned by the Ministry of Agriculture, it is likely that many animals will still suffer and die from this disease. Surely there is something intrinsically wrong in feeding meat waste to creatures that are exclusively vegetarian?

But the problem of disease doesn't end with cattle. Over the past couple of years, a kidney disease of lambs first reported in 1974 has become increasingly widespread. Nephrosis, or drunken lamb syndrome, causes young lambs to stagger and become unable to suckle. Eventually they collapse and die. The cause of the disease is unknown and, as yet, there is no cure.

In 1989, 1,500 farms were quarantined by the Ministry of Agriculture. All had given cattle food contaminated with lead to their livestock. The compound in question had come from a Dutch supplier and farms affected ranged from Liverpool in the north to Exeter in the south-west. Almost every month, it seems, there are new incidents. They show how vulnerable the food chain is to dangerous practices, and are bound to ignite public concern about food production. The malaise affecting modern agriculture may cast a shadow over the food we eat, but intensive farming methods also put the entire countryside at risk.

BRITISH AGRICULTURE – A SUCCESS STORY?

British farming has been transformed in the four decades since the end of the Second World War. Agricultural development suddenly accelerated. The desire to produce more of our own food, born of necessity during wartime, became the number one objective after the war. Government money was poured into agriculture with the single aim of maximizing production. According to the wisdom of the day, this meant one thing: specialization.

Wheat, barley and other cereals grow best in the drier eastern half of the country. So this was where grain was to be produced. The wetter west, where grass flourishes, was to be the base for the dairy industry. Livestock, such as pigs and poultry, once a free-ranging element in many farms, were destined to be reared *en masse* in purpose-built sheds. All manner of financial carrots were dangled in front of farmers, including grants for new buildings, hedgerow removal, land drainage and generous subsidies on fertilizers.

This policy was spectacularly successful. The all-purpose farm, producing cereals, meat, a few eggs, vegetables and dairy products, has all but disappeared. Huge prairie fields devoid of trees and hedgerows dominate the Midlands and eastern counties. Vast tracts of the sheep walks on the Downs have been ploughed up. Most of our wetlands have been drained to grow crops. Most of our pork, poultry and eggs come from factory farms. Use of nitrogen fertilizer rose from a mere 60,000 tonnes a year before the Second World War to more than 1.5 million tonnes today – a twenty-fold increase. Farmers propped up by a European Community (EC) payment support system are guaranteed a market however much they produce. Is it any wonder that Europe is awash with food surpluses? There can be no doubt that the objective has been achieved, but at what cost?

DANGER: SPRAYS AT WORK

Wildlife are in the front-line of the chemical war waged down on the farm. If there is uncertainty as to the safety of pesticides on human health, there can be no such doubts about the effects of pesticides on creatures and plants inhabiting Britain's farmland. They kill them. Unfortunately it is not only the pests that are killed. Bees collecting nectar from flowers are frequently poisoned by mistake. Insecticides intended for pests such as aphids (greenfly) are equally effective in killing ladybirds and other beneficial insects that prey on them. Slugs poisoned by pellets may be eaten by birds and hedgehogs, building up doses sufficient to kill them.

Insecticides kill insects whether they are pests feeding on farm crops or creatures living harmlessly in a nearby pond. If dead insects are eaten by fish the poison accumulates in their body tissue until it reaches a critical level. When these fish are eaten by larger fish or fish-eating birds, the pesticide is transferred to them. In 1986, this chain of events brought about the deaths of herons feeding on eels living in the River Avon in Warwickshire. More recently, alarm over the contamination of eels in Cornish estuaries and the consequent risk to human health, finally brought about the banning of the pesticide Aldrin. The Government took this action in May 1989, twenty-seven years after the biologist Rachel Carson had warned about this phenomenon in her book *Silent Spring*.

Though part of the pesticide screening process for new products requires that they be tested in the laboratory for their effects on wildlife, it is only when they are used outdoors that their true effects can be seen. The results are often unexpected. For example, fungicides sprayed against diseases affecting wheat and other cereals also kill harmless fungi living in the soil. These fungi represent an important part of the diet of predatory insects that eat cereal insect pests. Consequently, predator numbers decline, pest numbers soar and farmers are forced to use yet more pesticides.

FARMING POLLUTES

Pollution of water by nitrates is a major problem. More that 1.5 million people are currently drinking water contaminated with nitrates at levels that exceed the EC maximum permitted dose. Though nitrates get into water from a variety of sources

– ploughing up grassland, sewage, animal slurry from factory farms – most is thought to come from the use of artificial fertilizers. When a farmer spreads synthetic fertilizer onto the land, only part of it is used by the crop. Most of the remainder washes into the soil, ending up in deep underground water supplies. The Government is trying to solve the problem by setting up water protection zones in areas of greatest risk. Here, farmers must greatly reduce the amount of fertilizer they apply. When you consider that it may take up to forty years for nitrate, percolating slowly down through the soil and rock, to reach the water table, the high nitrate levels we are witnessing today may well be due to ploughing up and the use of fertilizers during the Second World War. We have yet to see the effect from the massive increase in the use of nitrogen fertilizers over the past few years.

Nobody knows what effect nitrates might have on human health. At high concentrations, they can produce met-haemoglobinaemia or 'blue baby syndrome' in newborn infants, although this is unlikely to occur until nitrate levels reach double the EC maximum. A number of water authorities have already made plans to cover this possibility. Bottling plants have been set up to distribute bottled water to nursing mothers. There is also a suggestion that high nitrates may lead to an increase in cases of stomach cancer. Although there is little evidence of this happening at present, the possibility cannot be ruled out, particularly if nitrate levels continue to rise.

Rivers and lakes also suffer from excess nitrate. Fertilizers promote plant growth in water just as effectively as they do on land. A thick scum of microscopic plants (algae) spreads over the surface, stopping light from reaching plants below and releasing toxic poisons into the water. As other plants die and decay, they use up the water's oxygen supply. In the resulting oxygen-starved water, fish and other aquatic creatures drown.

During 1989, a number of English reservoirs were stricken by a blue-green algal tide. Dog owners exercising their animals along the shores were warned to keep away, but nevertheless a number of pets died. The growth was blamed on the hot summer, but it is unlikely to have happened if nitrate levels hadn't been so high. These 'algal blooms' are increasingly common in coastal waters. Huge slicks, often many miles long, have been reported off Scandinavia and in the Adriatic. Quite apart from the damage done to marine life, the local tourist economies have been wrecked. Who wants to go for a dip in a sea covered with green slime?

Not all the blame can be laid at the door of agriculture. Synthetic fertilizers make a contribution to algal growth, but so do household detergents containing phosphate, that go down the drain, into the sewage works and from there, often untreated, into rivers or out to sea. Cleaning up our act in the kitchen and better control of sewage pollution must go hand in hand with agricultural reform if our waterways are to have any chance of survival.

A CRISIS OF CONFIDENCE?

If people were ill every time they ate an apple or a cooked chicken portion, there would be an outcry. The demand for change would be irresistible. But this isn't the case. How many of us believe that the attractively displayed and packaged food in the shops could possibly do us any harm? Short-term dangers can be dealt with, but what about the situation in ten or even twenty years' time? Food poisoning from salmonella and other bacterial organisms apart, the main worry is the possible long-term threat posed to health by minute traces of pesticides and other substances that may be present in our food.

Could the alarming increase in the number of people suffering from food allergies be anything to do with these contaminants? We already know that food additives can produce violent responses in sensitive individuals. Everyday substances such as bread, meat and milk are poisonous to a growing number of sufferers. Is it the food, or what is *in* the food, that's to blame? What can we do about it?

FOOD YOU CAN TRUST

Those of us who are not prepared to accept the statements and reassurances from industry and Government do have an alternative. We can choose to buy organic food produced without recourse to artificial pesticides, drugs, or potentially harmful substances. More and more consumers are demanding organic food although it is still relatively scarce in the shops. Some purchase on health grounds: if there is a question mark over the safety of food, why take the risk? Others do so because they believe that organic food tastes better. Yet others buy organic food because they see it as a way of supporting a farming system that is in tune with the environment: anti-social practices such as straw burning are forbidden under organic regulations; nitrate pollution of ground water is greatly reduced; the elimination of pesticides benefits wildlife, and the organic farming system helps to create and preserve habitats. Intensive rearing is forbidden and livestock are allowed to range freely.

Of course there are still enormous hurdles to overcome. Conventional farmers wishing to get off the 'chemical treadmill' are given no financial incentives to take them through the transition stage. Land needs at least two years without artificial chemicals before food grown on it can be sold as 'organic'. Crop yields drop while the soil is re-vitalized. And, so long as there is a scarcity prices will remain high. Only when there is a great deal more organic food produced will prices begin to come down.

There is also the need to improve labelling and standards. Far too often, organic food is sold without any verification whatsoever. The situation is ripe for exploitation as consumers clamour for 'additive-free' and 'natural' produce.

The lesson of ozone-friendly aerosols and phosphate-free detergents is that consumers have the power to change the way goods are produced. Food is no different. Industrial farming with its exploitative attitude to land and livestock has replaced traditional husbandry. There has been no public discussion over the rights and wrongs of this approach. It just happened. Now we are about to enter the brave new world of genetic engineering. The controversy over the growth-promoting hormone BST is just the beginning. We are told that this is progress. We are told that there is no alternative. Why not?

More and more people are now concerned about the prospects for agriculture. Output is high at the moment, but how long can it last? The price that all of us pay is polluted water, degraded soil, abused farm animals, a despoiled countryside and risks to health. That is too high a price. Just how bad does our drinking water have to get, how high must pesticide levels in our food become, before we call a halt? We are heading up a blind alley. Organic food and farming is one way – perhaps the only way – of producing safe food by methods that are in harmony with the planet. It is up to each of us to make sure that the future is organic.

ALAN GEAR
December 1989

PART ONE

Chapter 1

LEARNING THE LANGUAGE

WHAT IS ORGANIC?

Put simply, organic food is produced without recourse to pesticides or artificial fertilizers. This applies to farms, small-holdings, orchards and gardens alike. The term 'pesticide' encompasses a whole range of substances that literally kill pests: it includes fungicides, herbicides (weedkillers) and many other 'icides'. These substances are usually administered by spraying; they are aimed at the soil, at the crop while it is growing and are even applied while it is being stored before going to market. The organic way is different. It is a mixture of good science, good sense, ingenuity and an awareness of the inherent usefulness of many kinds of creature as biological pest controllers.

Artificial fertilizers, usually based on nitrogen, phosphorus and potassium, are poured onto the land by the tonne. Their effects are now recognized as long-term and potentially damaging to the environment. Organic growers reject them in favour of animal manure, seaweed and other substances. Organic farmers do use pesticides, but these are usually plant-based natural products such as pyrethrum or derris, which do not have long-term effects; they are used reluctantly, less often and in smaller quantities than conventional synthetic pesticides.

Organic farming challenges the apparent wisdom of conventional agriculture: crops are grown by rotation to maintain the fertility of the soil; all kinds of wildlife are encouraged, not treated as enemies; traditional varieties of fruit, vegetables and herbs, and rare breeds of livestock, are recognized for their true worth; and there is new technology and new science as well.

Above all, organic farming doesn't threaten the environment, and organic food doesn't threaten your well-being.

FREE-RANGE

Most people associate the term 'free-range' with eggs. It is a word that suggests the idea that creatures have been reared in the open, fed a natural diet, and allowed to live their days without stress. But is free-range the same as organic? Not quite. It is true that organically reared chickens, pigs and so on will 'range freely' in open territory for at least some of their time, and they will be kept in humane conditions; but the main difference lies in the pasture they live on and the food they eat. To be 'organic' an animal has to be fed a diet that is at least 80 per cent composed of organically produced ingredients. Needless to say, it must also be free of all drugs, medications and additives.

However, even 'free-range' can be less than it seems. It is clear that quite a number of the large, so-called free-range farms rearing chickens, guinea fowl and quail, are uncomfortably close to battery systems. The creatures may be let out for their obligatory time in the open – rather like prisoners in the exercise yard – but they are soon returned to conditions that are cramped and certainly not humane.

VEGETARIAN

There is a widespread belief among consumers that organic food is vegetarian. Something about unrefined quality and the notion of food produced in harmony with nature suggests that meat is taboo. In fact the reverse is true. Organic farming depends largely on the relationship between crops and livestock. In other words, organic farmers keep animals (see p.29). There will always be people who object to meat-eating – either for religious or moral reasons or simply because they do not like it. Much of this has to do with the deplorable system of intensive factory-farming that confines animals to cages and pens, force-feeds them a diet spiked with growth promoters and antibiotics, and demands that they develop at an unnaturally fast rate. Is it any wonder that there has been a mushrooming of vegetarian and wholefood shops, restaurants and cookery books since the late 1970s?

Organically produced meat is different. Animals reared with care and respect for their well-being result in better quality, more flavoursome food. Anyone buying genuine organic meat knows that it will contain no pesticide or drug residues and no additives. The escalating trend towards vegetarianism may well slow down once organic meat is better distributed and more widely available. Consumers will realize that there is a humane way of rearing livestock for food.

Having said that, much organic produce is firmly rooted in the wholefood tradition; the emphasis on fresh fruit and vegetables, cereals, grains and pulses is all in line with wholefood thinking and attitudes.

CATCHPHRASES AND LABELLING

Organic produce and ingredients can be labelled organic provided they conform to certain agreed standards (see p.64). The problem becomes more difficult with processed foods which contain organic ingredients. Bread is a case in point. It is quite common, nowadays, to see loaves labelled 'organic' when in fact they have simply been made with organic flour. True organic bread has to be made from entirely organic ingredients, from the flour to the oil. The same applies to other processed foods, from tomato ketchup to baked beans.

This may not be deliberate deceit on the part of the manufacturer, but other ploys are more contrived. In the wake of concern about 'E numbers', the food industry quickly learned that it could sell its products if they were marked 'additive-free'. But it was more subtle than that. The claim 'free of all artificial preservatives' may well be true, but it can be used as a convenient smokescreen to cover up the fact that the product is still loaded with colourings, stabilizers and anti-oxidants. The same is true of organic produce. You may see the claim, 'grown without sprays or insecticides', when in fact other 'icides' such as fungicides have been used.

'Additive-free' is another widely used slogan. Organic food should be additive-free, but not all additive-free produce is organic. The food industry, helped by its advertising and PR agencies and marketing departments, can conjure up all manner of persuasive catchphrases from 'farm fresh' to 'naturally traditional' in order to attract the consumer. Bucolic scenes of rustic farmyards appear on egg boxes and all kinds of packaging. But remember that behind those imaginary trees there is probably an intensive livestock unit or a shed crammed with thousands of scraggy, disease-ridden hens. Do not be fooled by the propaganda. Be on your guard.

Chapter 2

WORKING WITH THE LAND

ORGANIC FARMING IN PRACTICE

The key to organic farming lies in achieving a balance between crops and livestock. This may come as a surprise to those who associate organic food with vegetarianism. It may also be something of a disappointment to animal rights activists who object to the exploitation of farm animals and mistakenly see organic farming as an alternative. In certain parts of the country, notably the hills of Wales or the Scottish lowlands, some organic farmers keep only animals, whereas in the drier eastern half of the country one or two farmers are trying to develop so-called 'stockless systems'. However, the real potential for organic expansion is with a return to patterns of agriculture associated with mixed farming, i.e. both crops and livestock.

Successive generations have reinforced and refined the art and craft of farming. But in the last forty years, agriculture has lost touch with its roots. The immense power of chemicals has seduced us into believing that we can lord it over nature. Fundamental rules, such as not growing crops year after year on the same soil, are abandoned now that diseases and weeds can be blitzed with pesticides. A daily diet of 'in-feed' medication allows animals to be crammed together in sheds under conditions that invite diseases. Animal manure, once appreciated as a valuable fertilizer, is now considered only as a waste product. Instead of fertilizing the land, it is a pollutant to be disposed of – all too frequently into rivers, with disastrous consequences. The accumulated wisdom of countless farmers the world over has been jettisoned almost overnight.

Organic farming takes its cue from traditional agriculture. It makes use of the best ideas from the past and grafts onto them a scientific approach coupled with modern techniques that were unheard of in our grandfathers' day. Organic farmers are aware that – like their conventional counterparts – they have to feed their crops as well as control weeds, pests and diseases. What is different is that organic farmers choose to do all this in ways that are in sympathy with, not hostile to, the environment.

Another difference is that of 'sustainability', i.e. the ability of the land to produce food indefinitely. Modern farming methods exploit natural resources, particularly energy. Up to a tonne of oil may be needed to produce a tonne of nitrogen fertilizer. Overall, most conventional farming systems consume far more in the way of fossil fuel energy than they produce as energy contained in the crop. You could say that we are all eating oil. The fact that this squandering of a scarce resource is justified by present-day economics is yet another sign of our cavalier attitude towards future generations. Sixty years from now, our grandchildren will curse us when dwindling supplies make oil more expensive than gold. Organic farming, on the other hand, uses on average up to 60 per cent less energy from fossil fuels.

But it is not only energy that is wasted by chemical farming methods. Soil, the farmer's most precious resource of all, is disappearing at a steadily accelerating rate. Deprived of the organic matter that binds particles together, crushed by heavy machinery and exposed to the elements in vast open fields, Britain's soils are washing and blowing away. It is estimated that up to 44 per cent of the arable soils in England and Wales are currently at risk. Losses of topsoil from individual fields amounting to more than 100 tonnes per hectare are no longer uncommon.

Steadily worsening crop yields from degraded soil may be masked in the short term by even higher applications of fertilizer. But even this has its problems. Potassium and phosphorus (in the form of phosphate), both major plant nutrients, come from mined deposits; evidence suggests that these reserves may last only a hundred years or so at most. As for nitrogen, the disastrous effects of increasing the use of this nutrient are starting to show up in our contaminated water supplies. Farmers should be putting on less nitrogen, not more.

As more farmers change over to organic techniques, the landscape will change too. More land will be under grass. Livestock will return to graze in the fields. Hedges will be needed to keep in stock and trees planted for them to shelter under. Hedgerows will be cut less often with flail trimmers, because organic farmers realize their value as refuges and food sources for birds and other wildlife which in turn act as unpaid pest controllers. There will be a reduction in crop spraying, less risk of pollution from farm slurry, and fewer noxious smells from intensive livestock units. These are just a few of the immediate, visible benefits that will come about as chemical farming methods are gradually abandoned.

A TYPICAL ORGANIC FARM

What is an organic farm? How does it work? Without chemicals how can crops grow and pests be kept in check? There is no such thing as a 'typical' organic farm, because each one varies according to the crops grown and animals kept; and they are influenced by the type of soil, the amount of rainfall and geography. However, there are several obvious features that they share in common. Most have one or more livestock enterprises – a dairy herd, a flock of sheep, perhaps some free-range pigs and hens or, instead, a herd of beef cattle. Between half and three-quarters of the farm is likely to be grassland. Some fields remain in grass permanently, others stay in grass for only a few years at a time before being ploughed up. Most of the rest of the farm is used for growing crops such as cereals and vegetables for sale, or root and fodder crops for feeding livestock. The farm might have a few acres cultivated as a specialist market garden or orchard, but other areas are left uncultivated as a habitat for wildlife.

This system has many advantages. It uses resources efficiently because by-products from both crops and livestock are recycled. On conventional farms, for instance, straw left over after grain has been harvested has no use, so it is burned. On organic farms, straw is used in a variety of ways: it can be fed to animals or used as bedding; it can also be used for roofing – thatchers claim that straw from organic farms is easier to work and lasts twice as long as the same stuff grown conventionally. Finally, when straw is combined with manure and composted, it can be spread onto the land to return fertility to the farm. Any suitable vegetable waste is fed to livestock or recycled through the compost heap. Nothing is burned, wasted or thrown away.

All nutrients on the farm are recycled through farmyard manure. This is produced by livestock that are kept in covered yards over winter, and consists of a mixture of animal dung and urine plus a bedding material, usually straw. The use of large quantities of straw not only makes life more comfortable for the animals, but also cuts down the smell. Each day, fresh straw is strewn on top of the ever-thickening pile which, by the end of winter, can be several feet deep. In the spring, once the animals have been turned out into the fields, the manure is shovelled from the yards and composted. After the hay or silage has been made it is usually spread back onto the grassland, though farmers may use some of it direct on the crops if they are growing vegetables.

FERTILITY WITHOUT FERTILIZERS

In general an organic field spends two to four years as grass being grazed by livestock. It is then ploughed up and crops are grown for two or three years. After that, the land is returned to grass and the cycle repeats itself.

Clover is the key to the success of this system. All plants require nitrogen for growth, and plants growing organically are no exception. The difference is that conventional farmers look to artificial fertilizers to provide the nitrogen needs of their crops, while organic farmers turn to clover. A typical temporary field, or 'ley' of grass will contain a mixture of grasses, clovers and herbs. Clover, along with other species of legumes, is special in that it 'fixes' nitrogen. The plant rootlets secrete nutrients which nourish specialist bacteria that live in the nodules attached to the roots. In return, these bacteria are able to convert atmospheric nitrogen, absorbed through soil pores, into nitrate. The plant uses this nitrate to grow. In other words, the farmer has a source of 'free' nitrogen. Paradoxically, if nitrogen fertilizer is used on clover or other legumes, the bacteria stop working.

Every time clover is cut or grazed by animals, some of the nitrogen, now surplus to requirements, is released into the soil where it can be used by the grass. The result is good crops for grazing by cattle and sheep, as well as hay or silage for the winter.

When grass/clover mixtures have been growing for about three years, a considerable amount of fertility has built up in the soil. There is enough goodness to allow the farmer to plough up the field and grow cereals or root crops. Once this reserve of fertility has been exploited, it is time to return the land to grass.

WEED CONTROL WITHOUT WEEDKILLERS

Conventional farmers spend more money on weedkillers than any other pesticides. Yet, at a pest control conference in 1989, scientists were told that four of the major weed pests of cereals were out of control. Weedkillers were no longer having an effect on sterile broom and black grass, for example, as they had developed resistance to the chemicals. Farmers have only themselves to blame for this state of affairs. The problem is easily solved if they rotate their crops: wild oats, for instance, cannot survive in a field of grass. So, returning land to pasture every few years is far more effective than any herbicide in eliminating cereal weeds.

In addition to crop rotation, organic farmers have other methods of controlling weeds. Perennials, such as thistles and docks that grow in pasture, can be killed by repeated ploughing and harrowing during a fallow summer period. Each time the roots are brought to the surface, the sun dries and kills them. In between times they can be kept in check by topping with a mechanical mower.

Annual weeds of cereal crops are tackled by what is known as a 'weed strike'. The seedbed is prepared ten days to a fortnight before planting. This encourages the weeds to germinate. Then, when the crop is planted, the young seedlings are killed by off by the mechanical action of drilling and harrowing. Though some weeds may survive, and more may germinate, a well-sown crop of cereals will usually be able to suppress any that remain. Organic farmers tend to choose cereal varieties with long straw and sow them at seed rates slightly higher than normal. The greater height and denseness helps to crowd out any competition.

Horticulturists use somewhat different techniques. Weeds might be kept down mechanically with tractors or hand-powered cultivations. Alternatively, flame weeders attached to the back of tractors can be used to kill weed seedlings without harming the crop. Mulching materials such as straw or hay, or sheets of black polythene, can also be spread over the soil surface to prevent weeds from competing with crops.

CONTROLLING PESTS AND DISEASES

Crop rotations are not only useful in controlling weeds, they are also the organic farmer's most effective weapon against diseases, particularly those that live in the soil. Most diseases are specific to certain groups of plants. A root rot that might devastate peas and beans won't attack cabbages, and vice versa. Moving crops from field to field around the farm prevents reservoirs of disease from building up. The same is true for many animal parasites which are kept under control by moving livestock to different pastures. For example, worms that affect sheep are different from those that affect cattle.

Because organic farmers have few ways of *curing* diseases, the emphasis is on prevention. Crops are planted out into well-prepared ground at the right time of year so that they are able to grow strongly. Where possible, disease-resistant varieties are chosen. With animals, natural suckling, lower stocking rates and the elimination of stress play a major part in keeping diseases at bay.

Control of pests is left largely to their natural enemies such as insect-eating birds and predatory insects. Ladybirds, lacewing flies and hoverflies are but a few of the many beneficial insects that feed on greenflies and other pests. Vast armies of largely unseen parasitic wasps also exert their toll on pests. Larger animals such as frogs, toads, and hedgehogs all have their part to play in maintaining a balance between pest and predator. Since these are wild creatures, their presence on the farm cannot be guaranteed. However they can be encouraged if they are provided with suitable habitats, such as hedgerows, woodland, damp areas, unimproved meadows and ponds.

In recent years, scientists have increasingly turned their attention to breeding natural enemies for release into crops. This method of 'biological control' has already scored a few notable successes. For instance, a tiny parasitic wasp and a predatory mite are now routinely used for control of tomato and cucumber pests in commercial glasshouse production.

Researchers are trying to see if a predatory beetle might successfully control slugs. The possibilities are endless.

Health, rather than disease, is the natural birthright of plants and animals, despite what we have been led to believe from the propaganda put out by the pesticide companies. Growers who reject chemicals are not doomed. But this doesn't mean that organic farms are without pests and diseases. They *are* present, but usually at levels which do not adversely affect the crop.

Problems can arise when a farmer is in the early stages of converting from conventional to organic methods. Debilitated soil, no longer propped up by chemicals, is incapable of properly nourishing plants. And sickly plants – like humans – are more prone to pests and diseases. Because pesticide sprays kill friend and foe alike, there are not sufficient beneficial insects to protect the crops effectively. Fresh habitats need to become established.

Having said this, it is impossible to guarantee the kind of cosmetic 'perfection' enshrined in EC regulations and demanded by supermarkets, without resorting to massive use of chemicals. As much as half of all organic fruit and vegetables produced never leaves the field or orchard because it fails to pass the colour, size or blemish test. Are we really so obsessed by appearance that we are prepared to condone waste on such a scale?

Chapter 3

COUNTING THE COST

THE ECONOMICS OF ORGANIC FARMING

Critics of organic farming are fond of doomsday scenarios. Without conventional agriculture, they claim, there would be mass starvation and economic ruin. Some pessimistic forecasters have predicted crop yields of less than one-tenth of those achieved conventionally. There may be public sympathy for organic farming, but there is also a widespread view that it would be dangerous to rely on such methods for the nation's food supply. Many people still have painful memories of shortages and rationing during the Second World War. Nobody wants those days to return.

The other Achilles heel of the organic movement is cost. Organic food inevitably costs more. Prices can be anything from 10 per cent to 100 per cent above those of their non-organic counterparts. But why is organic food more expensive? Does it cost more to produce or are shops charging more because it is in short supply? Are prices ever likely to come down? And if prices fall, will it be profitable for farmers to produce food organically? Should farmers receive some benefit from higher prices to compensate for rejecting environmentally damaging practices? After all, it is the promise of higher prices – and profits – which lures many of them into abandoning chemicals.

In September 1989, Professor Wilson of the Edinburgh School of Agriculture, speaking at the opening of The Safeway Organic Farming Centre in Scotland said: 'Is organic farming an entirely new concept? For those with long farming memories the answer must be a definite "no". The use of the so-called "artificial inputs" into farming is relatively new, but before they were available farmers maintained, and sometimes increased, their soil fertility by such means as crop rotations, the return of crop and animal residues and by the use of "organic control measures" such as the use of naturally occurring substances such as pyrethrum and derris dusts. It is modern-day "inorganic farming" which is relatively new – organic farming was alive and kicking in medieval times and, in other parts of the world, long before that.'

Many people in conventional agriculture believe that organic farming is simply a return to the past. They conjure up images of 'fields full of folk', rooting out weeds by hand, tending livestock and working horse-driven ploughs. Medieval technology may have been safer for the environment, but it was unable to feed the people. Nowadays we live in an era of food surpluses and food mountains. But how, except by the use of the very latest agrochemical techniques, will we be able to grow sufficient food for a rapidly expanding world population, set to double by the year 2025? Can organic farming offer any hope of rising to this challenge?

DISASTROUS CROPS – A MYTH?

There are no more than 1,000 organic farms in the UK out of a total of 244,000. Even in Europe, where there is more official support for organic farming, there are less than 10,000 organic farms, mostly concentrated in France and West Germany. Because the organic sector is such a small part of farming as a whole, statistics are thin on the ground. Most research has looked at the yields of cereals – wheat, oats and barley. As a general rule, it seems that organic farmers can produce cereal harvests that are 10 to 20 per cent lower than their conventional counterparts. It is the same story for field vegetables such as potatoes. Fruit and salad vegetables have not been monitored, but it would be reasonable to assume a similar 10 to 20 per cent reduction in cropping. However, it's worth remembering that the intensive market gardens set up around Paris at the end of the last century, and fertilized entirely by horse manure, easily outperformed anything before or since.

Even if organic yields are somewhat lower, they are hardly likely to give rise to fears of mass famine. By coincidence, 20 per cent is roughly the amount of excess production of crops like cereals that currently gives rise to costly EC food mountains.

CONVENTIONAL VERSUS ORGANIC

Comparisons often show that around one quarter of the organic farms are able to achieve results that are as good as, or better than, their conventional counterparts. This point was brought out recently in a five-year study conducted by the prestigious National Academy of Sciences in the US. It looked at fourteen 'alternative' farms, including one in Ohio which had used no chemicals for fifteen years, yet achieved corn yields 32 per cent higher and soya bean yields 40 per cent higher than the local average. The report concluded that a reduction in the use of chemical inputs 'lessens agriculture's potential for adverse environmental and health effects without necessarily decreasing – and in some cases increasing – per acre crop yields and the productivity of livestock management systems.' So, why can't *all* organic farms achieve similar results?

There is no simple answer, but certainly soil is all-important. Organic farms sited on good soil are more likely to do well. Many organic vegetable holdings, for example, were set up in the 1970s in west Wales, where the weather and soil is more suited to rearing sheep and cattle. It would be very surprising if their crop yields could compete with those cultivated on the rich fen soils of eastern England.

Soils improve under organic cultivation and, as fertility rises, so do crop yields. It is a very different story with conventionally grown crops: soil fertility declines through continual cropping; no goodness is put back into the soil; and plants become more and more dependent on what they are fed from the fertilizer bag. Added to this, there is the serious problem of soil erosion (see Chapter 4).

Weeds are controlled conventionally by herbicides (weedkillers), but organic horticulture involves planting crops at wider spacings, so that machinery can be used to get in between the plants and physically remove weeds. Less dense plantings are bound to result in lower yields.

Conventional farmers put fertilizers onto grass as well as onto their crops. This enables them to increase their numbers of livestock. On average they can rear 25 per cent more beasts than their organic neighbours. Since output of meat or dairy produce is usually recorded as the amount coming from a hectare of farmland (a hectare is 2.5 acres – roughly the same as a full-size football pitch), it isn't surprising that organic livestock farms cannot compete with their conventional equivalents. Also, the concentrated feeds of imported fishmeal and soya which do most to boost milk and meat yields are generally shunned by organic producers, who tend to rely on grass supplemented by home-grown cereals. All of this affects outputs and yields.

The great increase in crop yields since the Second World War isn't simply due to chemicals. The efforts of plant breeders have resulted in even higher yielding varieties. Once a new variety has been developed, it is tested in the field using conventional growing methods, i.e. it is given a diet of artificial fertilizers and sprays. The winning variety will be the one that does best. The chances are that it will be a variety that is good at taking up water. Nutritional comparisons between food produced organically and that produced with artificial fertilizers usually reveals that the conventional crop has a higher water content – another reason why crop yields are higher. In other words, consumers are getting more water for their money.

This is all very well for farmers who use synthetic sprays but it discriminates against organic growers. Scientists should be looking for varieties that are suited to organic systems. However, with plant breeding concentrated almost entirely in the hands of the fertilizer and pesticide manufacturers this is not going to happen. Research should be the Government's responsibility, but UK plant variety breeding is being axed; the Plant Breeding Institute and The National Seeds Development Organisation were sold off to Unilever in 1988, The National Fruit Trials closed down in March 1990.

IS ORGANIC FARMING PROFITABLE?

Organic food costs more in the shops, but does the extra money find its way back to the farmer? Does the extra price (or premium) that the farmer might get compensate for lower yields? There will not be an expansion in the number of farms producing organic food unless farmers feel that it is worth

while to do so. No one is going to change over to a system
that might bankrupt them. So what are the real economics of
organic farming?

Conventional farmers believe that fertilizers and other
agrochemicals are justified so long as the returns from their use
exceed their costs. Organic farmers consider that lower costs of
production (i.e. savings on fertilizers, sprays, etc.) ought to
compensate for lower yields, even without the benefit of
premium prices.

Some definitions

Variable costs are those which apply to the growing of a
particular crop, and relate to the area of the crop: e.g. the
cost of seeds, fertilizers or sprays, casual labour etc. These
have to be set against the price the farmer gets for the crop.
The difference is an amount known as the **gross margin**.
Apart from his or her variable costs, the farmer also incurs
fixed costs. These are costs that are not directly related to
the size of the crop or livestock enterprise, e.g. machinery
servicing and fuel, depreciation, farm rent or mortgage plus
wages for the permanent workforce, including the farmer. It
is only when these are subtracted from the overall gross
margin that the ultimate profit – or loss – of the farm is
known.

A FARM IN PRACTICE

Barry Wookey farms 660 hectares in Wiltshire. He began
converting his farm in 1970, and by 1985 the entire farm had
been turned over to organic methods. In 1983/4, ADAS, the
Government's Agricultural Advisory Service, compared six
wheat crops on the organic farm with six conventional crops.
The results are shown in Table 3.1.

Seed costs are greater for the organic crop because one of
the ways of reducing weed competition in cereals is by sowing
more densely. The organic field doesn't receive any fertilizers
or sprays but the cost of cultivations is higher as more
preparation goes into creating a weed-free seedbed. The effect
of not using agrochemicals shows up in drastically reduced
variable costs – less than half of those used on the chemical
crop. 1983/4 was a bad year for cereals and yields were lower
than usual. The organic crop suffered worst of all and as a

Variable costs (£)	Conventional		Organic
Seeds	41		49
Fertilizer	118		-
Sprays	96		-
Cultivations	65		76
Harvesting	58		58
Total Variable Cost	378		183
Yields (tonnes per hectare)	7.4		4.4
		with premium	without premium
Price (£ per tonne)	110	160	110
Income (£ per hectare)	801	704	506
Gross margin (£ per hectare)	423	521	323

(*Note*: 1989 prices for conventionally grown wheat remained at £110/tonne whereas for organic wheat they were £220/tonne.)

Table 3.1: Organic and Conventional Wheat Crops

result the yield was only 60 per cent of the chemical crop. Even so, when sold at the organic premium, the gross margin was nearly £100 per hectare greater. Had the crop been sold at conventional prices there would have been a similar difference the other way. Of course, this represents only one growing season. In a different year, the figures might be quite different.

In Barry Wookey's case, all the crops were grown at the same location, on the same type of soil and subject to the same climatic conditions. If the researchers had used figures from a farm twenty miles away, there might have been a significant difference. Genuine comparisons can only come from carefully matched pairs of conventional and organic farms. Most studies of this kind have been done on the Continent and the results show that the lower variable costs associated with organic farming result in similar gross margins even *before* premiums are taken into account.

Organic farmers know that even if the bottom drops out of the organic market and the crop has to be sold at conventional prices, they should be no worse off than if they had used chemicals.

WHOLE FARM COMPARISONS

Organic crops don't grow by magic – they require fertile soil, which adds to the farm's costs. A conventional cereal farmer will get a crop off each field every year, but this is not the case for the organic counterpart. Most organic farms are mixed, i.e. they include crops and livestock (see also Chapter 2), and the system works by rotation. Any proper comparison has to look at the whole farm, since at any one time a field might be in either a fertility-building or a cropping phase.

Table 3.2 is a hypothetical comparison of a field over an eight-year crop rotation cycle. The figures are typical gross margins per hectare for the crop in question.

Even without a premium, the organic cycle gives a similar gross margin to the average conventional rotation. With a premium the total organic gross margin exceeds even the high output conventional equivalent. However, many arable farmers would be faced with large increases in fixed costs for buildings, fencing and labour if they were to re-introduce livestock. Their gross margins are not sufficient to cover these additional expenses. This is a major barrier for conventional cereal farmers who want to move over to organic growing.

THE COST OF LABOUR

Even if gross margins are impressive, any financial advantage can be wiped out by excessive labour costs. It is often assumed that organic farms require considerably more labour than conventional farms. This is only the case for some enterprises – usually involving jobs such as hand weeding of vegetables. Once organic cereal crops have been sown, they are not tended again until harvest, so labour requirements are not very different from a those of a conventional farm.

When an all-cereal farm converts to a mixed farm based on dairying, beef or sheep, more labour is needed to look after the

		Conventional			Organic	
		Gross Margins			Gross Margins	
					With	Without
Year	Crop	Average	High	Crop	Premium	Premium
1	Oil seed rape	480	650	Grass	315	315
2	Winter wheat	430	555	Grass	315	315
3	Winter wheat	430	555	Grass	315	315
4	Winter barley	345	450	Grass	315	315
5	Oil seed rape	480	650	Winter wheat	1005	532
6	Winter wheat	430	555	Milling oats	830	470
7	Winter wheat	430	555	Field beans	775	565
8	Winter barley	345	450	Winter wheat	1005	532
Total Gross Margin (£)		3370	4420		4875	3359

Notes:

1. Conventional gross margins from *Nix's Farm Management Handbook* (1989).
2. Organic gross margins from *Organic Farming* by Nic Lampkin (Farming Press, 1990).
3. Gross margin derived from organic grass phase is from meat sold off the farm.
4. Organic premiums are as follows: 100 per cent for wheat; 65 per cent for oats; 35 per cent for field beans.

Table 3.2: Hypothetical Whole Farm Comparison

animals. But this is only in the region of 10 to 20 per cent. (Biodynamic enterprises are an exception because more time is involved in making the various 'preparations' needed to comply with their standards.)

COSTS AND RETURNS

The first British study of organic farm profitability took place in 1981. It looked at 30 farms and concluded that any reduction in yields was not offset by lower costs and that financial returns suffered. A more recent study in West Germany compared 57 organic farms with 223 conventional medium-sized (25-30 hectare) farms. The organic farms achieved 82 per cent of the output of conventional farms. Total costs were lower by about 23 per cent. So, the final farm incomes were more or less identical.

In October 1989, the UK Government announced that it would be surveying every organic farm in Britain to determine costs and yields. Although this information will be useful, especially for advice, the government should be moving ahead with policy measures *before* the results are published.

WHAT PRICE ORGANIC FOOD?

There is no question that organic food costs more, largely because there is such a huge demand for it. And at the moment supply cannot keep pace with demand. Most of the organic fruit and vegetables on sale in the shops comes from abroad, where prices are high to begin with. Imports account for 60 to 70 per cent of all fresh organic produce – including basic crops such as potatoes and carrots, which could easily be grown in the UK. In the spring of 1989 demand was so great that imports were running at 98 per cent of the total. In such a situation prices always rise. Only when there is a significant increase in the production of organic food will prices come down.

THE FOOD BILL AND HIDDEN COSTS

Organic food may be more expensive in the shops, but at least the costs stop there. Conventionally produced food may seem cheaper, but it carries all manner of hidden 'extras'. You won't see them listed on your till receipt, but you will pay for them nonetheless.

Conventional farming pollutes. Drinking water is contaminated by pesticides and nitrates derived from fertilizers. Pesticides get into food, and this requires expensive monitoring. Wildlife habitats are destroyed, so farmers are paid to conserve them. And, of course, there is the EC.

Under the Common Agricultural Policy, farmers are guaranteed a price for every acre of wheat they produce. The 'intervention price' as it is called, is fixed in Brussels every year, usually at a level well above the world market price. In 1986, the difference was about £44 per tonne. A typical conventional wheat yield is 7.5 tonnes per hectare. This means that every hectare of wheat grown in the UK costs the consumer at least £330.

The higher the yield, the more it costs. EC support does not only run to wheat. It covers all of the major cereal and field crops, dairy products and some types of meat. The total cost of EC support to agriculture in 1987 was £40,000 million – which works out at £11 a week from every British family. By contrast organic farmers receive no EC subsidies and are able to sell all they produce on the open market.

We have yet to know the full cost of cleaning up Britain's water supply. Contamination from nitrates is so serious that the Water Authorities Association estimates that farming practices may have to change in over 4 million hectares (80 per cent of all farmland) in the water authority areas of East Anglia, Thames and Severn Trent. The bill is likely to be around £200 million, spent over ten years, plus an annual running cost of £10 million a year after that. You might think that under the 'polluter pays' principle that this cost would be borne by nitrate-using farmers, perhaps as a tax on fertilizers. Not at all. It is proposed that farmers forced to cut fertilizer use are to be compensated for any fall in yields that they might experience. The cost of cleaning up the supplies is to be borne by the consumer. Remember that, the next time your water bill drops through the letterbox. As for pesticide pollution, there is no suggestion as to how this might be dealt with, let alone the cost.

Our supposedly efficient, chemically-driven agriculture is not 'cheap' at all. When these hidden costs are added to shop prices, organic food does not seem to be a bad bargain after all.

CONVERTING BRITISH AGRICULTURE

The great stumbling block for any farmer wishing to convert a farm to organic methods is that yields are bound to fall during the conversion period. The farmer cannot sell the produce as 'organic' until the land has received no chemicals for at least two years. Since the farmer will be unable to get an organic premium during this time, income will suffer. This is a major hurdle, but other European countries have tackled the problem by providing conversion grants to their farmers. Denmark gives £375 per hectare per year for every field that undergoes conversion. This is payable for a three-year period; in Sweden conversion grants of between £175 and £625 per hectare are given over the same period; Germany pays £110 per year, over a five-year period. Each of these governments is also encouraging the development of organic agriculture through the provision of advisory and research facilities.

In July 1989, a group comprising British Organic Farmers, the Organic Growers Association and the Soil Association launched a campaign to convert 20 per cent of British agriculture to organic mixed farming systems by the year 2000. They calculated that such a conversion would result in 6 per cent less cereal production, 12 per cent less oil seed rape, 4 per cent less milk, beef and sheep meat. In order to achieve this, they called for conversion grants and more research and development. As yet, this call has not been answered.

Note: most of the figures quoted in this section are taken from *Organic Farming* by Nic Lampkin (Farming Press, 1990), from which orginal sources can be obtained.

Chapter 4

REPAIRING THE DAMAGE

ORGANIC FARMING AND THE LANDSCAPE

In October 1989, a deluge of acidic rain defoliated thousands of hawthorn trees in Lincolnshire. It might seem like a small incident, but it was yet another reminder of the insidious effect that environmental pollution is having on the British landscape.

It is worth remembering that well over 80 per cent of rural Britain is agricultural land. Over the last forty years, intensive agriculture has worked on the principle of maximum food production, whatever the cost – even if this means decimating wildlife and ravaging the countryside. The extent of this wholesale destruction and re-definition of the land showed up clearly in a nationwide survey conducted by the Institute of Terrestrial Ecology between 1978 and 1984. In the space of six years, 6 per cent of broadleaf woodland had been lost and 28,000 kilometres of hedgerow removed. At the same time, land under wheat increased by 66 per cent and acreage of oilseed rape increased tenfold. And there is no end in sight. The use of artificial fertilizers and pesticides seems set to continue, despite increased public concern over their safety. Although plans to relax controls so that new housing developments can take place on rural land have been scrapped, other schemes are going forward: new roads are likely to cut across national parks and unspoilt areas, and there is likely be an increase in conifer forests, paid for by grants and often planted in areas where trees don't grow well. Scotland will bear the brunt of this, but there are also plans to plant on moorlands in the north-east of England. Then there is the question of the quality of our water supply in the aftermath of privatization.

LAND TO BE PROUD OF?

Since the 1940s, 97 per cent of Britain's ancient meadowland has disappeared. These crucial areas were a unique habitat, providing refuge and food for countless small mammals, birds and insects, and were also precious sites for some of our finest wild flowers. In their place there are acres of arable crops, and hybrid grasses. Half our ancient woodland has been felled, burned or grubbed up since the Second World War, wetlands have been drained to provide arable fields, and the amount of hedges ripped up since 1945 in Britain alone would stretch six times round the equator.

Conventional agriculture can only function with chemicals. The Soil Association has estimated that one billion gallons of pesticides are applied in Britain each year. Apart from the mounting problem of residues in food (see Chapter 5), these substances have wreaked havoc with wildlife: wild flowers and butterflies have been destroyed; birds, mammals and reptiles have had their habitats poisoned, and all kinds of insects – both helpful and harmful to the gardener and farmer – have been wiped out. There is often a carefree attitude to the way pesticides are used on the land. Sulphuric acid – a corrosive substance known to every budding chemist – is now used for spraying on potatoes as an alternative to dinoseb, which was banned recently. The regulations state that livestock should be kept off these fields for three days after spraying, but there is no warning to prevent human beings exercising their legal rights of way. Two women, walking in north Yorkshire during the autumn of 1989, discovered this to their cost and had their legs severely burned.

Something like 1.5 million gallons of liquid nitrogen fertilizer are also poured onto the land each year. They leach out into our rivers and canals, poisoning pondlife and freshwater creatures and making miles and miles of disgusting uninhabitable waterways. Any nitrogen left in the soil is bound up with soil particles or released into the atmosphere where it helps to contribute to acid rain.

COMMON GROUND

Organic farming can help to repair some of the damage caused by years of intensive conventional agriculture. Its philosphy hinges on the relationship between those who live on the land

– both humans and wildlife – and the production of good, healthy food by a system that is in tune with the environment, not working against it. It assumes that humans have no dominion over nature, that the creatures of the world are our partners, not our servants. Organic farmers rely on natural ecosystems; they use nature without taking advantage of it. They control pests biologically, which means encouraging beneficial insects, birds and mammals, rather than treating all of them as potential enemies and a threat to crops. So, diverse habitats, from hedges and wild flower meadows to woodland and ponds, are deliberately created to encourage them. Mixed hedgerows can be used as a way of fencing and controlling livestock which are an integral part of most workable organic enterprises.

Organic farming is about the conservation of resources, yet until recently the organic movement and the conservationists and ecologists seemed to be working independently. What they have in common – apart from a commitment to the land – is the idea of 'self-containment'. Ecologists see this as a way of protecting natural systems. As long as fuel, water, fertilizers and the like come from the same place, *within* the system, and waste is returned to it, it is under control. Once that cycle is disrupted or broken, specialization sets in and the system starts to break down. This is what happens in conventional agriculture.

At last, it seems, the environmentalists and those in the organic movement are beginning to find some common ground. The immediate result of discussions and co-operation between leading bodies in both camps during 1989 was a series of *Guidelines for Conservation* issued by The Soil Association; these have been expanded as an Environment and Conservation Section in the Association's *Standards for Organic Agriculture*. The new guidelines focus on six areas: traditional field boundaries and hedge management; pasture management; moorland; drainage; tree and woodland management; and buildings and archaeological sites.

BOUNDARIES

Hedges are crucial to organic farming. They provide refuge and food for wildlife – birds, insects and the like, which can go out into fields to police crops and attack unwanted pests; they are also a very practical form of natural fencing and shelter for livestock.

Most modern cereal farmers cut hedges too harshly, too often and at the wrong time of year. As a result the hedges are weak, and they go into winter bare and fruitless – which is of no help at all to wildlife. The best way of conserving hedges and wildlife is to restrict trimming. It should only take place between January and March, and preferably once every three years. The current policy of cutting in the spring and summer each year should be banned.

If new hedges are needed to replace the damage of the past, they can easily be planted and will be sufficiently mature within a few years. Hedges were being created as early as the eighth century, and organic farmers can look to history for ideas and techniques. First of all, a hedge needs a spine of species that will provide support and be sturdy enough to keep out livestock: perhaps blackthorn, hawthorn and holly, put in as double rows for extra strength. Then a range of flowering plants that are attractive to insects: dogwood, wayfaring tree, rose. Elder is excellent as an attraction for predatory hoverflies and was used in the eighteenth century to provide a strengthening criss-cross latticework within the hedge itself. If the hedge is more than twenty yards long, farmers ought to include some slow-growing trees for the future. And it's worth looking at the possibility of adapting the medieval idea of 'linear orchards', in which fruit trees were planted in the hedge, thus providing a crop of apples or pears and giving the whole structure an added usefulness.

Conventional farmers are hamstrung by the system that they have created. For example, the only way to manoeuvre combine harvesters and the other bulky machines is to grub up hedges and leave unusable areas around the edges of fields. Organic fields need boundaries, but these can be used imaginatively. Although there might be a loss of cropping, a hedge or a raised bank is important. And the scrubby edges and margins of fields are potentially useful too. When William Cobbett was deep into his *Rural Rides* in the early years of the nineteenth century, he saw some unusual hedge borders in the Hertfordshire countryside:

The custom is ... to leave a *border* round the ploughed part of the fields to bear grass and to make hay from, so that, the grass being made into hay, every corn field has a close mowed grass walk about ten feet wide all round it, between the corn and the hedge. This is most beautiful! The hedges are now full of shepherd's purse, honeysuckles, and all sorts of wild flowers; so that you are upon a grass walk, with this most beautiful of all flower gardens on the one hand, and with corn on the other. And thus you go from field to field (on foot or on horseback), the sort of corn, the sort of underwood and timber, the shape and size of the fields, the height of the hedge-rows, and the height of the trees, all continually varying. Talk of *pleasure-grounds* indeed! What that man ever invented under the name of pleasure-grounds, can equal these fields in Hertfordshire?

This may sound like an agricultural Arcadia, but the idea of croppable hedge borders that can also be used as pleasurable pathways for walkers is something that organic farmers might do well to consider.

Hedges are also a good source of timber and firewood, but are not really important as protection against wind-blown soil. They are simply not tall enough, apart from the 20ft-high hedges which are a feature of the Weald landscape in south-east England. On the other hand, organic gardeners should remember that they can plant banks of sunflowers or Jerusalem artichokes as windbreaks.

Dykes and ditches are effective boundaries too. If it isn't practical to plant hedges, then drainage dykes or 'linear ponds' are just as good. These also provide a useful habitat for insects, birds, frogs, toads and other creatures; they may not be 'pest controllers' in their own right, but they form part of the ecosystem of the farm. It is important to ensure that a proportion of dykes and ditches remain uncleared each year, and that any routine clearing is done as a phased operation. This gives beneficial creatures of all kinds the best chance of survival, which, in turn, benefits the organic farmer.

HABITATS AT RISK

Every part of our countryside, every habitat, is under threat from conventional agriculture and its legacy of poison and pollution. We need to protect our landscape. Our ancient meadows have been ploughed up, vast tracts of moorland, lowland heath and wetland have disappeared, and much of our traditional woodland has been chainsawed and bulldozed. The only way to conserve these places is to prohibit the ploughing up of unimproved pastures of ecological interest and stipulate that manuring should be strictly controlled. Important wetlands should not be drained and any proposals for the 'improvement' of semi-natural vegetation should be approved by all concerned before any scheme goes ahead. There also needs to be restrictions on the clear felling of woodland or the felling of healthy, mature specimen trees.

LOOKING TO THE FUTURE

The link between organic farming and the landscape suggests all kinds of possibilities for the future. It can offer a new link between 'wild' and 'cultivated' land. For example, an organic farmer might wish to cultivate a few acres of ornamental flowers or lavender which could be used to attract bees and provide the basis for hives and honey. It might also be possible to create woody plantations of fruit trees that could be used to provide a crop. On a wider scale, all kinds of systems are possible: in the Far East, fish are humanely 'farmed' beneath the rice in paddy fields. In what remains of the Brazilian rainforests, an efficient system of producing Brazil nuts and rubber tapping works hand in hand. Vines can be trained on timber trees in some parts of the world – a kind of three-dimensional farming that grows upwards as well as outwards.

Research from Denmark published in 1989 suggested that birds survive better on organic farms. Not only were they more numerous, but species were more varied. Numbers and density of birds on conventional farms could be as much as 50 per cent less than on organic.

The relationship between organics and conservation is global, but one tiny example from England shows the way forward. Folly Farm, a nature reserve owned by the Avon Conservation Trust, will shortly be farmed organically. The outbuildings may need renovation, the land may need nurturing, but the message is clear. Ecology, conservation and organic farming belong together. Folly Farm is a small symbol for the future.

Chapter 5

SAFE TO EAT?

ORGANIC FOOD AND HEALTH

Recent food scares have alerted the public to the possible dangers from additives and diseases. Many consumers are also worried about the long-term effects of absorbing minute traces of pesticides in their daily diet. Two examples, sheep dipping and crop storage, give some indication of the extent of the problem.

DANGEROUS DIPS

Scab is a particularly nasty affliction of sheep, caused by a parasitic mite that lives on the surface of the skin under the fleece. In an attempt to control this problem, farmers are forced by law to dip their sheep every year in an insecticidal bath. Until 1985, most farmers used an organochlorine (O-Cl)-type insecticide, such as lindane or dieldrin; it was the Ministry of Agriculture's responsibility to check that farmers were carrying out these compulsory twice-yearly dips by conducting random inspections of fleeces for evidence of residues. But does the chemical get beyond the fleece and into the meat? According to the Ministry's own watchdog committee in its *Report of the Working Party on Pesticide Residues 1985-8*, in 1985 of 1,492 samples of sheep's kidney fat, 71 per cent contained detectable residues of gamma HCH (lindane).

Mounting fears about the persistence of gamma HCH led the Ministry to announce its voluntary withdrawal in January 1985. In its place farmers were recommended to use a different class of chemicals – the organophosphorus (O-P) group. These compounds were orginally developed as potent nerve gases by the Germans during the Second World War. It is hardly surprising that, by 1988, reports were beginning to come in of ill-health in farmers who had used O-P compounds. They complained of dizziness, weariness and depression. One farmer, former Devon County National Farmers Union Chair, Geoffrey Cleverdon, became so ill that he was forced to give up the use of this type of dip. Mr Cleverdon had been using organophosphorus-based pesticides for some time, and believed that their effects were cumulative: 'To me, this is a progressive type of poison that builds up over the years.' As a result of concern over the safety of workers using sheep dips, the Health and Safety Executive is currently investigating cases of 'post dipping flu' to establish how harmful the side effects might be.

Meanwhile, as residues of lindane (gamma HCH) are beginning to disappear from sheep meat samples, residues of new O-P compounds are taking their place. In 1987, 7 per cent of 287 samples of sheep's kidney fat analysed contained residues of the compound diazinon, and four samples (i.e. 2 per cent) exceeded the maximum residue limit (MRL) – which implies that for every 100 tonnes of sheep kidney sold in Britain two tonnes should not be eaten. However, so few samples are taken for analysis that we cannot tell whether this underestimates or overestimates the problem. We simply do not know how much of the meat we consume contains pesticide residues above the limit.

There might be some justification for this gamble with the nation's health if sheep dipping eliminated scab. For decades, farmers have been compulsorily dipping their sheep and the policy looks set to continue indefinitely. Yet, at least one flockmaster considers dipping to be not only a complete waste of time, but also cruel and traumatic for the animals concerned.

Writing in *Farmers Weekly*, David Griffiths asserted that: 'It is my firm belief that were sheep dipping not given the seal of approval by the Ministry, we would all be prosecuted for cruelty. Ewes with little wool to protect them are manhandled into a cold bath where they can scarcely avoid swallowing a liquid which must be foul to begin with and gets worse as the day wears on. Lambs in full fleece become sodden in the statutory minute and can easily sink below the surface with fatal results. I have been helping sheep dip for over forty years.

In this time the incidence of scab has fluctuated, *but it is now, I am sure, higher than it was then*' (Our emphasis). Not a great success story.

AFTER THE HARVEST

Once wheat is harvested, it is taken to large grain silos where it is stored until required. As a precaution against attack from insects and mites, it is routinely treated with pirimiphos-methyl or a similar chemical. The manufacturers recommend uniform spraying at a rate of 4-8 g for every tonne of grain. However, in the summer of 1988, Friends of the Earth was sent confidential Ministry papers which expressed grave concern at 'post-harvest' treatment of stored foods – in particular, the random way in which pesticides are applied. So-called 'bucket and shovel' methods, used instead of spreading the chemical evenly, can lead to patchy distribution and local 'hot spots'. Subsequent Government tests for pesticide residues in samples of bread revealed that more than half were contaminated. This, despite the fact that much of the pesticide on the outside of the grain is removed in the milling process.

If bread was bad, bran was worse. Out of 104 samples of bran tested, 97 contained residues. Although levels were below the MRL, it is hardly reassuring to know that it is almost impossible to buy bran that is not contaminated by pesticides.

Grain is not the only staple food to be sprayed with chemicals after it has left the soil. Potatoes come in for this treatment too. The problem isn't insects, but mould-forming fungal diseases. Potatoes also have a tendency to sprout, causing the tubers to shrivel. One chemical, tecnazene, alleviates both these problems. Its usefulness as a combined fungicide and anti-sprouting agent makes it extremely popular, and it is estimated that over 1 million tonnes of potatoes are treated with it each year. As with wheat, sloppy methods of application are leading to residues in excess of the recommended international standard. Indeed, in January 1989, tests conducted by Friends of the Earth for the Channel 4 television programme *4 What It's Worth* showed that potatoes bought from three major supermarket chains contained tecnazene at double the maximum residue limit. The Government's own tests for tecnazene on potatoes sampled between 1985 and 1986 found residues on three-quarters of them. The Ministry recommends that consumers wash tubers thoroughly and remove the skin. This runs contrary to advice from nutritionists, who state that a lot of the goodness in potatoes is found in, or just under, the skin. Surely the answer is not to allow potentially harmful chemicals to get into food in the first place, rather than having to remove them afterwards.

Consumers have a right to know what gets into the food they eat. Consider Table 5.1.

Chemical	Active ingredient	Problem	Frequency of spraying
Basudin 40 WP	Diazinon	Lettuce root aphid	Once
Draza	Methiocarb	Slugs	Once
Kerb 5OW	Propyzamide	Weeds	Once
Rovral WP	Iprodione	Botrytis mould	Once
Ronilan	Vinclozolin	Botrytis Mould, Sclerotinia rot	Once
Metasystox SS	Demeton-S -methyl	Greenflies	Once
Pirimor	Pirimicarb	Greenflies	Three or four times
Hostaquick	Heptenophos	Greenflies	
Dimethoate	Dimethoate	Greenflies	
Ambush C	Cypermethrin	Caterpillars	Two or three times
Zineb	Zineb	Downy mildew	Three or four times
Favour	Thiram and Metalaxyl	Downy mildew	
Thiram	Thiram	Ringspot, Botrytis	Three or four times

Note: Lettuces grown intensively under glass usually require even more chemical treatment. In Ministry-sponsored glasshouse experiments, lettuces sprayed with dimethoate and iprodione (both approved pesticides), at rates recommended on the labels, were found to contain levels in excess of the maximum residue limits.

Table 5.1: A Typical Spray Programme for a Commercial Crop of Outdoor Lettuce

HOW SAFE IS 'SAFE'?

Pesticide manufacturers are keen to point out that even if residues are detected in food, the amounts are so tiny that there can be no risk to human health. This assertion is based on the results of toxicity testing.

All pesticides have to undergo an elaborate series of experiments on laboratory animals to determine the dose at which there is 'no observable effect' (NOEL). The NOEL is then divided by an arbitrary factor of 100 to give an 'acceptable daily intake' (ADI). This is considered to be the amount of a chemical which can be safely consumed by a person every day of his or her life. Alongside the safety studies, there are field trials in which the pesticide is applied at rates recommended by the manufacturer. Crops are analysed for residues. From these figures the 'maximum residue level' (MRL) is set.

In theory, it ought not to be possible for a person eating food contaminated with pesticides close to the MRL to exceed the acceptable daily intake. Even if this happens, the levels of pesticide detected are infinitesimal – often of the order of one part per billion. As an industry handout puts it: 'This is the equivalent of the thickness of a credit card in the whole distance between London and Peru.' So is there cause for concern? Why should we worry?

The first thing to remember is that pesticides are designed to kill. We should be cautious even if the amounts involved are tiny. At the high doses used in laboratory tests it is not uncommon for rats, mice and other experimental animals to develop tumours or give birth to deformed offspring. The ADI is based on the assumption that people are ten times as sensitive as the most sensitive laboratory animals and that even the most sensitive person is ten times more sensitive than the norm – hence the safety factor of 100. Yet these figures are entirely arbitrary.

Even the experts don't agree on the interpretation of the experimental tests. The US Environmental Protection Agency (EPA) uses the data in mathematical models to help it gauge the likely effect of pesticide residues. On this basis, for example, it believes that 125,000 Americans will develop cancer from eating food contaminated with the zineb group of pesticides. Indeed, a voluntary ban was issued by the EPA in October 1989 and a statutory ban is likely to follow. The

British Government, meanwhile, disputes the validity of mathematical modelling. Maneb, mancozeb and zineb, which have been used for over forty years, may still be used by farmers in the UK.

One of the problems with trying to fix safety levels for the population as a whole is that they take no account of individual differences. Suppose a sensitive individual is not ten, but *one thousand* times more susceptible than the average person to a particular pesticide? Special groups – the sick, elderly, infants or nursing mothers – may be more at risk. In addition, ADIs are based on average consumptions of foodstuffs, and take no account of particular dietary needs or preferences. Vegetarians, for example, might be expected to eat more fruit and vegetables than meat-eaters, while wholefood devotees would probably eat more bran than the population at large.

ADIs can be exceeded. Ministry tests on samples of cows' milk during 1985-6 revealed two-thirds containing residues of dieldrin with three samples at, or near to, the MRL. These findings alarmed the Ministry and prompted them to issue the following warning: 'We are concerned at the levels detected and the frequency of occurrence of organochlorine residues in cows' milk, particularly as this may constitute a large proportion of the diet in infants and young children. We are concerned that intakes of dieldrin by infants consuming the most contaminated samples could exceed the ADI. The long-term effects, if any, of exceeding the ADI are unknown.' Permission for all agricultural, horticultural and veterinary uses of dieldrin were *officially* withdrawn in 1981, yet traces were still showing up in milk sampled as recently as 1987.

Even the most extensive experiments on laboratory animals cannot tell us the whole story about the likely effects on humans, particularly in the long term. Different types of animal may give completely different responses to the same chemical. The British Toxicological Society, in evidence to the House of Commons Select Committee on Agriculture stated: 'The evidence to date indicates that animal cancer studies are of value in detecting "strong" carcinogens but do not offer a simple means of discovering, nor are a reliable means of predicting, human hazards from "weak" carcinogens.'

Nor can we expect animal experiments to show up subtle effects that might alter our physiological or mental state. We know from homoeopathy that certain substances, diluted by a

Pesticide	Use	Suspected Risk	Date Banned
Aldrin	Insecticide	Carcinogen/ Teratogen/Mutagen	1989
Binapacryl	Fungicide	Teratogen	1987
Bitertanol	Fungicide	Teratogen	1985
Captafol	Fungicide	Carcinogen/ Teratogen/Mutagen	1989
Cyhexatin	Acaracide (kills mites)	Teratogen	1988
DDT	Insecticide	Carcinogen/ Teratogen/Mutagen	1964-84
Dieldrin	Insecticide	Carcinogen/ Teratogen/Mutagen	1989
Dinoseb	Herbicide	Teratogen	1988
DNOC	Insecticide	Teratogen	1989
Ethylene dibromide	Fumigant	Carcinogen	1985
Endrin	Insecticide	Carcinogen/ Teratogen/Mutagen	1964-84
Bromoxynil	Insecticide	Teratogen	*
Chlordane	Earthworm killer	Carcinogen/ Teratogen/Mutagen	1992
Ioxynil	Insecticide	Carcinogen/ Teratogen/Mutagen	*
Mercurious chloride	Fungicide	Environmental hazard, persistent poison	*

Notes:
* use severely restricted
carcinogen–may cause or promote cancer
teratogen–may cause reproductive problems, e.g. deformed offspring
mutagen–may damage genes and chromosomes; possible
abnormalities in future generations

Table 5.2: Pesticides that have been banned in the UK since 1984

factor of a million or more, are sufficient to promote healing. Is it not possible that poisons, diluted by similar amounts, might lead to sickness and disease? Perhaps there is no way of predicting the long-term risk from pesticides? Perhaps we can only wait and see what happens?

WHOM CAN WE TRUST?

The British Agrochemical Association, representing fertilizer and pesticide interests, has nothing but good words for their wares. What about antibiotics and other farm drugs fed to livestock? Are they unsafe? No, says NOAH (the National Office of Animal Health) – which is funded by the pharmaceutical companies. Whenever *anyone* raises the alarm about a product, you can guarantee that an industry-sponsored expert will be on hand to contradict the statement. Is this simply irresponsible mischief-making on the part of the environmentalists, or has the industry something to hide? How are we, the consumers, expected to decide between the conflicting claims of experts?

THE ORGANIC ALTERNATIVE

It is possible to grow crops and rear livestock without recourse to suspect chemicals, so there is no need to take risks with your health. Organic food is the safe alternative, it is the only positive and reliable answer for consumers who are concerned about what they put into their mouths.

In theory, if dubious chemicals aren't used on the farm, they won't turn up in food. In practice, things are not that simple. Even organic food cannot be guaranteed 'pesticide-free'. As early as 1964, scientists discovered DDT in the body fat of penguins living in the Antarctic. Traces of pesticides have been found in the flesh of coelacanths – fish living 600 feet down in the depths of the Indian Ocean. We live in a polluted world. Chemical residues may persist for decades, and they can travel on wind and water across the planet. Even if organic farmers do not use synthetic chemicals themselves, they may be affected by this stray contamination. However, if the soil has not had a past history of intensive chemical use and if the water supply is reasonably pure, the chances are that pesticide residues will not be present at all. This is borne out by the few chemical analyses of organic food that have been carried out.

The absence of unwanted chemicals is one thing, but does organic food *taste* better than conventionally grown produce? And is it nutritionally superior? Many people buy organic food simply for its taste. Organic gardeners have few doubts that home-grown produce has a better flavour than produce from the shops. However, vegetables picked fresh from the garden always taste better than those which have spent several days on the journey from farm to greengrocers, whether they are organic or not. The only accurate way of comparing organic and non-organic is to grow and harvest a single variety under identical conditions. Effects of soil, climate, and so on are the same; the key difference is the use of chemicals. On the rare occasions when such tests have been carried out, tasting panels have usually voted in favour of organic produce. The Potato Marketing Board, for instance, reported in its 1988 Annual Review that organic potatoes taken from store after 3 and 6 months had less 'off flavours' after boiling, compared with their conventional counterparts. Carrots usually do well, too, and are said to be sweeter and less coarse.

But the most convincing results of organic production show up in meat. There is simply no contest when it comes to comparing the flavour of organic meat and that produced by intensive livestock farmers. Quite apart from any moral objections people may have about factory farming, meat produced by such methods is simply inferior. It is hardly surprising that more people are becoming vegetarians when the quality of meat is so appalling: bacon containing so much water that it literally boils when being grilled, chicken that needs a stock cube to give it flavour, steak that is so tough that it is barely edible. Most meat is a disgrace. And the fact that most poultry, in particular, is likely to be infected with harmful bacteria only adds insult to injury.

The contrast with meat produced from animals that have ranged freely on naturally fertilized grass, with supplements from organically grown foodstuffs, has to be tasted to be believed. After visiting organic farms and seeing at first hand the way the animals are reared as well as sampling the produce, some vegetarians go back to meat eating.

When it comes to the question of nutrition, it isn't possible to give definitive answers. The EC has any number of regulations covering the size, shape and colour of the food we eat, but there are no laws determining minimum requirements for vitamins and minerals. It seems that cosmetic appeareance comes before nutrition. Scientific analysis is expensive; if it is not required by law, why waste money doing the tests? As a result we know precious little about the nutritional differences between organic and conventionally grown food. Processed food may be analysed for its calorific content to satisfy 'weight watchers', but try to discover whether Cara potatoes contain more vitamin C than Desiree and you will be unsuccessful.

However, it is possible to make a few general comments about the quality of conventional and organic food. Conventional food, produced with the aid of artificial fertilizers, usually has a higher water content – often as much as 20 per cent compared with organic equivalents. This might explain why so much conventional food is virtually 'tasteless' and may account for the 'concentrated' natural flavour of organic produce, which tends to have a higher sugar content, enhanced vitamin C and more magnesium. Organic food usually contains smaller amounts of potentially harmful nitrate too (except in the case of winter leafy crops such as lettuce).

There is a long way to go, and more research is needed, but anyone confronted with an organically reared chicken and a broiler hen can see and taste the difference. It should be obvious that a bird reared as naturally as possible, with access to fresh air and well-tended organic pasture, is healthier – and therefore better to eat – than a creature confined indoors. The message for consumers is clear; choose free-range, choose organic, choose the healthy alternative.

Chapter 6

READING THE SIGNS

HOW TO RECOGNIZE
ORGANIC PRODUCE

In 1989, during the run-up to Christmas, a consignment of potatoes found its way onto a market stall in the Midlands. They were labelled 'organically grown' and were soon selling well. Whether it was the suspicious bargain-basement pricing or the result of a tip-off isn't clear, but the local trading standards officer decided to investigate. When a sample was analysed, it was found that the potatoes had been treated with the fungicide tecnazene, which is applied to potatoes when they are stored as a way of preventing mould and reducing sprouting. Needless to say, its use is not permitted under organic regulations. In other words, the potatoes were being sold as 'organic' when they were clearly nothing of the sort. At the time of writing, a prosecution is pending.

Had the analysis failed to show the presence of tecnazene, but instead had revealed traces of the weedkiller atrazine, the position would have been more complicated. Friends of the Earth, in an investigation into pesticide pollution of drinking water (published in 1988), discovered widespread contamination, particularly from weedkillers. In the Thames region alone, one sample of atrazine was recorded at forty-five times the EC permitted limit. If an organic grower had used water drawn from such a supply to irrigate the cropland, some of that atrazine might well have found its way into the crop.

Another problem is that tiny droplets of pesticide spray applied on a conventional farm can be carried on the wind and may be taken up by an organic crop. Obviously this kind of stray contamination would be far less than if the farmer had deliberately used pesticides, but it *would* show up in analysis. It isn't possible to insulate an organic farm from air, rain and water, so there is no way of giving absolute guarantees about the lack of pesticide residues.

Does this mean that the consumer's position is hopeless? The food industry is prepared to use marketing, cunning and the subtle manipulation of words to give a misleading impression. It has already been noted that food labelled as 'insecticide-free' may still have been grown using fungicides, weedkillers and all the other 'icides' available to the conventional farmer. How can the consumer recognize genuine organic produce? And how can the genuine organic farmer be protected from unfair competition by unscrupulous growers and traders?

The answer to both these questions lies in the establishment of comprehensive standards defining precisely how organic food is produced. These should be backed up by independent inspections to ensure that farmers, market gardeners and the food processing industry are following the rules. Food grown to these standards should carry a symbol that consumers can look out for. Indeed no food should be sold as organic unless it carries such a symbol.

BRITISH ORGANIC STANDARDS

Since the mid-1970s there have been two organic standards schemes in the UK. The older and more widespread is that run by The Soil Association, a registered membership charity founded in 1946. The Soil Association started its symbol scheme in 1973. You can find its distinctive circular logo on most organic pre-packed fruit, vegetables, cereal and bakery products on sale in supermarkets and shops. Its standards for organic agriculture have been continuously updated since that time, and it has recently worked in conjunction with other organic organizations acting under the umbrella of the British Organic Standards Committee (see p.276). The latest edition of The Soil Association's *Standards for Organic Agriculture* runs to 80 pages and covers all aspects of growing crops and producing animal products, as well as food processing, packing and distribution.

The other scheme is run by Organic Farmers & Growers Ltd. OFG is a marketing co-operative of farmers set up in the mid-1970s. Members contract to sell their produce direct to the company. Until recently, OFG has tended to specialize in grains and their logo appears mainly on the 'Morning Food' range of breakfast cereals. Much of their output is sold abroad or used by companies that do not display the OFG symbol.

ORGANIC STANDARDS OVERSEAS

A great deal of organic produce sold in Britain comes from abroad. At certain times of the year imports of vegetables can be as high as 90 per cent of the total on sale. Any system of recognized standards has to take account of this foreign produce. The basis for this is an international organization known as the International Federation of Organic Agricultural Movements (IFOAM), which provides a set of minimum standards. These can be adapted by organizations in different countries depending on their needs and circumstances. Once standards have been drawn up, individual organic organizations become responsible for policing them and awarding their symbol. There is no IFOAM logo or symbol as such.

Organic growing flourishes in many developed countries worldwide. Currently Britain imports from Holland, France, Spain, Israel, Canada, and the US, with lesser amounts coming from Italy, Belgium, Denmark and Morocco. Each of these countries has at least one standard-setting body while some have as many as three or four separate symbol schemes. In France, there are eleven competing organizations, each with its own symbol.

Fortunately the British consumer is not faced with having to decide the merits of each foreign scheme. The Soil Association, acting in co-operation with other IFOAM members, has drawn up a list of approved overseas standards. Produce imported to the UK by approved companies is then eligible for the Soil Association's own symbol. Occasionally you may find foreign symbols on UK produce, e.g. avocados and citrus fruits from Israel bearing the 'Biotop' symbol of the Israel Bio-organic Agriculture Association. The Farm Verified Organic (FVO) scheme, which originated in the US, is associated with some

North American produce, especially cereals, sent to Britain. Also, the National Association of Sustainable Agriculture in Australia, and the Organic Crop Improvement Association (Nebraska, Ontario, NW. and S. Saskatchewan Chapters) in Canada have recently been added to the Soil Association's approved list. Otherwise, wine is the only exception to this rule; the labelling of French wine, in particular, can be baffling.

There is, however, one international symbol that regularly turns up on organic produce sold in the UK. This is the Demeter trademark certifying that produce has been grown biodynamically. Although it is largely international, Demeter produce is also grown in the UK on a small scale. It is not possible to explain biodynamic agriculture in detail here, but it is best described as 'organic-plus'. Rudolf Steiner, the Austrian philosopher, founded this variant of organic agriculture in the 1920s. It follows basic organic principles, but growers are required to use certain extra substances called 'preparations' and other practices which, it is claimed, harmonize the farm with the wider environment and the cosmos. Seeds and plants are sown according to instructions in a lunar and constellation calendar. Biodynamic standards are stricter than most organic standards in terms of what the farmer is allowed to use and the length of time taken in converting the farm. There is also an interim standard, called Biodyn, for farms in the process of conversion to full biodynamic status.

'NOT QUITE ORGANIC' PRODUCE

Nowadays more and more 'organic-style' foodmarks and symbols are starting to appear. These are not fully organic, but connect with one or two aspects of the subject. The RSPCA, for example, is planning to introduce an award for farms producing meat by methods that do not involve factory farming. Free-range eggs are well known, and the Free-Range Egg Association (FREGG) has its own standards, inspection scheme and logo. But unless the hens have been mostly fed grain that has been organically grown and have ranged over grass that has not been treated with artificial fertilizers, their eggs cannot be sold as 'organic'.

A more important symbol in the marketplace is that of The Guild of Conservation Food Producers. Under Guild regulations, members are allowed to use certain non-organic inputs to boost yields. A number of chemical weedkillers, banned under organic regulations, are also permitted. Their use is justified on the grounds that the substances break down readily in the soil and are unlikely to contaminate food. You will see the Conservation Grade symbol on the range of breakfast cereals sold by Jordan's (see p.78) and a few other products.

The Pure Meat Company produces all of its meat to Conservation Grade standards. Like organic regulations, these standards insist on proper welfare conditions for the livestock. The chief difference concerns medication. Most livestock can be prone to infection by parasitic worms. Organic standards recommend management practices such as clean grazing, strict hygiene and the use of drugs only as a last resort; however, drugs may be used as a preventative under Conservation Grade standards, although the routine use of antibiotics and growth promoters is not allowed.

Farmers who are changing their farms from conventionally run to organic sometimes produce a crop from land which is still in the process of conversion. At one time there was an 'in transition' grade of produce sold in the shops, but this is rarely seen now. Most cereals produced this way are sold as Conservation Grade.

STANDARDS FOR THE FUTURE

Until a few years ago, the amount of organic produce sold was so small that governments could afford to ignore it. Regulation of organic production was left largely to ad-hoc voluntary bodies. However, the increase in trade in recent years has heightened the possibility of abuse and illegal practice. It is tempting for unscrupulous traders to take advantage of high prices and the lack of an official 'organic' definition to pass off dubious produce.

In 1986, the EC announced that it was planning a Directive on the production and marketing of organic food. Spurred on by this, the British Government in 1987 set up the United Kingdom Register of Organic Food Standards (UKROFS). The idea was to create a single UK standard for organic food.

Farmers and food processors would have to register with an organic sector body such as the Soil Association (whose own standards had been approved by UKROFS), or with UKROFS direct if they chose to do so. In May 1989, after two years of deliberation, the UKROFS standards were finally agreed. In essence, they are little different from those of the Soil Association. Inspections of organic sector bodies will be carried out by the government's Agricultural Development and Advisory Service (ADAS).

UKROFS has its own logo which will be used by everyone who registers direct with it. But it won't become the only organic symbol on food. The Soil Association will continue to use its own symbol along with the words 'UKROFS Approved'. Organic Farmers & Growers Ltd will place its symbol alongside the UKROFS symbol. The Biodynamic Agricultural Association has yet to decide what it is going to do, but it is unlikely to drop the internationally known Demeter symbol. So, as far as British produce is concerned, the letters UKROFS (either as a symbol or alongside existing symbols) show that the farmer and food processor has conformed to an agreed set of organic standards.

In November 1989, the EC finally came up with a draft regulation aimed at harmonizing the definitions of organic production throughout the Community. At present, this falls some way short of current British standards, but eventually it will be illegal to sell food as 'organically grown' unless it has been produced to national standards acceptable to the EC. It is expected that this will become law late in 1990 or early in 1991. Trading standards officers will then have a strict definition to rely on when making prosecutions.

It may be confusing for consumers to see so many organic symbols on produce, but it is important that reliable organizations within the organic movement continue to exert an influence over government-run standards. It would be all too easy, given the mushrooming demand for organic food, for official bodies to cave in to commercial pressure for a relaxation of standards – perhaps to allow a little fertilizer use, or a shorter conversion period, or the occasional weedkiller spray. While there is a strong independent standard and symbol scheme, this is not possible. A range of symbols operating with proper regulation is, perhaps, not too high a price to pay for consumer confidence, guarantees and safety.

PART TWO

Chapter 7

ORGANIC PRODUCE

A SHOPPER'S GUIDE

CEREALS, BREAD AND BAKERY PRODUCTS

Before 1987 it was difficult to find a bag of organic flour in the shops. None of the supermarkets considered it worth stocking. Even wholefood shops specializing in bulk supplies of cereals couldn't be relied upon to sell organic grains. Now the consumer is spoilt for choice. All the major supermarket chains offer at least a couple of branded products and new lines are being added almost weekly.

This revolution has come about through the energy and enterprise of a small number of family milling firms. Most operate traditional stonegrinding mills. It is no accident that stonegrinding millers have taken the lead: though the bulk of British wheat is processed in roller mills, quality millers have always chosen stone. The reason is simple. The gentle crushing action of the slowly rotating millstones stops the wheatgrain from overheating. By contrast, huge steel rollers spinning at up to 1,000 revolutions per minute get so hot that the natural oils present in the wheatgerm could easily become rancid if they were not taken out. Vitamins and minerals – which are destroyed by high temperatures – have to be put back later in the bread-making process. There would be little point in subjecting a quality product such as organically grown wheat to the punishing treatment of a roller mill. It has to be stoneground.

Flour

Doves Farm is, perhaps, the best known organic flour mill in the country. It is run by husband and wife team, Michael and Claire Marriage, from their headquarters in Hungerford, Berkshire. Doves Farm make a range of four flours. Look for their 100 per cent strong wholemeal, 100 per cent extra fine wholemeal, 100 per cent self-raising wholemeal and unbleached white flour. You will find them in most branches of Tesco, Gateway and Budgen and in many good food shops. In 1989, Doves Farm won the food products section of 'The Green Grocer Awards'.

By the banks of the upper reaches of the River Avon near Tetbury in Gloucestershire, John Lister, owner of picturesque Shipton Mill, produces a range of organic flours. As you might imagine, Shipton was originally driven by the force of the river, but now the stones derive their power from electricity rather than water. A great deal of the flour from Shipton is sent to supermarkets for their in-store baking or to Master Bakers, for turning into bread sold by small family shops. John also supplies flour to Cranks, the London-based chain of vegetarian wholefood shops/restaurants. However, in 1989 Shipton Mill launched a range of organic flours aimed at the domestic market. Their stylishly designed bags can be bought through many wholefood shops, but not from supermarkets.

Shipton Mill produces five kinds of flour: two white, and three 100 per cent wholemeal. Home-grown wheat mixed with wheat from North America is the basis of two of their breadmaking flours, a strong white and a 100 per cent wholewheat. Another wholemeal flour, made entirely from American organic wheat, is especially good for bread rolls. For cakes there are two flours made entirely from English wheat: a white cake flour and a fine milled 100 per cent pastry and cake flour.

Pimhill is the trade name of the other nationally distributed organic flour. At their Shropshire farm, the father and daughter partnership of Richard and Ginny Mayall is continuing a tradition of organic growing that was started by Richard's father, the late Sam Mayall, in the 1940s. Indeed it was Pimhill's boast that it was the very first organic farm and mill in the country. There are five Pimhill brands: a 100 per cent wholewheat flour available either as plain or self-raising; an 85 per cent extraction fine brown flour, also plain or self-raising; and a speciality Shropshire brown flour which is a blend of their fine brown flour, toasted malt flour and malted wheatflakes. Pimhill cereals are sold by many wholefood shops, top-class grocers and delicatessens. You can also buy them in bags direct from the farm shop. Most of the flour is grown on the farm, though supplies may be topped up with grain from other Soil Association registered organic farmers.

Marriages is a name you might see on bags of organic flour in supermarkets, particularly Safeway and Sainsbury. The Marriage mill is based at Chelmsford, Essex (Michael Marriage of Doves Farm is a relative). Though most of its output goes to commercial breadmakers, the company does make a 100 per cent wholemeal bread flour for shoppers.

In addition, an ever-growing number of small mills around the country are buying in organic grain for turning into their own brands of organic flour. If you are lucky enough to have a mill in your area, ask if they sell organic flour. They may also produce 'speciality' flours like barley, rye and oatmeal, though you are more likely to find these in wholefood shops. Some of the better known organic mills include:

The Watermill, Little Salkeld, Cumbria
Downfield Windmill, Soham, Cambridgeshire
Crowdy Mill, Harbertonford, Totnes, Devon
Charlecote Mill, Hampton Lucy, nr. Stratford-upon-Avon, Warwickshire

Flour made from wheat and other cereal grains may not be eaten by people suffering from gluten intolerance or coeliac disease. Fortunately, most good quality wholefood shops now stock a range of non-cereal based organic flours, such as maize, buckwheat, soya and brown rice flour.

Whole grains, flakes and rice
If you can buy your own grain mill or a milling attachment for your food processor, you can grind your own flour. Most good wholefood shops can easily obtain organic wheat grains and also buckwheat, millet and bulgur (cracked wheat). Check with retailers that their bagged grains are truly organic.

Organically grown barley is available in a number of different forms: grains, pearl barley and barley flakes. Flakes of other cereals such as wheat and rye can generally be obtained from wholefood shops.

Organic rice, as short- or long-grain and as flakes, is quite common. It comes from Italy and is usually broken down from large sacks into small bags by the wholefood retailer or distributor. At present very few supermarkets stock organic rice, though some Safeway stores sell tins of Witte Wonder pre-cooked organic brown rice. Whole Earth Foods market something similar for sale in wholefood shops.

Bread

Tradition has it that you can't make bread from English wheat. It is too soft. North American wheat, on the other hand, is hard. Whether or not a wheat is classified as soft or hard depends on how much protein – specifically gluten – it contains. Gluten is what makes bread rise. If you want a light airy loaf you either use a flour made entirely from North American wheat or the same wheat mixed with home-grown grain. This is what commercial bakers used to do before Britain joined the EC. Suddenly bread manufacturers were faced with an import tax on North American wheat and, desperate to keep prices competitive, turned to new methods of getting loaves to rise. These included the addition of gluten powder and 'improvers'. The industry's favourite white bread improver used to be potassium bromate. This was banned in France, Italy, Switzerland and West Germany some years ago, but its use was not prohibited by the British Government until November 1989.

Organic bread made to Soil Association standards must not include gluten powder, bleaching agents, flour improvers, emulsifiers, colourants, preservatives or any other chemical additives. Only yeast and natural leavening agents are allowed. All other ingredients, such as herbs, spices, oils and fats must be organic. Doves Farm 100 per cent wholemeal loaf is the only nationally distributed organic loaf to carry the Soil Association symbol. You can get it from branches of Waitrose, Safeway, and Sainsbury.

Both Hovis and Allinson have recently started producing bread made from organic flour (which is not quite the same as fully organic bread). Neither carry an accredited organic symbol. Most leading supermarkets stock both brands. Safeway and Sainsbury compete for the best range of bread made from organic flour. Sainsbury also sell a white sliced and wholemeal bread under the Nature's Choice label. Wheat from these loaves comes from organic farms in Canada, though the remaining ingredients are not necessarily organic. They also stock organic wholemeal rolls and an oven-bottom loaf from Justin de Blank's renowned London bakery.

Safeway is now selling freshly baked organic bread at all its in-store bakeries. It is made from organic Canadian flour, organic soya flour, organic malt, yeast and sea salt. There are two types on sale: a 400g Farmhouse Loaf and a 300g batch. Safeway also sell Hovis organic bread and two loaves baked by Goswells for Doves Farm (at present these are only found in selected stores in the south of England). Branches of Waitrose also stock Goswell bread, as well as excellent 'heavy' wholemeal loaves from their own bakeries made with organic flour from Shipton Mill.

Sourdough bread enthusiasts have a choice of two types of loaf from Sunnyvale, based in Aylesbury, Buckinghamshire. Their bread, made using natural yeasts present in the atmosphere (rather than breadmaking strains), is much denser than normal and is something of an acquired taste. The flour – either 100 per cent wheat or rye – is organic, but other ingredients are not. People allergic to gluten can choose the Sunnyvale mixed grain bread, made from maize flour, rice, linseed and sunflower oil. All Sunnyvale breads are vacuum-packed and have a long shelf life.

Rushall is a 100 per cent wholemeal loaf made entirely from grain grown on Barry Wookey's Wiltshire farm and puts the lie to the myth that you can't make bread from English wheat. Though denser than the usual shop-bought loaf, it is one of the best brands around. Unfortunately it is not that easy to find. The bakery only produces bread on Tuesdays and Fridays, and it is only sold through the mill shop at Upavon and at one or two shops in the south-west. In addition to bread, the Rushall bakery does a good line in garlic croutons, scones and rolls; you can also get Rushall wholewheat flour direct from the mill, if you want to make your own bread.

Breakfast cereals

Gone are the days when wholefood breakfast cereals simply meant muesli. Now there are plenty of alternatives. At Tesco you can get Wholewheat and Raisins or Puffed Cereals, blended from three whole grains without any added sugar or salt. Both are manufactured from organically grown ingredients by W. Jordan (Cereals) Ltd at Holme Mills, near Biggleswade.

Jordan's waterpowered mill differs from most other mills that grind organic cereals because it uses steel rollers rather than stone. However, the rollers turn much more slowly than conventional mills (200 revs per minute), limiting damage to the nutritional content of the grain. Jordan's cereals are stocked by supermarkets and wholefood shops throughout Britain.

Lima organic cornflakes are harder to find, but well worth the effort. They are made in Germany and contain only maize and sea salt; packets bear the European Nature et Progrès organic symbol. Most good food shops ought to sell them. The same is true of Kallo puffed rice cereal, made from 100 per cent organically grown brown rice.

Recently, Doves Farm launched three new organic breakfast cereals: cornflakes, branflakes and wheel-shaped cereal made from maize, oats and wheat. You can buy these from the same outlets that stock Doves Farm flour.

For those who like porridge oats, there are several to choose from. The brands you are most likely to see are made by Morning Foods. Their Mornflake Pure Organic Oats is sold by Tesco, Asda, branches of Holland & Barrett, Sainsbury and some branches of the Co-op and many other wholefood shops. Organic jumbo oats, oatmeal and toasted oats are also sold under the Mornflake label. All Morning Food products carry the Organic Farmers & Growers symbol.

Jordan make a porridge oats, available at Safeway, and Rushall Farms sell whole and rolled oats. But for the best choice, organic oat enthusiasts need look no further than the Pimhill range. They sell three grades of oatmeal: coarse, medium and fine jumbo oats as well as a porridge oats and groats.

Pamela Stephenson, writing in the November 1989 issue of *Green Magazine*, complained that she could not find an all-organic muesli. The cereals may have been organically grown, but not the nuts and fruit. Pimhill, for example, sell an organic muesli base made from oatflakes and wheatflakes, but their muesli is not fully organic. However, in the near future, Organic Farmers & Growers are planning to launch a nationally available, completely organic muesli. Several of the major wholefood distributors make up their own organic mueslis, so it is worth checking in your local wholefood shop.

Bran is the most heavily pesticide-contaminated of all cereal products, so it makes sense to buy organic. Doves Farm,

Pimhill and Shipton Mill each sell their own brand.

Cakes, biscuits and snacks

The Village Bakery at Melmerby in Cumbria has far and away the best selection of organic cakes and pastries. English wheat milled at the nearby Watermill at Little Salkeld is baked in a wood-fired brick oven by Lis and Andrew Whitley. Their bread and bakery products are sold locally and in good food shops around the country. Only organic flour is used, along with free-range eggs, raw cane sugar and sea salt. Other ingredients need not necessarily be organic, but no artificial colours, flavours or preservatives are used. Examples from their range are Christmas pudding (including a vegan version made without eggs); various types of fruit cake and cake slices; local specialities include Borrowdale teabread and Cumberland Rum Nicky. There is also a range of rolls, buns and a dozen different types of bread for those fortunate enough to live locally.

The Village Bakery makes various types of biscuit though these are not always easy to find. Doves Farm makes two digestive biscuits, a plain wholemeal and a carob-coated wholemeal. Both are sold in branches of Waitrose and in many wholefood shops.

The Edinburgh company that makes Healthy Life biscuits has now started producing a range of biscuits and cookies using organic wholemeal flour. Their selection includes ginger and orange, carob wholemeal digestive, muesli and honey flavoured varieties.

Organic crispbread made by Molen Aartje, a Dutch company, is sold in most branches of Safeway. The Origina range of rice cakes is also sold by Safeway and by many delicatessens and good food shops. This Belgian company manufactures four different types – either salted or unsalted: one with sesame, one with corn and a mixed grain version with millet and buckwheat, as well as a plain version. All are suitable for those on a gluten-free diet. Kallo foods produce a similar range of cakes made from rice, barley, wheat or rye.

The various crunchy bars made by Jordan with Conservation Grade cereals are the nearest to an organic snack available at present. Some wholefood shops sell bags of organic American popcorn, as well as taco shells made with stoneground organic maize from California. These are sold under the Little Bear Organic Foods label.

If you have difficulty in obtaining any of the products mentioned above, contact the manufacturers for your nearest stockist.

Doves Farm
Salisbury Road, Hungerford, Berkshire RG17 0RF
Tel: (0488) 84880

Shipton Mill Ltd
Long Newton, Tetbury, Gloucestershire GL8 8RD
Tel: (0666) 503620

Pimhill
Lea Hall, Harmer Hill, Shrewsbury, Shropshire SY4 3DY
Tel: (0939) 290342

W. & H. Marriage & Sons Ltd
Chelmer Mills, New Street, Chelmsford, Essex CM1 1PN
Tel: (0245) 354455

Rushall Farms
The Manor, Upavon, Pewsey, Wiltshire
Tel: (0980) 630264

W. Jordan (Cereals) Ltd
Holme Mills, Biggleswade, Bedfordshire SG18 9JX
Tel: (0767) 318222

Morning Foods Ltd
North Western Mills, Crewe, Cheshire CW2 6HP
Tel: (0270) 213261

The Village Bakery
Melmerby, Penrith, Cumbria CA10 1HE
Tel: (0768) 81515

Kallo Foods Ltd
Sunbury on Thames, TW16 7JZ

Molen Aartje
Distributed by: The Organic Trading Company
PO Box 916, Brighton, Sussex BN1 3GB

Sunnyvale (previously Springhill)
P.M. Corporation, Gatehouse Close, Aylesbury, Buckinghamshire HP19 3DE

Mitchellhill Healthy Life Biscuits
OF1, 90 Peffermill Road, Edinburgh

PASTA

There is now a very large market for wholewheat pasta of all
kinds, and organic pasta is starting to make an impact.
Although very few supermarkets stock it at present, there is
nonetheless a good choice available elsewhere.

Wholefood shops usually sell the Italian Euvita range of
lasagnes, macaroni, shells and spaghetti. Ugo, a British
company, make tagliatelle and noodles. Some shops also sell
organic buckwheat noodles.

FRUIT

Throughout the expansion of organic production in the
1980s, one area has been conspicuously neglected: top fruit
growing. The number of British producers of apples and pears
can be counted on one hand. A major reason for this is the
difficulty in attaining the EC quality standards which apply to
all fruit sold in the Community. Yet again, quality is expressed
only by what can be measured – size, shape, colour, uniformity.

For an apple to gain the coveted Class I status, for example,
it must have a minimum diameter of 60mm measured across
its middle if it is a large fruited variety such as Bramley or
Golden Delicious, or at least 55mm for small varieties such as
Cox's. The authorities allow 1mm tolerance either way. (If you
happen to like small apples – as many young children do – you
will have to make do with second best.) Having passed this
hurdle it will fail if the stalk is missing or badly damaged
(which might cause premature rotting) or if the shape is a little
too elongated (more than 2cm greater than normal). Surface
damage is tolerated inasmuch as skin defects must not exceed 1
sq cm, and any speckling should cover not more than 0.25 sq
cm over the entire surface of the apple.

Varieties designated as 'red' must have at least half of their
surface coloured, though 'mixed red' varieties need only have

red over one-third of their surface. Striped varieties such as Cox's are more tricky to assess, but the rules state that at least one-tenth of the surface of the apple must be speckled with red. If the apples are packed in individual 'cell trays' there should be no more than than 5mm difference in size between any of them, though this is relaxed to 10mm if they are jumbled loosely in a crate. Nowhere is the question of taste, surely the most important attribute of all, mentioned.

In order to produce apples that satisfy these requirements, conventional growers have to resort to more than forty pesticide sprays. Despite this, you have only to visit an orchard after harvest to see the colossal number of reject apples that are left on the ground to rot. Even organic growers have to resort to a certain amount of spraying if they have any hope of competing or meeting the criteria. Donald Cooper, who supplies supermarkets with organic apples from his Kent orchards, reckons to spray his trees half a dozen times a year. He uses a mixture of seaweed – which acts as a preventative – and sulphur, which attacks fungal diseases whilst leaving beneficial insects unharmed. Even so, up to half of all organic apples never leave the orchard or reach market at all. They may be slightly too small, or have too many surface markings. Clearly, these ludicrous rules lead to pesticide use and waste on a scale that is impossible to justify.

Temperate fruits

Specialist greengrocers and some wholefood shops will usually stock some organic *apples* and *pears*, although there is not much choice in the way of varieties. Most come from Holland or France. Apples are available all year round, apart from June and July. Pears have a much shorter season: Williams, Comice and Conference are only available from September to December. If you doubt the difference in flavour between conventionally and organically grown food, try an organic Golden Delicious apple.

Yellow and white-fleshed *peaches* are grown in France and Spain and are exported to Britain in June and July. White-fleshed varieties have a better flavour and are more expensive. Neither type keeps well and for this reason a lot of smaller shops avoid them. *Plums* are another summer crop with an even shorter season. They are sent from France and the US in June. You can occasionally find English grown plums, but they are not as tasty as those from France. America, along with France, also supplies the UK market with organic *cherries*. Recently, Italy has also begun to export this crop. You can buy black and white varieties, but they are expensive. American cherries have the best flavour.

Soft fruit, such as *strawberries, raspberries* and *blackcurrants* are not traded on any scale because they are too perishable and their shelf life is too short. Your best bet is to go direct to the farm or look out for shops that specialize in produce from local organic growers. The problem is that punnets are unlikely to carry any symbol of organic authenticity. A similar problem exists with *rhubarb* – either in-season or forced. However, the chances are that synthetic chemicals are unlikely to have been used on this crop.

Citrus and other tropical fruits

It may seem strange, but organically grown citrus fruits are more common in the shops than home-grown UK produce. This is mainly because of strong export drives from the countries involved: Israel, Spain and the US. You can get *oranges* and *lemons* all year round, often from supermarkets as well as from shops specializing in organic produce. Blood oranges are sent from Sicily. For a brief period either side of Christmas, there are also organic *clementines* and *satsumas* sent from France, Corsica and Spain. Over the winter and early spring, you will find Israeli grown *grapefruits*, both pink and yellow types. During the same period you can also get organic *kiwi fruit*. As they are finishing, supplies of *melons* appear. Honeydew and canteloupe types are the most popular and they have a very good flavour. Good quality *figs* from Israel are now available for most of the year.

Both Israel and the Canaries send *bananas*. Those from the Canaries are small, but have an exceptionally strong, almost overpowering flavour. Many Israeli bananas are still green when they arrive here. If you are not careful they will blacken on the outside before their flesh has ripened properly. The trick is to put them in a paper bag with a ripe banana and keep at 12-14°C until they are ready for eating. You can buy organic bananas all year round, except February and March. They are expensive, but are worth it as a special treat.

Other organic fruits in the shops include *avocados* (from October to March), *pomegranates* (Christmas time only) and *mangoes*. From July to October you can also buy black or green *grapes*. Quite a few countries supply this market, but Italian ones taste best.

Dried fruits

Wholefood shops that sell apricots, apple rings and diced pineapple cubes that have not been treated with sulphur, may also sell a selection of organic dried fruit. Quite a few lines have appeared in the UK over the past few years. Turkey is the main supplier, with whole apricots and figs. It also sends sultanas, but not raisins, which come from California.

Consumers may find difficulty in verifying the authenticity of fruit sold in shops. Much of it arrives in unlabelled crates and is distributed loose. The position should improve in the future as nationally accepted standards, backed up by EC law, begin to take effect.

VEGETABLES

What is true of fruit is also true of vegetables: cosmetic appearance comes before quality and flavour. Breeders can produce tomatoes that are perfectly red and perfectly round, with skins that do not split, but they have no flavour. Commercially grown lettuces need an extensive course of pesticide treatment to make them acceptable for the supermarket shelf. Organic growers are hard pressed to match this drive for uniformity. As a result there is a huge amount of wastage from produce that does not meet the standards demanded by buyers and wholesalers operating for the big chains. Added to this, vast quantities of organic vegetables are imported. Many of these are basic crops that could be supplied by growers in the UK if they were given support and incentives. As it is, around 70 per cent of organic vegetables come from abroad, and there are occasions when this can rise to more than 90 per cent.

Vegetables were among the first organic foods to find their way onto supermarket shelves. Safeway introduced them into a few of its stores in 1981. These days, almost all the major supermarket names have some organic vegetables in at least some of their stores. Wholefood shops are increasingly offering them in addition to their traditional cereals and other dried goods, and a number of forward-looking greengrocers are selling them alongside conventionally-grown produce.

Basic crops such as potatoes, carrots, swedes and cabbages do come from UK growers, but there are also massive imports, particularly from Holland. Other vegetables, from onions to fennel and asparagus, can appear from various countries, depending on supply and distribution. One or two enterprises – such as Somerset Organic Producers – can also offer beansprouts and alfalfa shoots.

As a rule, consumers should support their local producers and buy locally if possible. The vegetables are likely to be fresher than those that have been transported through the wholesale system. Also, local support helps to ensure that local growers stay in business.

One crop which UK producers are cultivating with increasing success is mushrooms. There are at least two well established enterprises: Barkston Heath Mushrooms in Lincolnshire and Chesswood Produce, based in Pulborough, Sussex. Both produce organically-grown brown-capped mushrooms and supply wholefood shops as well as branches of Sainsbury, Tesco, Gateway and Marks & Spencer. However, these are not always sold as 'organic' although they have the Soil Association symbol.

We would always recommend buying fresh vegetables, but it's worth noting that there is one producer of canned organic vegetables with the Soil Association symbol: Foresight Canning, based in Essex.

HERBS

For centuries, cooks, gardeners and physicians have been extolling the virtues of herbs and their usefulness as flavourings, decorative plants and medications. It's ironic that most commercial growers nowadays resort to the use of artificial chemicals to produce their crops. But there is mounting interest in organic herbs and several growers are operating very successfully in the marketplace.

John and Caroline Stevens are typical of the new breed of herb grower. Their Suffolk nursery is run as a healthy mixed environment by using soil-based compost, bonemeal and chicken manure as fertilizers, and applying some ingenious methods of pest control (anything from planting marigolds to discourage whitefly to experimenting with garlic sprays). They grow herbs for culinary use, for fragrance and for their medicinal properties. Part of their strategy is to preserve old varieties and ancient names such as alexanders, wood avens and vervain; they have also established a vast catalogue of old vegetable varieties, as well as oriental vegetables, cottage garden plants, even mixtures of grasses and wild flowers for different soils. Their seeds are available from many good shops, you can order direct from their catalogue, or visit the farm for plants.

Also in Suffolk, Caroline Holmes produces a wide range of culinary and medicinal herbs. She is also an expert on the subject and, as a member of the Herb Society and the Royal Horticultural Society, gives talks and runs special courses on all aspects of herbs. Her produce is also available direct or by mail order.

Although fresh herbs are usually the best, good quality dried herbs can be very useful. Mike Brook runs Hambleden Herbs, the country's leading grower and supplier of dried organic herbs. His range includes up to 100 different varieties, all grown to Soil Association standards, and his produce is available from wholefood shops and delicatessens around the country. You can also order direct.

Geoff Mutton's organic nursery north of Bromyard in Herefordshire is one of the best wholesale suppliers of vegetables and unusual salad crops. He also specializes in growing a range of different herbs to Soil Association standards, and supplies herb packs. Each one contains five culinary herbs cut and ready for use in the kitchen. They are individually packed in an attractive cardboard display box. The design and presentation won Geoff Mutton an award at the 1989 Royal Show.

Suffolk Herbs
Sawyers Farm, Little Cornard, nr. Sudbury, Suffolk CO10 0NY Tel: (0787) 227247

Caroline Holmes Herbs
Denham End Farm, nr. Bury St Edmunds, Suffolk IP29 5EE
Tel: (0284) 810653

Hambleden Herbs
Hambleden, Henley-on-Thames, Oxfordshire RG9 6SX
Tel: (0491) 571598

Muttons Organic Growers
Lower House Farm, Thornbury, nr. Bromyard, Hereford and
Worcester HR7 4NJ
Tel: (08854) 204

PULSES

A good range of organically grown beans, lentils and other
pulses are imported into the UK. These are usually distributed
by the large wholefood wholesalers such as Suma and Infinity
Foods, and individual shops tend to make up their own packs
for sale. As a result they don't normally have any accredited
organic symbol.

Most pulses come from the US, which exports aduki beans,
mung beans, haricot beans, green lentils, pinto beans, red
kidney beans and soya beans. Chick peas come from Turkey,
while some field beans and marrowfat peas are produced in this
country.

Tins of baked beans, made from organically grown haricot
beans (complying with the California Organic Food Act) are
sold under the Whole Earth label. The recipe contains no
added sugar and other flavourings are natural.

NUTS

Organically produced nuts are still quite difficult to find in
wholefood shops, and supplies can be spasmodic. The most
common are almonds and hazelnuts from Spain and Italy and
walnuts from California.

Organic peanuts, in the form of peanut butter, appear in
most good wholefood shops including Holland & Barrett. The
best known brand is Whole Earth, made with roasted peanuts
and sea salt. Meridian also produce a peanut butter from
peanuts that have been certified by an organization recognized
by IFOAM.

DAIRY PRODUCTS

Milk

All dairy produce begins with milk, but the quality of what we
drink has become a political issue. In 1985, the Government

attempted to ban the sale of unpasteurized 'green-top' milk. This has been given a reprieve, but for how long? Supplies of green-top are quite localized, mostly in parts of Yorkshire and other rural areas in the north of England. Recently, a more sinister issue has come to light: the use of BST (bovine somatotrophin), a hormone used to increase a cow's yield of milk.

The alternative is organic milk. Some farmers supply milk to wholefood shops in their area, but on a bigger scale, Safeway has introduced Pastures Pure Organic Milk from Unigate Dairies. This comes from farmland in the Channel Islands and carries the Soil Association symbol.

Butter

A small number of organic farms produce and sell butter, usually as a small part of their other dairy-based activities such as cheese-making. The best known, and one of the richest in flavour, comes from Rachel's Dairy in Borth, Dyfed. It is available in selected wholefood shops and delicatessens.

Yoghurt

Organic yoghurt is now quite widely available. Once again, the most well-known brand is from Rachel's Dairy in Borth, which produces both plain and fruit, in a range of eight flavours. As yet, supplies are confined to wholefood shops.

A number of supermarkets now stock organic yoghurt and yoghurt flavoured with organic fruit. The BioBest range is stocked by Safeway and Asda; Onken Bioghurt from Germany is also on the shelves at Safeway, as well as at branches of the Co-op (Leo) stores and Gateway. Live yoghurt from Busses Farm, East Grinstead, is sold by Safeway and Sainsbury.

Also look out for pots of fruit-flavoured *fromage frais* made by Onken and sold at branches of Safeway.

Cheese

Apart from salmonella, the most publicized food scare of the 1980s was listeria. The disease listeriosis is caused by *Listeria monocytogenes*, an organism that lives naturally in the soil and can get into animal feed, particularly through badly stored silage and root feeds. Most cases of listeria come from dairy produce (apart from the much less publicized – but potentially more serious – threat from 'cook-chill' foods). Back in 1983,

49 cases of listeria in the US were attributed to pasteurized milk. In 1986, the US Food & Drug Administration removed supplies of imported French Brie, because they were found to be contaminated (these were factory-made cheeses produced from pasteurized milk). But the most publicized incident was in the winter of 1987–88, when seven deaths were traced to supplies of Vacherin Mont d'Or, a pasteurized cheese made in Switzerland. Samples of unpasteurized Vacherin made at neighbouring farms were not infected.

Although it has not been clearly spelled out, there is more chance of finding listeria in pasteurized rather than unpasteurized cheeses. The campaign to outlaw unpasteurized cheese has affected many farmhouse dairies, but – ironically – cheesemongers have reported increasing interest in unpasteurized cheese since listeria made the headlines.

Most problems with listeria occur *after* pasteurization. And it seems that the crucial factors in producing good wholesome cheese free from harmful organisms are careful husbandry, hygienic milking and skilful cheesemaking. Farmhouse cheesemakers generally take more care with their craft, and their products can be trusted.

Around half a dozen organic cheeses are in general circulation. Many come from Wales, especially Dyfed, where there has been a spectacular revival in local food enterprise. The best known are Pencarreg – a buttery soft cheese made from organic milk and vegetarian rennet – and its 'hard' cousin Cardigan, both of which are distributed by Organic Farm Foods (Wales) Ltd, Lampeter. Also in Lampeter, Dougal Campbell produces Tyn-Grug – a Welsh version of Cheddar. At Castle Morris, Leon Downey makes Llangloffan cheeses, including one flavoured with chives and garlic.

Supermarkets are starting to stock some of these organic cheeses. Safeway have Pencarreg and an English cheese called Wiltshire White; Sainsbury also stock Pencarreg; Asda and branches of the Co-op (Leo stores) sell Pencarreg and Cardigan.

Several other cheeses are stocked by wholefood shops and delicatessens and are available direct from the farm. In particular, look out for Staffordshire Farm Cheese, from the Deavilles' farm, near Newcastle-under-Lyme; herb flavoured Botton Cheeses and Danbydale, produced to Biodynamic standards at the Camphill Village Trust, Danby, North

Yorkshire; goat's cheeses from Malthouse Cottage Farm, Ashington, Sussex; and Devon Dell ewes' milk cheeses from Lower Turley Farm, Cullompton, Devon.

(Details of specific producers can be found in the Directory).

MEAT

Since organic farming depends on the balance between crops and livestock, there is a great future for organic meat. As evidence about the realities of intensive livestock farming started to come to light, and as consumers became aware of exactly how most of today's meat is produced, there was bound to be a backlash. The vegetarian trend has been one sign of this. Many people have simply stopped eating meat altogether over the last ten years. Organic meat probably won't change *their* minds, but if it is widely available, others may find meat eating acceptable.

The production of additive-free meat from naturally reared livestock has been the first stage in this process. Two enterprises in particular are well known in the marketplace. The Real Meat Company was formed by Richard Guy and Gillian Metherell 'to provide meat and meat products for consumers wanting to avoid the over-use of chemicals and unacceptable welfare conditions used in intensive livestock production'. It now has a national delivery and distribution system to wholesalers and retailers for its range of pork, beef, lamb, poultry, ham and bacon. The company is based at Heytesbury in Wiltshire and now owns three retail shops at: 7 Hayes Place, Holloway, Bath BA2 4QW; 61 Chelsea Manor Street, London SW3 5RZ and 3 Nugent Terrace, St John's Wood, London NW8 9QB.

The Pure Meat Company, based in Moreton Hampstead, Devon, is a group of West Country farmers producing meat to Conservation Grade standards. Their range includes beef, pork, lamb and poultry as well as bacon, ham and up to seven kinds of sausages (made with organic brown rice instead of rusk); their butchers will also produce ready-prepared dishes, such as beef olives, to order. The business is primarily a nationwide special delivery service to the door; there are also retail shops in Moreton Hampstead and Taunton.

Organic meat is subject to stricter standards regarding

husbandry, feedstuffs and the use of medications – particularly growth promoters and antibiotics. It is also more difficult to obtain. The problem is one of supply and distribution. Most organic livestock farmers still have to sell direct from the door or from their own farm shops. The Young family, who run Kite's Nest Farm in Broadway, are perhaps the best-known organic livestock farmers in the country. Their organic beef is highly rated, but they rely on supplies to restaurants, established retail outlets and individual customers for business. There are a few organic butchers, such as Wholefood Butchers and Unique Butchers in London, and Ray Cornmell in Bolton (see entries in Directory), plus a handful of other outlets, such as Ryton Gardens, that stock organic meat, but it has yet to make a real impact on the high street. The situation is similar to organic vegetables in the mid-80s, before farmers, growers and retailers had worked out an effective system to deal with consumer demand.

However, there are signs that the situation is improving. More farmers are obtaining the Soil Association symbol for their meat, and there is also a much better distribution system. Greenway Organic Farms, based in Edinburgh, is an example. They offer a home-delivery service throughout the United Kingdom, and can supply fresh chilled organic beef and lamb produced to Soil Association standards. They also deal in French organic chickens, ducks and guinea fowl.

In January 1990, organic meat reached the supermarket. Safeway announced that it was introducing supplies of organic beef into ten of its stores in London and the south-east of England. The farmer at the centre of this experiment is Evan Owen Jones, who has 228 acres in Llanwrda, Dyfed. He now supplies the supermarket with his own meat and additional quantities from other farmers in the area. All of his produce conforms to Soil Association standards. This is a very encouraging sign and hopefully Safeway will be able to extend the scheme if there is sufficient interest and demand from consumers (as well as guaranteed supplies from the farmers).

As well as meat, there are a number of organic meat products available from farmers and butchers. Look for the bacon and ham from Ray Cornmell in Bolton, Ian Miller's haggis and black pudding (from James Field Farm in Fife), and Kite's Nest Farm beefburgers. For further details of these and other meat products, see entries in the Directory.

The Real Meat Company Ltd
East Hill Farm, Heytesbury, Warminster, Wiltshire BA12 0HR
Tel: (0985) 40436/40060

The Pure Meat Company
Coombe Court Farm, Moreton Hampstead, Devon
Tel: (0647) 40321

Kite's Nest Farm
Broadway, Hereford & Worcester WR12 7JT
Tel: (0386) 853320

Greenway Organic Farms
FREEPOST, Edinburgh, Lothian EH1 0AQ
Tel: (031) 557 8111

Evan Owen Jones
Briwnant, Plumsaint, Llanwrda, Dyfed SA19 8UT
Tel: (05585) 410

POULTRY

The publicity given to salmonella and the battery system made very little mention of similar – and even worse – problems in the broiler industry. It has been estimated that up to 60 per cent of all chicken carcasses destined for the table are infected with salmonella. And the production system itself is iniquitous.

Broilers are the result of intensive A1 selection for maximum feed conversion. They are fed up to weights of 10-12 lbs; as a result many birds cannot stand up and heart attacks are frequent due to fat pressing on the heart. They are fed on pellets or mash containing animal protein or the waste from slaughterhouses; they are routinely inoculated and fed antibiotics and growth promoters. There is little chance of them developing any flavour since they are generally slaughtered at 12 weeks. After a long, and often traumatic journey, they are killed, plucked, eviscerated, washed and wrapped up in minutes – a process guaranteed to prevent any flavour developing.

It isn't surprising that more people are demanding free-range chickens. But how different are they? At a time when the words 'free-range' can guarantee premium prices in the shops, many farmers are rearing their so-called free-range birds intensively. The chickens spend most of their lives indoors, on floor space often no bigger than a battery cage. Of course, they are allowed outside, but not for long. They may well be fed a similar diet to their caged relations, and they can be crammed in as densely as 4,000 birds per acre.

A few free-range poultry farms, such as Cracknells in Somerset, really do live up to their name, but supplies of their chickens are limited. Now the supermarkets are starting to choose their free-range birds with more care. Tesco have introduced free-range corn-fed chickens from France. These birds are the real thing. They have unrestricted access to the million acres of pine forests in the Landes, south of Bordeaux, and they are fed locally grown maize to eat. Tesco also sell free-range turkeys from the same co-operative of Landais farmers.

Most other supermarkets, such as Safeway and Waitrose, tend to sell free-range and corn-fed chickens from the firm of Moy Park.

Greenway Organic Farms, a wholesale distributor of organic meat based in Edinburgh also offer French free-range poultry, from a group of twenty or so poultry breeders in the South Vendée. Their range includes poulet noir, Barbary duck, guinea fowl and turkeys, all free-range and organic. The birds are fed a mixture of wheat, maize, barley, peas, sunflower seed cake and seaweed. They are also allowed unlimited access to the Vendéean meadows. The business is certified by the Fédération Nationale de Defense de la Culture Biologique – an organization recognized by the Soil Association.

Greenway Organic Farms
FREEPOST, Edinburgh, Lothian EH1 0AQ
Tel: (031) 557 8111

EGGS

In December 1988, Edwina Currie appeared on national television and announced to the British public that most eggs were contaminated with salmonella. Although few people realized it at the time, this was the spark that ignited a consumer revolution. Suddenly people became aware of the way in which their food was produced. They began to ask questions and, perhaps for the first time, the food industry became accountable to the people. It was front page news in all the tabloids, egg jokes were traded in pubs and the word 'salmonella' entered the popular vocabulary.

Consumers learned about the realities of the battery system, about the strain of salmonella called *Salmonella enteridis* that was passed on because of overcrowded conditions and because hens were being fed offal and dead carcasses from infected chickens. In this climate, free-range eggs seemed like the safest option. But shoppers are still confused by the different terms used to describe eggs and the way in which they are produced.

There are four main categories laid down by EC standards.

Free-range
The birds must have continuous daytime access to open-air runs, covered with vegetation and with a maximum stocking rate of 1,000 per hectare (or 450 per acre). Conditions in hen houses must follows the stipulations for the 'deep-litter system' (see below).

Semi-intensive
The birds must have continuous daytime access to open-air runs as above, but more are allowed per hectare – up to 4,000 (or 1,619 per acre). Hen house conditions should follow the 'deep litter system'.

Deep-litter
Birds are kept in hen houses at a maximum stocking rate of 7 birds per square metre of floor space. At least one-third of the floor space should be solid, covered with straw, wood shavings, sand or turf. At least one-quarter of the floor area should be used for the collection of droppings.

Barn (perchery)
This is the least reliable and vaguest category. It is a variation of the deep-litter system which uses a series of perches and feeders at different levels so that the farmer can cram in more birds – up to 25 hens per square metre.

Clearly the free-range system is the most humane, although it still allows farmers to pack as many hens as they wish into the hen houses once other conditions have been met.

The Free-Range Egg Association has its own standards which

are stricter. It also has its own registration system, independent inspectors and a 'blue triangle' logo which is issued to producers and suppliers of eggs that meet their standards.

Genuine organic eggs are much harder to find. Standards require that at least 80 per cent of the hen's feed must come from organic ingredients, in addition to the other rules about rearing conditions, the use of drugs and additives.

In the wake of the salmonella scare there has been an upsurge of interest in free-range eggs, and supply can hardly keep pace with demand. However, we are eating fewer eggs than we did ten years ago. The industry may stage lavish advertising campaigns to persuade us otherwise, but to little effect. And as the battery system comes under attack, as energy costs and the cost of pharmaceuticals rise, it seems inevitable that the industry will be forced to produce fewer eggs by a system that is more humane.

You will need to look hard for genuine organic eggs, but free-range eggs are widely available. Almost all the supermarket chains sell them, although mark-ups can be high. They are also available in most good wholefood shops across the country.

The Free-Range Egg Association
37 Tanza Road, London NW3 2UA

OILS
When buying oils look for 'cold-pressed' and 'unrefined' on the label. These not only have the best flavour and quality, but are nutritionally the best too. Vitamins and enzymes are destroyed by the high temperatures created by most pressing machinery, and the refining process also results in a loss of nutrients.

Organic oils of this type are quite common. Olive oil, sunflower oil and sesame oil are the most widely available and can be bought from most good wholefood shops. Meridian and Suma are the usual brands: Safeway sell Meridian organic olive oil.

PRESERVES, CONDIMENTS AND VINEGARS
Now that organic fruit and vegetables are widely available, more organic preserves, pickles and chutneys should start to

appear on the market. A number of jams are prepared from organic fruit. The best known is Whole Earth's Golden Plum jam, made from Claudia de Tolosa fruit grown in Spain and cooked with Alar-free apple juice and pectin from limes (which acts as a gelling agent).

Organic marmalades are produced by several manufacturers. Duerr's fine-cut and thick-cut Seville orange marmalades are some of the best. The fruit comes from groves on the Isla de Cartuja where the oranges are grown without pesticides or artificial fertilizers. Vida Sana, the Spanish organic agricultural organization, certifies the fruit and its production. Whole Earth also produces a Seville orange marmalade made with organically grown fruit, from the orchards of Señora J. Gahona near the River Guadalquivir; these, too, are verified by Vida Sana. Also look for a medium-cut Seville orange marmalade from West Country Organic Foods (who also supply honey).

Some organic growers are starting to make their own pickles and chutneys on a small scale (see entries later). In addition there is at least one widely available organic pickle: pickled beetroot slices from the Apples Co-operative, sold under the William's Favourite label. The vegetables are preserved in a mixture of organic cider vinegar and apple juice with no added salt or sugar. It is also worth looking out for chutneys made by Clare Benson in Gloucestershire and sold under the Clare's Kitchen label. From further afield, there are organically grown black olives, which are preserved in brine and sold under the Euvita label. Some wholefood/macrobiotic shops also stock heavily salted Japanese umeboshi plums, pickled radish and sauerkraut (fermented cabbage), made with organic ingredients.

We haven't heard of a genuine organic mustard, although there are plenty of excellent additive-free products on the market. But there is an organic version of tomato ketchup, produced by Whole Earth. The tomatoes are grown organically in Europe and verified by agronomists from the Swiss VSBLO and the Nature et Progrès in France. The recipe is an intriguing one, with cider vinegar, tamari, organically grown brown rice meal and kelp among the ingredients; it also has no added sugar.

The best known organic vinegar is the 'cyder' vinegar from Aspall in Suffolk, produced as a sideline by cider maker John

Chevallier-Guild at Aspall Hall (see p.122). It is widely distributed and now appears in some supermarkets as well as wholefood shops. Martlet also produce organic cider vinegar, and Boots sell a similar product under their own name. There is no organic version of malt vinegar and there doesn't need to be. However it should be possible for an organic wine grower to produce a decent organic wine vinegar as part of his operation.

Whole Earth Foods
269 Portobello Road, London W11 1LR

F. Duerr & Sons Ltd
Old Trafford, Manchester M16 9LH

West Country Organic Foods
Braeside Farm, West Horrington BA5 3EH

William's Favourite
Apples Co-operative, Valley Road, Hebden Bridge, West Yorkshire HX7 7BZ

Clare's Kitchen
Aycote Farm, Rendcomb, Gloucestershire GL7 7EP
Tel: (028583) 463/555

Aspall Cyder Vinegar
Aspall Hall, Debenham, Suffolk IP14 6PD
Tel: (0728) 860510

SOYA PRODUCTS
The soya bean is extremely versatile and can be turned into all manner of products. Organically grown soya beans can be bought from wholefood shops, but that is just the start.

Soya milk is quite widely available although questions have been raised about its high aluminium content and low levels of zinc. Granose, Provamel and So Good are the most common brands.

Soy sauce in its various forms is also available as an organic product. A few specialist wholefood retailers, such as Real Foods in Edinburgh and Clearspring Natural Grocers in

London can supply the Japanese version called 'shoyu' as well as the top-of-the-range 'tamari' (made with no added wheat or cereal).

Tofu, tempeh and miso are the three most unusual soy products. Tofu is basically 'bean curd', produced by a very elaborate process; tempeh is a South-East Asian variant which is often fermented; miso is fermented soya bean paste and is most commonly associated with Japanese cooking. A few shops and producers, such as Full of Beans in Lewes, are making these products on their premises in the UK, and various tofu-based products are distributed by wholesalers.

There is also a tofu-based mayonnaise called Soyanaise, produced under the Infinity label and available in quite a number of wholefood shops.

HONEY

Is there such a thing as 'organic' honey? The Soil Association Standards state that 'due to the difficulties in ensuring that bees forage only on organic crops, it has been decided that the Symbol will not be licensed for honey producers in the UK at the present time. However, certain parts of the world may be isolated enough from conventional food production systems for the provision to be guaranteed.'

A bee will usually travel no more than three miles from the hive. During its flight it will be attracted to any flowers in bloom, some of which may have been sprayed with pesticides. Since the pesticide in question is likely to have been an insecticide, and given that a bee is an insect, the visit will probably prove fatal. Even so, it is possible for a bee to receive a less than fatal dose and still be capable of delivering contaminated nectar to the hive.

West Country Honey Farms market a natural organic honey sold in branches of Safeway and Holland & Barrett and by many independent retailers. There are two types: clear and set. Their label states: 'All pure unprocessed honey is organic in the true sense of the word as it is a pure naturally produced food.' They go on to stress the importance of their manufacturing process which involves cold-pressing instead of the usual high temperature process of most honey manufacturers. Their honey is in fact blended from 'supplies from regions and flora where artificial fertilizers and agricultural chemicals are not normally used.' There is a proviso, however, 'due to the free foraging nature of the honey bee we can make no claim regarding each flower visited.'

New Zealand Natural Food Co. make a raw organic honeydew which comes from bees working in the beech forests of the southern mountains of New Zealand. The honey is very dark and runny and simply delicious. In such a remote wilderness, the company's claim that the bees will never come into contact with agrochemicals is almost certainly true.

West Country Honey Farms Ltd
Braeside Farm, West Horrington, BA5 3EH

New Zealand Natural Food Co. Ltd
London N10 3HW

JUICES

For years, parents thought that apple juice was one of the healthiest drinks to give a child. Revelations about the pesticide Alar in 1989 changed all that. Although this substance has been withdrawn by the maunfacturing company Uniroyal, it hasn't yet been banned by the Government. Although Alar residues are often present in apples themselves, it is at its most toxic when the fruit is processed or turned into juice.

Organic apple juice is the safe alternative. The best known brand is Aspall, which has been produced in Suffolk for many years as a sideline to John Chevallier-Guild's cider making enterprise. All Aspall products are made from organically grown, unsprayed fruit, and they have the Soil Association symbol. Peake's, based near Colchester, have also been making apple juice (and other fruit juices) under the Copella brand name for a long while. Devora and Bill Peake set aside an area of their land for organic husbandry and this is now paying dividends. They can now produce an organic apple juice without sweeteners, preservatives or added water. It is pressed on the farm and carries both the Soil Association and Organic Farmers & Growers symbols.

Fruit and vegetable juices are also produced by a number of European companies who distribute in the UK. Three names, in particular, appear regularly on the shelves: Rabenhorst, Eden and Biotta. The Rabenhorst range includes Rabenhorst Red (a grape juice made from the first pressings of three varieties); Cherry Nectar produced from Morello cherries and three vegetable juices – carrot, beetroot and tomato. Eden also produce three organic vegetable juices – carrot, beetroot and celery, as well as a mixed juice. They carry the Demeter symbol for biodynamic cultivation. Organic juices from the other company, Biotta, include orange, grapefruit, carrot and beetroot, as well as a mixed vegetable cocktail. In addition there is a biodynamically-produced apple juice from the Dutch company Bionova, distributed by Vinceremos Wines.

Organic red and white grape juices are also produced by French wine makers. Guy Bossard has a light white juice made from 60 per cent Muscadet grapes and 40 per cent Gros Plant; Pierre Arnaud does a red juice, made from southern Rhône grapes. These are also distributed by Vinceremos Wines. Some supermarkets, in particular Safeway and Asda, are beginning to stock organic juices, but at the moment the best choice is to be found in good wholefood shops and delicatessens across the country.

Aspall Apple Juice
Aspall Hall, Debenham, nr. Stowmarket, Suffolk IP14 6PD
Tel: (0728) 860510

Peake's Organic Foods
Hill Farm, Boxford, Suffolk CO6 5NY
Tel: (0787) 210348

Haus Rabenhorst
Importer: John Powell Wines
Harding Way, St Ives, Cambridgeshire PE17 4WR

Eden-Waren
Distributor: Leisure Drinks
Castle Donington, Derbyshire

TEA AND COFFEE
Some supermarkets claim that they test samples of tea for pesticide residues, but consumers should be pleased to learn that organic tea is now available in the UK. It comes from a

single estate 7,000 feet up on the slopes of the Livingstonia Mountains of Tanzania. No artificial fertilizers or pesticides are used, and the bushes are allowed to develop slowly to produce tea of a much fuller flavour than usual. Organic tea is marketed by The London Herb and Spice Company under the Natureland brand name. It comes in packets of 40 sachets and is sold throughout the UK in most supermarkets such as Tesco, Sainsbury and Waitrose, in branches of Holland & Barrett and many independent wholefood shops.

Less common are macrobiotic teas from Japan. A few specialist shops sell organic Kukicha Bancha Twig tea loose or in bags, as well as organic green tea.

Organic herb teas are sold under the Pompadour label and are mainly distributed by Suma Wholefoods to shops around the country. At present there are five flavours: peppermint, fennel, chamomile, limeflower and rosehip.

Organically grown coffee is available from a few shops in various parts of the country. The most common is Café Organico; there is also Yannoh Grain Coffee for those who want a macrobiotic brew. These are worth knowing about, although they may not impress coffee connoisseurs.

Natureland Teas
The London Herb and Spice Co. Ltd, 18 Selsdon Road, South Croydon, CR2 6PA

BABY FOODS

The Government Report of the Working Party on Pesticide Residues, 1985-88 recommended that 'efforts be made to reduce residue levels in infant foods as much as possible.' Commenting on this, Heather Paine of the manufacturers' Infant and Dietetic Food Association stated that 'The levels of pesticide in commercially prepared baby foods are the lowest quoted in the report and are well within maximum residue levels set by the Government ... At the present time organically produced crops are not a viable alternative for the manufacture of infant foods.' And three years earlier, in response to HJ Heinz USA requiring its suppliers to ban the use of twelve common pesticides, the National Farmers Union announced 'We have never heard of any specific problems with residues affecting babies.' Thankfully, there is a way out of this uncertainty and confusion. A good selection of organic babyfoods has appeared on the market, although they are not always easy to find. Wholefood shops, rather than supermarkets, are the places to look for bottled purées, ground cereals and fruit juices.

Two brands of pre-cooked, ready-to-use bottled baby food are readily available: Granose and Johanus. Both come from West Germany. Of the two, Granose (with eight varieties such as carrots with apples and vegetables with wholewheat noodles) is the more widely distributed. The Johanus brand carries the Demeter biodynamic seal of approval and offers a similar choice ranging from mixed vegetable purée to apple, oats and blueberry. No salt, sugar or preservatives are added to any of the products. Johanus also make three types of 'junior' babyfoods: mixed vegetables and barley, vegetables with noodles, and root vegetables with wheatflakes.

Thursday Cottage, best known for their high quality jams and marmalades, also market a selection of finely ground organic cereals in 'baby' size 4oz packets. They are sold under the Thursday's Child label and are intended for babies aged 4 months or over. There are five varieties: millet, rice, oats, barley and a mixed cereal containing barley, oats and soya.

Holle is another company manufacturing cereal-based foods for infants. They have a starter babyfood that can be mixed with milk and eaten from a spoon or thinned and put into a feeding bottle. For older children, there is a follow-on food. Babies who find difficulty in taking wheat and may be showing first signs of gluten allergy can be tried on Holle's rice food. There is also an organic rusk to help with teething. The company also makes a mildly sweet pure cane sugar which can be used for sweetening cereal dinners. This may discourage the 'sweet tooth' that so many babies develop as a result of taking sugar early in their lives.

When it comes to organic drinks, the choice is more limited. Johanus make three juices for babies: carrot; carrot with apple and honey; and a mixed fruit drink with honey. For older children, Voelkel – another German company – sells a junior juice made from a mixture of six fruits and carrots selected to provide a good balance of vitamins and minerals.

Granose Foods Ltd
Stanborough Park, Watford, Hertfordshire WD2 6JR

Caradoc Ltd
121 Bath Road, Worcester, Hereford and Worcester WR5 3AF
Tel: (0905) 353130
(distributors of Johanus, Holle and other biodynamic foods)

Thursday Cottage
Spaxton, Bridgwater, Somerset TA5 1DD
Tel: (0278) 67330

Biodynamic Supplies Ltd
Woodman Lane, Clent, nr. Stourbridge, West Midlands
Tel: (0562) 886858
(distributors of Voelkel fruit juices; available by mail order)

CRISPS AND SNACKS

There is one brand of organic potato crisps on the market, sold under the name of Hedgehog. The potatoes are grown with organically based fertilizers (although the label says nothing about the use of pesticides); they are unpeeled and thickly sliced. The crisps have a variety of natural flavours: sea salt and cider vinegar; vegetarian cheese and tomato; yoghurt and cucumber to name but three. A proportion of the profits from sales go to the British Hedgehog Preservation Society. Hedgehog crisps are widely available in wholefood shops and branches of Holland & Barrett, as well as Asda, Safeway and Sainsbury supermarkets.

Hedgehog Foods Ltd
Welshpool, Powys SY21 7DF

MISCELLANEOUS PROCESSED FOODS

While we would always recommend cooking food fresh as required, convenience food does have its uses. Frozen wholefood meals, made with organic ingredients, can be good. The best supplier is the firm Organic & Natural, based in Cheltenham. Their range takes in about 20 vegetarian and vegan dishes, from lentil dhal with organic rice to aubergine moussaka; they also produce savoury crêpes and wholewheat pizzas.

A number of wholefood shops and delicatessens also

produce ready-made meals. The following are good outlets.

Brewer's Basic, Leominster, Hereford and Worcester
Cook's Delight, Berkhamsted, Hertfordshire
Hockeys – Naturally, Fordingbridge, Hampshire
Wye Organic Foods, Stow-on-the-Wold, Gloucestershire

Organic & Natural
317 High Street, Cheltenham, Gloucestershire GL50 3HW
Tel: (0242) 241070

Chapter 8

THE ORGANIC DRINKER

WINE, CIDER AND BEER

WINE

Growing vines, harvesting the fruit and transforming the grapes into wine sounds like a perfectly natural process. But is the end result a glass of your favourite claret or a cocktail of chemicals? You certainly won't find out by reading the label, because manufacturers are not required to list ingredients. In the US it is obligatory to print the words 'contains sulphites' and many Australian wines have 'contains preservative E220' (the E number for sulphur dioxide) on their labels. But this isn't the case for European wines.

Many commercially produced wines – especially the bulk, high volume, cheaper varieties – are as 'processed as peas'. The drinks industry is big business and the wine department is in the thick of it. This doesn't mean that all the wine we drink is laced with diethylene glycol (the chemical also found in anti-freeze, which was discovered in some Austrian wines a few years ago); or worse, methyl alcohol, which appeared in some cheap Italian wines in 1986 resulting in several deaths. Nor does it mean that your favourite Italian white is made from 'water, sugar, ox blood, and the sludge from banana boats' as was alleged in the unresolved case that rocked the Italian wine trade in the 1960s.

However, we should be concerned. And we should ask questions. Just what chemicals are permitted in the vineyard and the winery? Are they harmful or not? And, if they end up in the wine we drink, why isn't the information listed on the label?

Additives in wine

Vineyard practices vary enormously from country to country, and from region to region. Synthetic chemicals are commonly used in fertilizers and in pesticides of various kinds – to deal with insects, mould and specific diseases that affect the vines. Where these chemicals are 'systemic' (i.e. they are taken into the internal system of the plant itself) they can all too easily appear in the grapes – and hence in the wine we drink.

Once the grapes have been picked and are being turned into wine, various permitted additives can be introduced. The most common and well-known is sulphur dioxide – the winemaker's standard sterilizing and preserving agent. It is very rare for anyone to make wine without it these days, for fear that the wine will oxidize and turn to vinegar. High levels of sulphur are potentially dangerous to health and produce unpleasant effects. If you ever drink a wine that has a slightly 'stinky' smell and a distinctly metallic aftertaste, it has too much sulphur in it. This is frequently noticeable in cheap red wines, but more often in bottom-price dry and sweet whites. More important, excessive sulphur – along with other chemical additives – is often the chief culprit and the main cause of hangovers, headaches and stomach complaints; some people, notably asthmatics, can also suffer allergic reactions.

If sulphur dioxide in small quantities is virtually unavoidable, what about calcium carbonate, potassium tartrate or potassium bicarbonate added to counteract an overly acidic wine? Or citric acid, ascorbic acid or potassium sorbate used to give acidity to a rather flabby product? While none of these additives is known to be harmful, they do add to the artificiality of the flavour. Labelling and legislation are vital, because substances can easily slip through the net; one potentially hazardous chemical – potassium ferrocyanide (a synthetic anti-caking agent) is banned in the US, but legal in Europe. The London Food Commission lists numerous potentially harmful chemicals which can legally be used in the production of wine in the EC: it claims that insecticides sprayed in vineyards could contain up to 49 substances that might cause cancer and 61 that might lead to birth defects.

Why is organic wine different?

Organic winemakers are required to use natural techniques.

Their vines are grown without the use of pesticides or artificial fertilizers, and their wine is made without additives. The only exceptions to this rule are the strictly limited use of sulphur dioxide, and of Bordeaux mixture (a lime and copper sulphate spray used on the vines to prevent mould and disease). It is also encouraging that organic winemakers often use fewer applications of Bordeaux mixture and sulphur dioxide than the strict organic regulations permit. For example, Pierre Frick, producer of really top-notch organic wines in Alsace, is legally allowed to add 225 milligrammes of sulphur dioxide per litre of wine; under the organic regulations, he could add only 100 mg/litre. In practice, he will only use 50–80mg/litre, depending on the vintage.

In the vineyard, growers shun chemicals. Fertilizers are natural – animal manure or powdered minerals. Weeding is either done by hand or machine, not chemical spray. Diseases can be counteracted with Bordeaux mixture or herbal or mineral sprays; but in any case they are generally less of a problem for organic growers because the vines are naturally healthier, stronger and more resistant to diseases. The philosophy is one of prevention rather than cure.

Organic wine: standards and symbols

Two of the biggest issues surrounding organic wine are those of recognition – how can you tell if it is really organic; and guarantee – how do you know it is really what it claims to be? Most good organic winemakers belong to an independent association which stipulates the 'do's and don'ts' of organic production, and also checks that growers are adhering to the regulations. Producers belonging to such a certifying body can put the logo of the organization on their wine labels as an identifying mark. Unfortunately there isn't yet a single European organic standard, nor a single European logo. In fact, France – the largest supplier of organic wines – boasts no less than eleven different standards organizations, all with different logos. The three biggest and most frequently seen on French wine labels in the UK are *Nature et Progrès*, *Terre et Vie*, and *Unia*.

The problem of identifying organic wines is further complicated by the existence of 'independent' organic producers – people who, for various reasons, refuse to join an organic certifying organization, even if they are making genuinely organic wines. At present their labels may carry the key word *biologique* (French for organic), but this is soon to be phased out by the French government. Only producers who are members of approved organic organizations will be able to use the word *biologique*. The government has also introduced its own organic standard under the name *Agriculture Biologique* in the hope that it will become the universally recognized symbol. At present this logo cannot be used on processed products (including wine), but the future beckons.

To be sure of an organic wine, stick with those that have an independent guarantee and logo. If there's nothing on the bottle, but the retailer tells you that the wine is organic, be sceptical.

Taste and cost

But do organic wines taste different? Are they better? The truth is that organic wines are not immediately identifiable by their taste – though many professionals say that they are generally fresher, fruitier and more individual in character. The point is that organic wines don't need to taste *better* – simply as good as those made conventionally. After all, if the same quality can be achieved without using a host of chemical crutches, why use them in the first place?

Most wine writers and experts now acknowledge that organic wine has come of age and that many of its best vintages can compete on equal terms with their non-organic counterparts. Business is booming and The Henry Doubleday Research Association now organizes the National Organic Wine Fair at Ryton Gardens – an annual showcase for growers, distributors and merchants, which also provides members of the public with an opportunity to sample the range of wines now available. The 1989 event, sponsored by Safeway, attracted more than 2,000 visitors, and it seems set to continue.

Organic wines are often more expensive than their chemical counterparts, but if they do cost more, it is only by about 10 per cent. It is important to compare like with like. For instance, a good quality domaine or château bottled Muscadet de Sèvre et Maine Sur Lie (organic or not) is likely to cost £4.50-£5 from most independent wine merchants in the UK. However, a basic non-vintage Muscadet in a supermarket may cost as little as £2.25. But the two wines are as different as chalk and cheese.

Forty recommended organic wines
This selection covers the major organic wine-producing countries and the range of styles available. At present these wines are not available from supermarkets or off-licence chains, but can be purchased from independent retailers and/or mail order companies (see p.118–120).

In addition to this list, several very good wines are stocked by supermarkets, especially the Vignoble de la Jasse Côtes du Rhône, Château de Prade Bordeaux Supérior, and Muscadet de Sèvre et Maine from Guy Bossard, all of which represent terrific value and are of consistently excellent quality from vintage to vintage.

Explanation of symbols
= drink now
= can be drunk now, but will improve if kept for several years
VN = vegan wine (i.e. no animal products in the winemaking process; this means principally no isinglass or egg white for fining). All wines are believed to be vegetarian.

Standards and control organizations
The organization whose standards the wine maker adheres to is indicated by the following:

NP = Nature et Progrès
FESA = Fédération Européene des Syndicats d'Agrobiologistes
UNIA = Union Nationale Interprofessionelle de l'Agrobiologie
BIO = Bioplamac
DEM = Demeter (Biodynamic Method)
DYN = Dynorga (Biodynamic)
FNAB = Fédération Nationale d'Agriculture Biologique
VS = Vida Sana
SES = Suolo e Salute
AN = Anog (Arbeitsgemeinschaft für Naturnahen Obst-, Gemuse-, und Feldfruchtanbeu)
SEC = Stichting Ekomerk Controle (and Biokultura)
BG = Bio-Grow (New Zealand Biological Producers Council)

CCOF = California Certified Organic Farmers
NASAA = National Association for Sustainable Agriculture, Australia
IND = Independent Organic

FRANCE

WHITE WINES

Muscadet de Sèvre et Maine Hermine d'Or, Guy Bossard, AC, 1987
▪▪▪ FESA VN
A specially selected cuvée awarded the prestigious Hermine d'Or, indicating that it is one of the very best Muscadets in the region. Dry and elegant.

Domaine de Grand Loup, AOC Blayais, Didier Eymard, 1988
▪ FESA
From the Blaye district of Bordeaux, a very quaffable wine for everyday drinking. Soft, fruity character from the Ugin Blanc grapes. Good value.

Chardonnay, Vin de Pays de l'Aude, 1988
▪ UNIA
A real find. The current popularity of the Chardonnay grape shows up well in this good value wine. Dry and well-balanced; elegant, fresh and friendly on the palate, with a nice finish.

Château Balluemondon, Bordeaux AC, 1988
▪ FESA VN
Dry, with a full and complex flavour. Guy Ballue's wine is predominantly Semillon with some Sauvignon and a small amount of Muscadelle. Excellent value.

Châteauneuf du Pape, Pierre André, AC, 1988
▪▪▪ FESA VN
Not over-oaked, fabulous golden colour, rounded, good length with fresh flowery flavour. From the Rhône's Bourboulenc, Roussane and Grenache grapes. Silver Medal winner, Macon 1989. Exquisite.

Château Canet Entre Deux Mers, AC, 1988
IND

A rich bouquet of succulent pears leads on to a deliciously fresh, vivid mouthful. A dry, light and easy wine of great appeal ready for immediate drinking.

Château le Barradis Monbazillac, AC, 1982
NP

Similar to a Sauternes, predominantly Semillon with a little Muscadelle, this is a rich dessert wine of real quality. Beautifully sweet, not at all cloying, the wine is aged for two years before bottling and has a lovely yellow hue. The exceptional 1986 vintage, also available, promises to be as good. Can also be drunk chilled as an aperitif.

Gewürztraminer AC 1988, Pierre Frick, Alsace
DEM VN

The best known quality grape from Alsace, M. Frick's Gewürztraminer is classic and distinctive; spicy and aromatic on the nose, full and tangy on the palate with a powerful finish. Top quality.

RED WINES

Jougla Vin de Table
UNIA

A very good value, full-bodied southern French red. Good fruit and body, just what you need for everyday drinking.

Domaine de Clairac Joubio, Vin de Pays de l'Herault
UNIA

Aged for at least eighteen months in the impressive large old oak casks at the Domaine, this is a surprisingly smooth and full flavoured wine. From Carignan, Cinsault, Grenache and Syrah grapes. Good value.

Domaine de Clairac Syrah, Vin de Pays de l'Herault 1987
UNIA

Fresh, intense Syrah fruit; strong, rich and dark. The wine has a very full bouquet – almost reminiscent of an Australian Shiraz in the forcefulness of its flavour.

Château la Chapelle Maillard, Bordeaux AC 1987
NP VN

Jean-Luc Devert's excellent, rich wine is ready for drinking now. Packed with fruit, good body, smooth flavour and good length. Merlot, Cabernet Franc and Cabernet Sauvignon grapes. Further proof that 1987 was not a uniformly poor year in Bordeaux.

Château Renaissance Bordeaux AC 1988
NP VN

A fine, medium-bodied claret made from Merlot and Cabernet grapes in the St Emilion region. Nice fresh fruit with some tannin allows drinking now and some improvement with keeping.

Château Jacques Blanc St Emilion Grand Cru 1986
NP

A cuvée of exceptional quality; the wine will open up with a few years' storage. Rich, meaty flavour.

Cave la Vigneronne, Villedieu du Rhône AC 1988
NP

A medium bodied Côtes du Rhône with a spicy aroma, light and fruity on the palate. Juicy and succulent, a wine made for early drinking. Bags of character.

Crozes-Hermitage, Albert Begot, AC, 1985
FESA

100 per cent Syrah grape, a big, rich, powerful wine with lots of finesse. A nice combination of depth of character and ease of drinking.

Châteauneuf du Pape, Pierre André, AC, 1986
FESA

From selected old vines, oak-aged, well-rounded, full and rich. A top quality producer of an exquisite wine. It is bottled after clarifying without filtration, so a slight natural deposit may appear with ageing.

Domaine de Jas D'Esclans Cru Classé, Côtes de Provence, AC, 1985
IND

Made from traditional Provençal grapes and aged for three

years in large oak barrels, this wine has a lovely deep red colour
and rich, weighty body. From one of the 23 best (cru classé)
estates.

**Domaine Richeaume, Cuvée Tradition, Côtes de Provence,
AC, 1987**
📖 FESA
Grenache, Cinsault and Carignan grapes enhanced with some
Cabernet Sauvignon produce a superb, rich, well-structured
wine. Big jammy fruit, good length.

**Domaine Richeaume Cabernet Sauvignon, Côtes de Provence,
AC, 1987**
📖 FESA
A truly remarkable wine, supremely rich and well-rounded;
long lingering flavour. Oak-aged. Exquisite.

Bourgogne Rouge Hautes Côtes de Nuits, A.Verdet, AC, 1986
📖 FNAB
Alain Verdet is renowned as one of France's leading organic
wine makers and this wine enhances his reputation. Classic
Pinot Noir, intense ripe fruit. Excellent value Burgundy.

SPARKLING WINES

Clairette de Die, Achard-Vincent
NP VN
Jean-Pierre Achard-Vincent makes excellent sparkling wines
from Muscat and Clairette grapes in the Drome Valley to the
east of the Rhône. The best are a fine Brut Méthode
Champenoise from the Clairette grape, and a succulent, richly
textured 'Tradition' from 80 per cent Muscat and 20 per cent
Clairette. The Tradition is fermented once and is only 7 to 8
per cent alcohol.

Champagne Brut, Cuvée Reserve, Jose Ardinat
NP VN
From the first pressing of the grapes, an excellent wine made
from Pinot Meunier and Pinot Noir grapes only (no
Chardonnay). Described by Robert Joseph of *Wine Magazine*
as 'Richly nutty and mature tasting, and would suit anyone
who – like me – enjoys old-fashioned fizz.'

LOW ALCOHOL

Petillant de Raisin, Domaine de Matens Gaillac
NP VN

From the Manzac grape, naturally sweet and sparkling, less than 3 degrees alcohol. Lovely grapey flavour and ideal if you want to avoid too much intoxication.

ITALY

Tenuta San Vito Chianti DOCG Roberto Drighi, 1988
SES VN

A bright ruby-red colour, medium body, fresh and fruity with plenty of zest. A delightful well-balanced wine from Sangiovese, Canaiolo and Trebbiano grapes. The wine is stored in oak casks prior to bottling. Top quality.

Tenuta San Vito, Verdiglio, Roberto Drighi, 1988
SES VN

Made from Verdicchio grapes, this wine has the colour of dark straw and the flavour is correspondingly full-bodied and strong. Dry and well integrated, complex and highly individual.

SPAIN

Biovin Valdepenas DO, 1988
VS VN

A typical medium bodied wine from La Mancha, dry, warm and fruity. The strong, almost rubbery, bouquet of the Cencibel grape is not dissimilar to that of the Syrah in southern France.

GERMANY

Bacchus Kabinett, Flonheimer Klostergarten, 1987
AN VN

From Dietmar Werner in the Rhine Valley, this is a medium white where the natural acidity of the Bacchus grape nicely balances the natural sugars in the wine. Fresh, clean and ripe; certain to win over lovers of dry French wines!

HUNGARY
SEC VN

The three Hungarian wines available in the UK come from the Szekszardi region and are included here for their value for money and general interest. The white – from the Leanyka grape – can lack acidity, but it is a friendly and easy-to-drink wine, almost medium dry with a strong flavour.

Of the two red wines, the Kekfrankos grape makes a lovely light red that could pass for a generic Beaujolais any day – the bouquet and flavour are very similar. The other red is from the Zweigelt grape and is fuller, richer and more earthy. It has a good jammy bouquet and a soft ripe flavour.

These wines are worth sampling: ask for them by their grape types. All are suitable for immediate drinking, and they are guaranteed organic according to the standards of a Dutch organization called Stichting Ekomerk Controle, along with the Hungarian Biokultura GT.

AUSTRALIA

Crouchen, Botobolar, 1988 (White)
NASAA

A little-known grape in the UK, the Crouchen is well suited to the cool vineyards of Mudgee. Pale colour, a hint of tropical fruit in the bouquet, and a full tangy flavour.

St Gilbert, Botobolar, 1986 (Red)
NASAA

Oak-aged for at least two years, this is a big punchy wine from a blend of Shiraz and Cabernet Sauvignon grapes. A real mouthful, dark red colour and rich peppery nose. Bronze Medal Winner in the International Wine Challenge 1988. Excellent.

NEW ZEALAND

All white, the wines of James and Annie Milton's small

vineyard on the east coast of North Island are very fine. Limited production is matched by top quality. Biodynamic.

Riesling, 1988
BG VN

Dry, but with strength of body, this is strongly typical of the grape type but in a very special New Zealand style. Much fuller flavour than most European Riesling, excellent weight and length.

Chenin Blanc, 1988
BG VN

Deeply coloured with complex voluptuous flavours. Quite unlike French wines from the same grape, where Chenin Blanc can be unacceptably dry and tart, this is dry, but mellow, beautifully balanced and rich.

Chardonnay, 1988
BG VN

Barrel-fermented like the Chenin Blanc, the honeyed, almost creamy flavour of the grape is well brought out while maintaining the balance with some acidity. Excellent.

USA

Zinfandel, Frey Vineyards, 1986
CCOF VN

A fabulous red wine, strong, dark, powerful flavour with just the right amount of tannin. Drink now or keep to advantage.

Cabernet Sauvignon, Frey Vineyards, 1985
CCOF VN

Oak-aged, a big Cabernet Sauvignon wine. Smooth, intricate and well-structured; its character will continue to develop for some time. One to remember.

WHERE TO BUY

RETAILERS
A large number of independent retailers now sell organic wines

and spirits – too many to list here and too changeable to remain reliably up to date. In restaurants and hotels, wine merchants and wholefood shops, organic wines are beginning to make their mark. Ask the companies listed under Wholesalers and Producers (p.118–120) to tell you whom they supply – you need to seek out the independents for an extensive range. Two of the very best are Ryton Gardens (run by The Henry Doubleday Research Association) at Ryton-on-Dunsmore, near Coventry, and Cook's Delight, Berkhamsted. Several wine merchants also stock some organic wines: Augustus Barnett (larger stores), Thresher, Wine Rack, Berkeley Wines and Oddbins.

The following supermarket chains told us that they sell a selection of organic wines. The wines of the enormous Listel company are included as independent organic products although the precise nature of their production methods is not absolutely clear at present. Vintages and availability are correct at the time of going to press.

Asda (all stores)
Muscadet de Sèvre et Maine sur Lie, Guy Bossard, AC, 1988
FESA VN
Organic Claret, Château Vieux Georget Bordeaux, AC, 1988
UNIA

Co-op (selected Leo stores only)
Blanc de Blancs, Guy Bossard
FESA VN
Château Le Barradis Bergerac Sauvignon
NP
Chianti Putto, Tenuta San Vito DOCG, 1988
SES VN
Vignoble de La Jasse Côtes du Rhône, AC, 1988
NP VN

Safeway (all stores)
Petillant de Listel
IND
Domaine Anthea, Cepage Merlot, Vin de Pays d'Oc
UNIA
Château Tour de Beaupoil Bordeaux AC
FESA

Château de Caraguilhes, Corbières AC
●— UNIA

Sainsbury
Domaine Coursay-Village, Muscadet de Sèvre et Maine Sur
Lie
▌ IND VN
Domaine St Apollinaire Côtes du Rhône, 1987
●— DYN

Tesco (selected larger stores)
Château de Caraguilhes, Corbières, 1983
●— UNIA
▌ Muscadet de Sèvre et Maine Sur Lie, Guy Bossard, 1988
▌ FESA VN
▌ Petillant de Listel Raisin (2.8 per cent vol)
▌ IND
▌ Petillant de Listel Pêche (4 per cent vol)
▌ IND
▌ Petillant de Listel Framboise (4 per cent vol)
▌ IND
Orfeno dell'Uccellina, Italy
Redola dell'Uccellina, Italy

Waitrose (all stores)
Château de Prade Bordeaux Supérior, 1986
●— BIO
▌ Gros Plant du Pays Nantais Sur Lie, 1988
▌ FESA VN

WHOLESALERS AND PRODUCERS
The following companies are the main specialist importers and
distributors of organic wines. Most offer wines for sale by the
case (12 bottles which can be mixed) by mail order;
alternatively they should be able to tell you of retailers they
supply near to your home where you can purchase organic
wines by the bottle.

Haughton Fine Wines
Row's Ground, Chorley Green Lane, Chorley, Nantwich,
Cheshire CW5 8JR
Tel: (0270) 74537

HDRA (Sales) Ltd, Ryton Gardens
National Centre for Organic Gardening, Ryton-on-Dunsmore,
Coventry CV8 3LG
Tel: (0203) 303517

Organics
290 Fulham Road, London SW6 6HP
Tel: (071) 381 9924

The Organic Wine Company
PO Box 81, High Wycombe, Buckinghamshire HP13 5QN
Tel: (0494) 446557

Real Foods
14 Ashley Place, Edinburgh, Lothian EH6 5PX
Tel: (031) 554 4321

Rodgers Fine Wines
37 Ben Bank Road, Silkstone Common, Barnsley, South
Yorkshire S75 4PE
Tel: (0226) 790794

Vinature
16 Cotton Lane, Moseley, Birmingham, West Midlands B13
9SA
Tel: (021) 449 1781/7472 (24 hrs)

Vinceremos Wines
Unit 10, Ashley Industrial Estate, Wakefield Road, Ossett,
West Yorkshire WF5 9JD
Tel: (0924) 276393 (24 hrs)

Vintage Roots
25 Manchester Road, Reading, Berkshire RG1 3QE
Tel: (0734) 662569 (24 hrs)

West Heath Wines
West Heath, Pirbright, Surrey GU24 0QE
Tel: (04867) 6464 (24 hrs)

In addition, the following are making commercial quantities of
organic wine in the UK:

Avalon Vineyard
The Drove, East Pennard, Shepton Mallett, Somerset BA4
6UA
Tel: (0749) 86393

Sedlescombe Vineyard
Robertsbridge, East Sussex TN32 5SA
Tel: (0580) 83715

APPLE WINE

Sometimes called cider wine, this is a unique beverage. It has
the smoothness and body of a robust wine, with the crisp,
refreshing taste of cider. Dr Howard Tripp produces it as a
sideline at the Avalon Vineyard in Somerset, using Bramley
apples.

SAKÉ

Japan's most famous drink, saké (rice wine) is made
commercially in huge quantities using white rice as its starting
material. However, there is one producer making it from
organic brown rice. Sasanoi Gyozo is a third-generation
organic wine-producing family based in South Island. They
ferment the rice for two months using a 'koji' (a seed which
acts as the starter yeast). No sulphur is used in the process;
instead the saké is sterilized by passing it through a small tube
and steaming it (rather like pasteurization).

Three grades of saké are available with increasing alcohol
content, and they should be drunk warm. Supplies are
spasmodic, but a few independents stock it. The best bets are
shops with a macrobiotic bias, such as Clearspring Natural
Grocers in London and Cook's Delight in Berkhamsted; Real
Foods in Edinburgh and Vinceremos Wines also have
occasional supplies.

COGNAC

Organic spirits and liqueurs have yet to appear on the market
in a big way, but supplies of organic cognac are now available
in the UK from Vinceremos Wines and a few independent
retailers, including Ryton Gardens. The front runner is from

Maison l'Heraud, one of the few organic and single vineyard cognac estates. The produce is of exceptionally high quality. Look for the Speciale Trois Etoiles (3 years old) and the 5-year-old VSOP. Both are 40 per cent alcohol.

Maison L'Heraud also produces two Pineaux de Charentes. These are not strictly cognac but consist of unfermented grape juice blended with cognac. They are served in France as an aperitif and have a superb bouquet. Both the Blanc and Rosé are 8 years old and 17 per cent alcohol.

Other Pineaux de Charentes and cognacs are produced by Jacques and Dany Blanchard, and Georges and Guy Pinard, both in Charente.

CIDER AND PERRY

Cider began as Celtic firewater, but by the seventeenth century it was an elegant brew sipped like wine. More recently its traditional image has been of rough 'scrumpy' swigged by West Country farm workers. But in the 1960s, things began to change. The large cider makers, such as Bulmers and Taunton, turned their attention to producing a drink that was fashionable, appealing and completely standardized. Like their colleagues in the brewing industry, they were convinced that 'keg' was the answer. They began to filter, pasteurize and carbonate their brews; they added preservatives, enzymes, artificial colourings and sweeteners, and packed the stuff into pressurized metal 'kegs' so that it would keep almost indefinitely.

As it turned out, traditional cider was waiting for a well-timed revival. Since 1973, CAMRA (the Campaign for Real Ale) has been enormously successful in changing public tastes and the attitudes of the brewers. In the wake of the 'real ale' movement, traditional cider has found a new lease on life. The same is true of perry, cider's potent pear-based relative, which was all but extinct in the 1970s.

But what exactly is 'traditional cider'? In 1989, CAMRA formed APPLE (The Apple and Pear Produce Liaison Executive) – its national sub-committee for the promotion of traditional cider and perry, and issued its own set of guidelines.

Category 'A' Traditional Cider and Perry must:
• Not be pasteurized

- Not be filtered
- Not receive enzyme treatment
- Not contain preservatives
- Not have the natural yeast replaced by a cultured yeast
- Not have a nitrogen source added unless essential to start fermentation
- Only contain sweeteners if it is labelled 'medium' or 'sweet' and only safe ones to be used
- Not contain apple concentrate
- Not contain extraneous carbon dioxide

There is also a Category 'B' 'Not to be actively discouraged', which is less rigid and much less reliable. It simply states that draught cider or perry 'should not be made entirely from concentrate' and 'must not contain extraneous carbon dioxide'. The 'Big Three' cider producers make small amounts of this kind of cider, which is distributed mainly in the traditional cider areas of the West Country and Hereford.

This is fine as far as it goes, but it makes no mention of the apples and the way they are cultivated. Most apples used in cider-making – especially by the large companies – come from large orchards which are dependent on artificial fertilizers and an arsenal of sprays. (Apples are notorious for their treatment with pesticides, hormones and the like.) It is also no secret that most of the big commercial cider makers use apple concentrates imported from all parts of the world to boost their supplies of home-grown fruit. Clearly there is no guarantee that the fruit is free of contaminants.

The Soil Association recognizes this problem, and will only award its organic symbol to cider makers who conform to their standards of fruit growing without artificial fertilizers or pesticides. For many years, John Chevallier-Guild was the only cider maker with a Soil Association symbol. He has been making cider (as well as apple juice and cider vinegar) at Aspall Hall in Suffolk using a recipe first devised by his family ancestors in 1728. He has some 60 acres of organically maintained orchards including traditional cider apples such as Dabinett and Yarlington Mill, as well as dessert Bramleys. These are blended to produce a medium-sweet and a still dry cider. Aspall Cyder is available from licensed wholefood shops around the country, as well as some wine merchants in East Anglia.

John Reddaway has been making cider in Devon since the mid-1970s and was until recently a Soil Association symbol holder. Economics forced him to relinquish this accolade, but his cider is still made organically, he uses no sprays and the orchards – planted in his father's day – are still grazed by animals to provide fertility. You can buy his traditional farm cider and scrumpy direct from the farm.

In 1989, Dunkertons Cider Company also gained the Soil Association symbol for some of its products. Ivor and Susie Dunkerton are the new champions of traditional cider in Herefordshire. Not only do they work organically and eschew additives of all kinds, but they are preserving and – in some cases – resurrecting classic old varieties of cider apple and perry pear. Their concern for varieties is in tune with the organic philosophy. Dunkertons didn't inherit ancient orchards, but have collected, grafted and planted out several thousand trees, including Kingston Black, Breakwells Seedling, Court Royal and Strawberry Norman, Bloody Turk and Sheeps Nose, Frequin and Roi de Pomme. They are doing the same for neglected perry pears such as Merrylegs, Red Horse and Painted Lady and have established an avenue of Moorcroft and Thorne for future generations of perry drinkers.

Their range is remarkable: four blended ciders ranging from traditional dry to sweet; three extraordinary 'single variety' ciders made from Breakwells Seedling, Court Royal and Kingston Black respectively; two still perrys and three sparkling brews (Old Adam and Sweet Adam Cider and Eve's Perry). Because no water is added to any of their products, they are high in alcohol. Their basic blended cider is more than 6 per cent by volume, while the single variety brews weigh in at 8 per cent; compare this with most of today's strong lagers, which are between 5 per cent and 6 per cent. In other words, Dunkertons cider should be drunk the old way – like wine – not quaffed by the pint.

Dunkertons products are well distributed in licensed wholefood shops and delicatessens from Sussex to the Lake District. They also appear in a number of pubs, cafes and restaurants around Herefordshire.

Other organic ciders are tied in with vineyards. In particular Avalon at East Pennard, near Shepton Mallet in Somerset, and Yearlstone at Tiverton in Devon. At the Avalon Vineyard, Dr Howard Tripp makes about 1,500 gallons of cider each year from traditional varieties of cider apple, matured in oak rum barrels and packed into corked wine bottles. There are two types: a dry still cider and a naturally conditioned dry sparkling cider that is fermented for a second time in the bottle so it has a sediment. It is sealed distinctively with a heavy Normandy-style wired-down cork and requires careful handling and decanting. Avalon Cider can be obtained from the farm shop, from other shops and wine merchants in the area; it is also distributed nationally by Vinceremos Wines.

Gillian Pearkes also makes two 'Cyders' (as she calls them) at the Yearlstone Vineyard. The fruit comes mostly from her own ancient orchards, which are grazed by sheep and planted with traditional varieties such as Somerset Redstreak, Brown Snout and Cornish Gilliflower. Yearlstone Gold is a still, dry cider with a crisp, fragrant character; Yearlstone Cyder Royale is a deep-golden colour, medium-sweet and made using selected apples from a single ancient orchard in the Exe Valley.

Compared with giants such as Bulmers and Taunton, organic cider makers produce relatively small quantities of cider. Supplies are limited and, as yet, they simply cannot produce enough to attract interest from the supermarket chains. However, their products are well distributed through off-licences, wholefood shops and delicatessens. Most also sell direct from the farm. For more details see entries in the Directory.

Aspall Cyder
The Cyder House, Aspall Hall, Debenham, Suffolk IP14 6PD
Tel: (0728) 860510

Avalon Cider
The Drove, East Pennard, Shepton Mallet, Somerset BA4 6AU
Tel: (0749) 86393

Dunkertons Cider Company
Hays Head, Luntley, Pembridge, Hereford and Worcester HR6 9ED
Tel: (05447) 653

Reddaway's Cider
Lower Rixdale, Luton, Ideford, S. Devon TQ13 0BN
Tel: (06267) 5218

Yearlstone Cyder
Chilton, Bickleigh, Tiverton, Devon EX16 8RT
Tel: (08845) 450

BEER AND LAGER

The dictionary definition of beer is an alcoholic beverage made by fermentation, from malted barley flavoured with hops. Nowadays, however, most draught, bottled and canned brews contain a great deal more than that. The chances are that you won't know about these additives and adjuncts, because – like wine – beer is a special case. It is designated as food, but is excluded from the labelling legislation which requires the listing of ingredients used in its manufacture.

Alarming information concerning possibly harmful ingredients has come to light in recent years due mainly to the work of consumer groups in the US. They are aided by the Freedom of Information Act, which gives access to files that would be marked 'secret' in Britain.

The increasing concentration of ownership in the American brewing industry – and in Britain too – has meant that a handful of giant companies now dominate the market and use that domination to lower quality and standards in the pursuit of greater profits. The natural processes of brewing are too slow and too labour-intensive for the giants. Chemicals are used to speed up the germination of the barley. During fermentation anti-foam agents are pumped into the vats to cut down on the size of the yeast head: the smaller the head, the greater the amount of liquid that can be fermented. And foam stabilizers are used in the finished beer to create that thick head of foam which is the delight of brewery marketing departments.

The giants have also been cutting back drastically on the levels of barley malt used in beer. The American giant Schlitz reduced the malt content of its beers to such an extent that it had to use massive amounts of silica gel containing enzymes to induce some fake sparkle and taste into the finished product. But by reducing the malt content, the company saved itself 50 cents on every barrel brewed.

In Britain, independent research, fiercely resisted by the brewers, has shown that the following cheap cereal adjuncts are used in brewing: corn grits, corn starch, rice, sorghum (a cereal used mainly in Third World countries which produces a fermentable syrup), wheat, torrified (i.e. scorched) barley, potato starch, tapioca and triticale. Liquid adjuncts include corn syrup, barley syrup and sugar syrup.

The brewer's chemistry set

Brewing is a chemical process, but today's brewery chemists have a whole arsenal of adjuncts, additives and enzymes to modify their products. At various stages of the process they might include amyloglucosidase, aspergillus niger, hypochlorite, hydrogen peroxide (i.e. common bleach), ozone and giberellic acid. Such additives are used in small amounts and the brewers claim that the levels are too low to be harmful. But that did not stop forty people dying from heart attacks in North America in the 1960s, when brewers experimented with small doses of cobalt sulphate in order to create a lively (sic) head on their brews.

In some cases, the brewers are the victims, not the villains. One brewer at Boddingtons Brewery in Manchester has been forced to use enzymes in his brewing process to counteract the increasingly high levels of nitrates used by barley farmers. As yet, only one 'micro-brewer' is using organic barley; nearly all the barley supplied to the brewing industry comes from the duopoly (Pauls and Munton & Fison) that dominates the industry. Hops are also heavily sprayed, though one spray – Cytrolane – was withdrawn in Britain in 1989 on the advice of the US government, when it was found to be carcinogenic.

The absence of labelling in Britain means that drinkers have no idea what they are drinking – or why they are suffering. Many people are allergic to certain cereals and they should be told if the beers they drink contain wheat. Sulphites are harmful to asthma sufferers, while benzoates can inflame the mucous membranes. Both are widely used in brewing, but never mentioned.

Attempts to introduce labelling for beer in EC countries have been bogged down for years as each country attempts to continue the cover up. Meanwhile the European Court has declared that the West German *Reinheitsgebot* – Pure Beer Law – is 'a restraint of trade'. German brewers are allowed to use just malt, water, hops and yeasts in their beers brewed for domestic consumption and, until the court intervened, banned the import of beers from other community countries that used additives. Now, in the name of the free market, West Germans can be subjected to beers full of chemical pit-props. There is nothing to prevent British brewers from labelling their beers. They can do so independent of any EC ruling and consumers should demand that they reveal their ingredients and clean up their vats.

Additive-free and naturally brewed beers are starting to appear in Britain, and a few independent breweries are producing the real thing from malted barley, hops and water. Look for the following: Goacher's of Bockingford, near Maidstone, Kent; Sarah Hughes Brewery at the Beacon Hotel near Dudley, West Midlands and – the front runner – the Pitfield Brewery, The Beer Shop, 8 Pitfield Street, London N1 which produces Pitfield Bitter, Hoxton Best, Dark Star and London Porter. The Yorkshire brewery, Sam Smith's, is also phasing out the use of sugar and moving over to all-malt beers.

Genuine organic brews are still a rarity. Only one is widely available: Pinkus Lager from Munster in West Germany, a strong lager (Original Gravity 1055) that is matured for up to six months before bottling. Some off-licences and wine distributors sell it (especially if they also stock organic wines) and it is sold in some licensed wholefood shops. Supermarkets have yet to include it on their shelves.

There are, however, signs that the situation is improving. Lincoln Green, Britain's first organic lager, is due to go into production in Lincolnshire before the end of 1990.

Chapter 9

A SURVEY OF THE HIGH STREET

We buy something like three-quarters of our food from supermarkets, so it is hardly surprising that their involvement is crucial to the future of organic produce in the high street. They have the commercial power to respond to consumer demand, once they recognize that it is more than a passing fashion. Although it might seem as if they are able to offer more choice than ever before, in fact they are the arbiters of choice, because their buyers and representatives get to see and sample the range before we do as consumers.

Some supermarkets have been much quicker to respond than others, but now all the major high street names are interested, and are keen to include at least some organic produce on their shelves. But they are faced with several problems. Demand for organic food outstrips supply, many growers are small enterprises that are simply not geared up to producing the quantities needed by supermarkets; as a result prices are high; there is a great deal of wastage because much organic food doesn't meet the standards of appearance and uniformity traditionally demanded by supermarkets, in the belief that they are providing the consumers with what they want. But attitudes may be changing. Speaking at a workshop organized by The Guild of Food Writers in September 1989, Ross McLaren, Departmental Director of Sainsbury (responsible for fresh produce), had this to say about the price of organic food.

We are faced with what I can only describe as horrendous

on-costs. We have packhouses taking tiny amounts from lots and lots of little suppliers, with an extremely high wastage. It can be as high as 30–40 per cent in terms of damage to the product which is acceptable to the consumer. Things may change as the years roll on, people will accept the different standard. But at the moment we have to guard against using the word organic linked with a dilution of standards... We are in it for the duration so we are actually extending the product and demanding that farmers grow more...We actually are making an investment in that market by taking a significantly lower margin on organic produce than we do on other produce. So in a sense we are already subsidizing.

Three supermarket chains in particular have shown a great deal of support for organic produce: Safeway, Tesco and Sainsbury. Safeway started selling organic vegetables in 1981, and since then has developed a vast range of products, from organic milk to wine, as well as cheese, bread and cereals. In January 1990 it also launched organic beef in a few of its stores in the south-east. Safeway has also involved itself with other projects: it sponsored the course in organic agriculture at Worcestershire College of Agriculture, it supports the National Organic Wine Fair at Ryton Gardens, and has recently set up an organic research centre in Scotland.

Both Tesco and Sainsbury are keen to be associated with 'green' issues, from lead-free petrol to environmentally-friendly packaging and protecting the ozone layer. Tesco took the lead some years ago in providing consumer information about health and nutrition.Both now have an extensive range of organic products, from fruit and vegetables to wine.

Other supermarkets, such as Waitrose, Asda and the Co-op also stock some organic produce, although supplies can be patchy and are often limited to a few of their bigger stores. It's worth pointing out that supermarket supplies and lines can change very quickly. A product that is tried out regionally one month, may be on sale nationally two months later. Other lines may be dropped if supplies cannot be maintained. The picture is always changing, so references to supermarket products should be treated as general guidelines.

Wholefood shops, large and small, are usually a decent source of organic products. The large chains, such as Holland

& Barrett, tend to concentrate on dried goods and wholefoods, although they are looking into the possibilities of bread and dairy produce. Before long they may even begin to sell fruit and vegetables. Independent wholefood shops can have a surprisingly good range of high quality products, from cheese to wine, and they deserve to be supported. You will also find organic produce on some market stalls, in delicatessens and in specialist shops such as bakers and greengrocers.

While many organic products such as bread, jams and marmalades are available in the shops, it is still worth making your own if you can get hold of good quality organic ingredients. And if you have a piece of earth – whether it's an allotment or a window box – make use of it to grow some organic produce. (There are some recommended organic gardening books in the list at the back of this book.)

Chapter 10

WHERE TO BUY ORGANIC FOOD

A DIRECTORY

The addresses listed in this section cover a vast range of producers and suppliers of organic food, from comprehensive mixed farms and big wholefood retailers to one-acre small-holdings producing a few vegetables, and local greengrocers. All of them produce or sell organic food of quality. It is worth pointing out that some of the best addresses are the small operations, and these deserve to be encouraged: a vast range and a high profile do not *necessarily* add up to quality.

We have attempted to make the listings as varied as possible, but inevitably we have missed some places. If your local outlet isn't mentioned, it may simply be that we didn't know about it. We are keen to expand coverage, so if you have any comments or recommendations, please make use of the form at the back of the book.

ABOUT THE ENTRIES

Entries are listed alphabetically by town, divided up into England, Scotland, Wales, the Republic of Ireland and Northern Ireland. If the address is difficult to find or some distance from the town itself, we have given general directions for finding it.

Opening times: these are times when callers are welcome to purchase supplies. Quoted comments come from the establishments themselves. Remember that many of these places are working farms and it is courteous – as well as sensible – to telephone before embarking on a journey.

Retail/wholesale: we have put the emphasis firmly on places that sell to the general public. In a few cases, the outlets are wholesale, but are happy to sell to individual customers, especially if they are given a couple of days' notice. There is a list of Wholesalers and Distributors at the end of this section.

Range: details about the range of items produced or sold were provided by the outlets. But it's worth remembering that many crops are seasonal, and new lines may be added or discontinued quite quickly. So, the entries should be used as a general guide to what is available.

Symbols: these have been included for producers and growers only. Many shops and retailers sell produce from symbol holders, and this is usually mentioned in the entry. Some places only have a symbol for part of their output – say, vegetables or soft fruit – and this is mentioned in the entry. The symbols are as follows:

ENGLAND

ALDRIDGE
HARVEST HEALTH FOODS
34 The Square, Aldridge Shopping Centre, Aldridge, West Midlands WS9 8QS
Tel: Aldridge (0922) 51219
Open: 9 a.m. to 5.30 p.m. Mon to Thur (to 6 p.m. Fri and Sat)
Closed: Sun and bank hols
Wholefood shop specializing in organic vegetables, top fruit, bread and bakery products. Much of the produce is from symbol holders.

ALRESFORD
BLUEGATES FARM
Alresford, nr. Colchester, Essex CO7 8DE
4 miles SE of Colchester on the B1027

Tel: Alresford (020622) 3656
Open: Ring first
Organic vegetables, soft fruit and additive-free meat are available from the Leylands' Essex farm.

ALVECHURCH
SUNNY BANK FARM
Stoney Lane, Alvechurch, Hereford & Worcester
Tel: (021) 445 1106
Open: 'any reasonable time, but telephone first'
Mrs Senior rears goats and can supply both organic and additive-free goat meat as well as dairy produce. She also sells honey.

ASHBOURNE
ACRE FIELDS FARM
Wyaston, Ashbourne, Derbyshire DE6 2DR
Open: 2 p.m. to 6 p.m. Mon to Fri
Other times by arrangement.
The Hadfields grow seasonal organic root vegetables. Some of their field work is still done by horses. They also produce rye straw which is sold to a Derbyshire thatcher.

ANGELA HUGHES
The Priory, Woodeaves, Fenny Bentley, nr. Ashbourne, Derbyshire DE6 1LF
3 miles N of Ashbourne off the A515
Tel: (033) 529238
Open: 'by telephone only'
Angela Hughes specializes in traditionally reared, additive-free meat, without chemicals or pesticides. Some non-organic barley is included in the feeds. Organic vegetables are available in season.

ASHBURTON
C. STANILAND

The Gardens, Buckland in the Moor, Ashburton, Devon TQ13 7HN
3 miles NW of Ashburton
Tel: Ashburton (0364) 53169
Open: 9 a.m. to 6 p.m. May to mid-Oct.
Closed: mid-Oct. to Apr.
Charles Staniland grows organic fruit and vegetables in a two acre walled garden on the edge of Dartmoor. His strawberries

have a high reputation, and he also specializes in unusual salad crops and fresh cut herbs; goat's cheese and yoghurt are also available.

ASHFORD
BURSCOMBE CLIFF FARM
Egerton, nr. Ashford, Kent
6 miles NW of Ashford off the A20
Tel: Ashford (0233) 76468
Open: by arrangement, telephone call appreciated
Hilary Jones grows organic vegetables, but specializes in additive-free beef and lamb. She delivers free of charge within a 15 mile radius, and small packs of her frozen meat are also available from Parkwood Trout Farm, Goddington Lane, Harrietsham, Kent.

P. J. ZEEN
Pollards Dane, Canterbury Road, Charing, Ashford, Kent TN27 0EX
Tel: Charing (023371) 2580
Open: 8 a.m. to 8 p.m.
Closed: Wed
A reputable grower of organic vegetables, produced to Soil Association standards.

ASHINGTON
MALTHOUSE COTTAGE FARM
Malthouse Lane, Ashington, nr. Pulborough, West Sussex RH20 3BU
6 miles E of Pulborough on the A24
Tel: Pulborough (0903) 892456
Open: 10 a.m. to 5 p.m. daily
The Ferris family's range of goats' cheeses includes mould-ripened, mature pressed Cheddar-style and cheese marinated in olive oil; their goats also provide milk and yoghurt, and they rear sheep for meat.

AYLESBURY
EVERFRESH NATURAL FOODS
Gatehouse Close, Aylesbury, Buckinghamshire HP19 3DE
Tel: Aylesbury (0296) 25333
Open: 8 a.m. to 4.30 p.m. Mon to Fri

Closed: Sat, Sun and bank hols
Produces a range of breads (including some gluten-free and yeast-free) from organic flour freshly milled on the premises. Their products sold under the brand name, Sunnyvale, are now available nationally. Cakes include some made without eggs and sugar.

BAKEWELL
THE HONEY POT
Hebden Court, Bakewell, Derbyshire DE4 1EE
Tel: Bakewell (062981) 4332
Open: 9.30 a.m. to 5 p.m. (from noon Sun) all week
Wholefood shop offering a wide range of organic produce, much of it from Soil Association and Organic Farmers & Growers symbol holders. There is a branch in Chesterfield.

BALSALL COMMON
BRANTWOOD ORGANICS
Waste Lane, Balsall Common, nr. Coventry, West Midlands CV7 7GG
3 miles W of Coventry on the A452
Tel: Coventry (0203) 469097
Open: 'all sociable hours'
The Whiteley's farm is fully organic and specializes in supplying regular customers with vegetables, soft fruit and top fruit. The Henry Doubleday Research Association at Ryton Gardens sells their produce.

BARNARD CASTLE
EGGLESTON HALL

Eggleston, Barnard Castle, Co. Durham
Open: 10 a.m. to 5 p.m. all week
The garden at Eggleston Hall grows organic vegetables and can supply soft and top fruit in season.

BARNHAM
D.R & M.N. WHEELER

44 Hill Lane, Barnham, West Sussex PO22 0BL
Tel: Barnham (0243) 552852
Open: 'please telephone first'
The Wheelers are growers and suppliers of organic vegetables and soft fruit.

BARROW UPON HUMBER
WHEELBARROW FOODS
3 Thorngarth Lane, Barrow upon Humber, South Humberside DN19 7AW
Tel: Barrow upon Humber (0469) 30721
Open: 'almost all the time, but telephone first'
Betty Whitwell runs this wholefood and organic enterprise from her house. She markets produce from a group of local organic growers (some symbol holders) and specializes in unusual vegetables such as salad leaves, pickling cucumbers and chicory. She also stocks organic wholefoods including cereals, pulses and biscuits from Doves Farm. At present she supplies four shops in Humberside.

BATH
HARVEST NATURAL FOODS
37 Walcot Street, Bath, Avon BA2 6AA
Tel: Bath (0225) 465519
Open: 9.30 a.m. to 5.30 p.m. (from 11.30 a.m. Mon)
Closed: Sun, bank hols and Christmas
Often known as the Bath Wholefood Co-operative, this wholefood shop has an impressive organic range, from vegetables, fruit and dairy produce to cereals, tofu and fruit juices. Eggs are from Martin Pitt's farm near Marlborough. The shop also stocks organic seeds and fertilizers as well as books and alternative medicines.

RADFORD MILL FARM
Timsbury, nr. Bath, Avon BA3 1QF
6 miles SW of Bath off the B3115
Tel: Timsbury (0761) 72549
Open: 'by arrangement, please telephone first'
The farm produces organic vegetables and top fruit, organic beef and lamb as well as additive-free pork. Meat is sold retail from the farm; all products are available wholesale. There is a farm shop in Bristol (see entry).

BEAWORTHY
MR W. L. ROBLEY
Little East Lake, East Chilla, Beaworthy, Devon EX21 5XF
Tel: Beaworthy (040922) 417
Open: 8 a.m. to 8 p.m. (telephone first)

Mr Robley supplies organic meat and has recently begun to grow vegetables and soft fruit.

BECCLES
HUNGATE HEALTH STORE
4 Hungate, Beccles, Suffolk NR34 9TL
Tel: Beccles (0502) 715009
Open: 9 a.m. to 5.30 p.m. (to 1 p.m. Wed)
Closed: Sun and bank hols
Also Mail order
This health food/wholefood shop aims to supply organic produce wherever possible. Seasonal fruit and vegetables are from a local supplier, eggs are free-range and other staples include grains, flours, cider vinegar and juices, as well as wines (including organic champagne). There are plans to open a cafe/restaurant in 1990.

BERKHAMSTED
COOK'S DELIGHT OF BERKHAMSTED
360-364 High Street, Berkhamsted, Hertfordshire HP4 1HU
Tel: Berkhamsted (0442) 863584
Open: 8.30 a.m. to 5.30 p.m. Tue; 8 a.m. to 1 p.m. Wed; 8 a.m. to 9.30 p.m. Thur and Fri; 8 a.m. to midnight Sat; 8.30 a.m. to 5 p.m. Sun
Closed: Mon, bank hols and Christmas
Rex Tyler's 'natural grocer's' stocks an uncompromising range of organic and additive-free produce. No animal products are sold, but there are seasonal fruit and vegetables grown to Soil Association standards (Rex doesn't sell imported produce out of season), dried wholefoods including rice, millet and barley, over 90 organic wines, organic cognac and saké as well as a vast selection of Japanese and other oriental foods. There is a tearoom/restaurant attached (See entry in Part Three).

BIDEFORD
MARSHFORD NURSERIES
Churchill Way, Northam, Bideford, Devon EX39 1NS
Tel: Bideford (02372) 77160
Open: 9 a.m. to 7 p.m. ('or dusk, whichever is the latest')
Closed: Tue, Wed and Sun from Oct. to Mar.
The Ebdons supply organic vegetables and top fruit as well as dried wholefoods, bread and bakery products.

BIRDHAM

WHITESTONE FARM
Birdham, nr. Chichester, West Sussex PO20 7HU
4 miles S of Chichester on the A286
Tel: Birdham (0243) 512416
Open: 9 a.m. to 4 p.m. Mon to Sat
Closed: Sun
Michael Young produces organic vegetables and lamb on his
farm near Chichester.

BISHOP'S CASTLE
HARVEST WHOLEFOODS
Glebe Farm, Lydham, nr. Bishop's Castle, Shropshire
SY9 5HB
2 miles N of Bishop's Castle on the A488/A489
Tel: (0588) 638298
Open: 9 a.m. to 5.30 p.m. Mon to Sat
Closed: Sun, bank hols and Christmas
Sue Jones operates from a converted farm building in the
Shropshire countryside. Her main lines are organic vegetables,
fruit, dairy produce and dried wholefoods, plus bread and
bakery products.

BLACKPOOL
E. H.BOOTH & CO. LTD
Highfield Road, Marton, Blackpool, Lancashire
Tel: Blackpool (0253) 67852
Open: 9 a.m. to 6 p.m. Mon to Wed (to 8 p.m. Thur and Fri;
to 5 p.m. Sat)
Closed: Sun, bank hols and Christmas
This branch of Booths is a conventional greengrocers with a
good organic section. It stocks mainly fruit and vegetables,
including produce from Low Carr Nursery, near Preston.
Juices and baby foods are also available.

THE MARKET GARDEN

Green Lane, Preesall, Blackpool, Lancashire FY6 0NS
Tel: Blackpool (0253) 811644
Open: 9 a.m. to 5 p.m. (wholesale and orders only)
Mr Ward and Yvonne Thompson supply organic vegetables on
a wholesale basis. There is no retail outlet.

BLANDFORD
RIVERMEAD FARM
Childe Oakford, Blandford, Dorset DT11 8HB
Tel: (0258) 860293
Open: 'all day, every day'
This farm produces organically grown vegetables to Soil
Association standards.

BODIAM
BRAMLEY ORGANIC FARM
Staplecross Road, Bodiam, East Sussex TN32 5UJ
Tel: Bodiam (058 083) 566
Open: weekends in summer
John Rigby and Yvonne Dhooge operate a genuine farm shop
selling only fresh vegetables, apples and strawberries from their
own land.

BODMIN
CAMEL VALLEY NURSERY
Nanstallon, Bodmin, Cornwall PL31 1BQ
Tel: Bodmin (0208) 831958
Open: 10 a.m. to 7 p.m. Tue to Sun during May.-Aug. (other
times by appointment only)
Closed: Mon
Iain Tolhust is a well-known grower of organic vegetables, soft
fruit and top fruit. Strawberries are his speciality. See also
Hardwick Organic Gardens, Reading.

HIGHER WAY FARM
Demelza, St Wenn, nr. Bodmin, Cornwall PL5 5PD
6 miles W of Bodmin off the B3274
Tel: St Austell (0726) 890489
Open: 'people are welcome to call'
Sarah Bolt does not have a shop or retail outlet, but is happy to
sell her organic vegetables and fruit to callers.

D.K. & C.E MATTHEWS
Turfdown, Fletchers Bridge, Cardinham, nr. Bodmin,
Cornwall PL26 4AN
4 miles NE of Bodmin
Tel: Bodmin (0208) 77293
Open: 8 a.m. to 1 p.m., 2 p.m. to 7 p.m.

Closed: Sun, Mon, bank hols and Christmas
The Matthews are growers of organic vegetables and soft fruit.
In 1990 they plan to start making pickled cucumbers, beetroot
and tomato chutney with organic ingredients.

BOGNOR REGIS
THE COTTAGE NURSERY
Shripney Road, Bognor Regis, West Sussex PO22 9PA
Tel: Bognor Regis (0243) 860324
Open: Ring first
Mr Baillie's nursery supplies organic vegetables, apples and
pears.

BOLTON
RAYMOND CORNMELL LTD

459 Halliwell Road, Bolton, Greater Manchester BL1 8DG
Tel: Bolton (0204) 46844
Open: 9 a.m. to 5.30 p.m. (to 1 p.m. Wed)
Closed: Sun, bank hols
Raymond Cornmell is one of the few organic butchers in the
country. All his meat is from Arthur Hollins at Fordhall Farm,
Market Drayton (see entry). He can supply beef, lamb and
pork, as well free-range turkeys, geese, game fowl, ducks and
chickens (fresh and smoked). In addition you can buy
traditionally cured and smoked bacon and hams (the dry-
salting is done by Mr Sadd of Spalding). Meat is butchered and
packed as required. Cornmells have a nationwide overnight
delivery service of vacuum-packed produce, and will shortly
have their own logo.

K. & M. WEST
2 Carlisle Street, Bolton, Greater Manchester BL7 9JF
Tel: Bolton (0204) 591780
Open: 'telephone first'
The Wests operate from their home on a non-profit basis as an
outlet for organic produce bought from a wholesaler. Their
range includes vegetables, soft and top fruit and eggs.

BOSTON
BRIGADOON
Midville Lane, Stickney, nr. Boston, Lincolnshire PE22 8DN
7 miles N of Boston on A16

Tel: Boston (0205) 480559
Open: 'by arrangement'
The Dohertys are commercial growers of vegetables and salads.
They have no retail outlet, but will occasionally supply
customers direct.

FINE HERBS
Rose Cottage, Station Road, Leake Commonside, Boston,
Lincolnshire PE22 7RF
6 miles NE of Boston off the B1184
Tel: Boston (0205) 870062
Geri Clarke specializes in dried culinary and medicinal herbs
grown organically. She also sells by mail order.

BRADFORD
BRADFORD CITY FARM
Illingworth Fields, Walker Drive, Bradford, West Yorkshire
Tel: Bradford (0274) 543500
Open: 8 a.m. to 4.30 p.m. Mon to Sat, 10 a.m. to 3.30 p.m.
Sun
Closed: bank hols
The farm can supply organic vegetables, gooseberries, black-
and redcurrants, as well as free-range eggs and poultry.

BRADFORD WHOLEFOODS
78 Morley Street, Bradford, West Yorkshire BD7 1AQ
Tel: Bradford (0274) 307539
Open: 9 a.m. to 5 p.m. Mon to Sat
Closed: Sun and bank hols
A well-stocked wholefood shop with a good range of organic
fruit and vegetables. Vegetarian and vegan snacks are made
with organic flour.

BRIDGNORTH
ACORN NATURAL FOODS
64 St Mary's Street, Bridgnorth, Shropshire WV16 4DR
Tel: Bridgnorth (07462) 761896
Open: 9 a.m. to 5.30 p.m. (to 1 p.m. Thur, to 5 p.m. Sat)
Closed: Sun
Wholefood co-operative offering a limited range of organic
vegetables, including potatoes, onions and carrots, as well as
free-range eggs and locally milled organic flour from Pimhill.

BRIDPORT
FRUITS OF THE EARTH
Victoria Grove, Bridport, Dorset DT6 3AA
Tel: Bridport (0308) 25827
Open: 9 a.m. to 5.30 p.m. Mon to Sat
Closed: Sun and bank hols
Soil Association symbol vegetables, plus dried wholefoods, pasta, tofu and olive oil are the main organic lines in this wholefood shop.

R.F. WILLIAMS & P.F. BAILEY
c/o 15 Victoria Grove, Bridport, Dorset DT6 3AD
Tel: Bridport (0308) 24839
Open: stall on Bridport Market 8.30 a.m. to 3.30 p.m. Wed and Sat
Richard Williams sells his produce on Bridport Market and boasts that his range of organic vegetables takes in anything from asparagus to zucchini. He also supplies fruit.

BRIGHTLINGSEA
CORNFLOWER
49 High Street, Brightlingsea, nr. Colchester, Essex CO7 0AQ
Tel: Colchester (0206) 304854
Open: 9 a.m. to 1 p.m., 2 p.m. to 5 p.m. Mon to Sat (to 1 p.m. Thur) *Closed*: Sun, bank hols and Christmas
Wholefood shop selling organic vegetables, fruit, breads and dried foods as well as free-range eggs.

BRIGHTON
BEAUMONT ORGANIC
363 South Coast Road, Telescombe, Brighton, East Sussex BN10 7HH
Tel: Brighton (0273) 585551
Open: 8.30 a.m. to 5.30 p.m. Tue to Thur; to 8 a.m. Fri; to 2 p.m. Sat
Closed: Sun and Mon
This outlet stocks a wide range of organic produce including meat and wine, as well as dried wholefoods. Gardening products are also available.

GINGER'S WHOLEFOODS
25 Nursery Close, Shoreham-by-Sea, Brighton, East Sussex BN4 6GJ
Tel: Brighton (0273) 453128

Open: 8 a.m. to 6 p.m. Tue to Fri
Closed: Sat, Sun, Mon, Christmas to New Year's Day
A delivery-only retail business, supplying organic fruit and vegetables and dried wholefoods, as well as tofu, nuts, oils, herbs. Free delivery of orders over £10 in Brighton and Worthing area. No personal callers.

INFINITY FOODS CO-OPERATIVE LTD
25 North Road, Brighton, East Sussex BN1 1YA
Tel: Brighton (0273) 603563/690116
Open: 9 a.m. to 5.30 p.m. (to 2 p.m. Wed; to 7 p.m. Fri)
Closed: Sun, bank hols
Infinity Foods is committed to organic produce, ranging from Soil Association standard fruit and vegetables (delivered four times weekly) to Italian brown rice, olive oil and wines. Free-range eggs and additive-free dairy produce are also available. A bakery on the premises supplies all kinds of breads and takeaway snacks. True to the principles of the enterprise, even the baking tins are oiled with cold-pressed oil. Gardening supplies, cosmetics and books are sold as well.

BRISTOL
BARTRAMS WHOLEFOODS
12 Clevedon Terrace, Cotham, Bristol, Avon BS6 5TX
Tel: Bristol (0272) 241183
Open: 9.30 a.m. to 7 p.m. Mon to Fri (to 6 p.m. Sat)
Closed: Sun and bank hols
Stocks the usual range of dried wholefoods, organic vegetables and fruit in season, as well as free-range eggs from Martin Pitt. Organic takeaway snacks available.

BEANS AND GREENS CO-OP
88 Colston Street, Bristol, Avon BS1 5BB
Tel: Bristol (0272) 268961
Open: 8.30 a.m. to 6 p.m. Mon to Fri; 9.15 a.m. to 5 p.m. Sat
Closed: Sun and bank hols
Organic produce includes top fruit, beansprouts, alfalfa, yoghurt and cottage cheese, as well as cereals and wholefoods.

RON ELLIOTT
9 Regent Street, Clifton, Bristol, Avon BS8 4NW
Tel: Bristol (0272) 735223

Open: 9 a.m. to 6 p.m. Mon to Fri, 8.30 a.m. to 5.30 p.m. Sat
Closed: Sun, bank hols and Christmas
Organic fruit and vegetables, dairy produce, dried wholefoods,
bakery products and free-range eggs are the main lines in this
shop. Ron Elliott also sells tofu.

LEIGH COURT FARM
Abbots Leigh, Bristol, Avon BS8 3RA
Tel: Pill (027581) 5308
Open: 10 a.m. to 4 p.m. Mon to Thur
Closed: Fri to Sun
Leigh Court Farm specializes in growing and supplying
organic vegetables.

THE MANGO TREE
224 Gloucester Road, Bristol, Avon BS7 8NZ
Tel: Bristol (0272) 246589
Open: 9 a.m. to 5.45 p.m. (to 5.30 p.m. Sat)
Closed: Sun, bank hols
Dried wholefoods, a range of dairy produce, breads and bakery
products are the main organic lines in this shop.

RADFORD MILL FARM SHOP
72 Picton Street, Bristol, Avon
Tel: Bristol (0272) 245360
Open: 9 a.m. to 6.30 p.m. Mon to Sat; 10 a.m. to 1 p.m. Sun
Closed: bank hols, Christmas
The retail outlet for produce from Radford Mill Farm (see Bath).
Vegetables, top fruit, free-range eggs, dairy produce and meat.

REAL FOOD SUPPLIES
Kingston Road, Southville, Bristol, Avon
(36C Gloucester Road, Bishopston, Bristol BS7 8AR)
Tel: Bristol (0272) 232015
Open: 9 a.m. to 6 p.m. Mon to Sat
Closed: Sun, bank hols
Phil Haughton stocks virtually everything for the organic
consumer, from Soil Association standard fruit, vegetables and
meat to free-range poultry, wine, gardening supplies and
ecologically sound cleaning products. He is planning to open
three more shops in Bristol, London and Dublin in the near
future.

ST WERBURGHS CITY FARM
Watercress Road, St Werburghs, Bristol, Avon BS2 9YJ
Tel: Bristol (0272) 428241
Open: 9 a.m. to 5 p.m. all year
The farm produces some organic vegetables in season, as well as goat dairy produce, free-range eggs and additive-free meat.

WINDMILL HILL CITY FARM
Phillip Street, Bedminster, Bristol, Avon BS3 4DU
Tel: Bristol (0272) 633252
Open: 9 a.m. to 6 p.m.
Closed: Mon
One of a cluster of urban farms dotted around Bristol. Produce includes vegetables, soft fruit, additive-free meat, dairy produce from goats as well as herbs. The farm also grows flowers and bedding plants organically.

BROADWAY
KITES NEST FARM
Broadway, Hereford and Worcester WR12 7JT
Tel: Broadway (0386) 853320
Open: Ring first
Perhaps the most famous organic farm in Britain, run by Richard and Rosamund Young and their parents. The livestock are allowed to range free in natural family groups. The farm shop sells organic meat from the cattle and pigs reared on the farm. Kites Nest beefburgers are exquisite.

BROCKENHURST
MRS C. ASHBY
Coronation Cottage, Main Road, East Boldre, nr. Brockenhurst, Hampshire SO42 7WU
5 miles E of Brockenhust off the B3055
Tel: Lymington (0590) 65336
Open: 'daylight hours'
Mrs Ashby sells additive-free pork and sausages from her home. Her produce is also available from the Organic Alternatives stall on Lymington Market all day Saturday.

BROMLEY
BROMLEY HEALTH CENTRE
54 Widmore Road, Bromley, Kent

Tel: (081) 460 3894
Open: 9 a.m. to 5 p.m. Mon to Sat
Closed: Sun, bank hols and Christmas
The Health Centre sells Soil Association standard organic vegetables and top fruit, as well as cereals, dried wholefoods, herb teas and soya milk ice cream.

BROMSGROVE

BADGERS MOUNT FARM
Mount Road, Fairfield, nr. Bromsgrove, Hereford and Worcester DY9 9QG
1 mile N of Bromsgrove towards the A491
Tel: Bromsgrove (0527) 36727/ also (0562) 730556
Open: 9 a.m. to 5 p.m. Fri and Sat
Closed: Sun to Thur
John Davenport grows organic vegetables, soft fruit and top fruit, and supplies a range of different herbs.

BROMYARD

MUTTONS ORGANIC GROWERS
Lower House Farm, Thornbury, nr. Bromyard, Hereford and Worcester HR7 4NJ
4 miles N of Bromyard off the B4214
Tel: Kyre (08854) 204
Open: 9 a.m. to 5 p.m. Mon to Sat (telephone first)
Closed: Sun
This is essentially a wholesale nursery specializing in a wide range of organically grown vegetables, unusual salad crops and herbs. Geoff Mutton's five-herb pack won The Food From Britain Award for 'Best General Presentation' at the 1989 Royal Show.

J. & M. WAKEFIELD-JONES
Batchley, Grendon Bishop, nr. Bromyard, Hereford and Worcester HR7 4TH
Tel: Bromyard (08854) 83377
Open: 8 a.m. to 1 p.m., 2.15 p.m. to 5 p.m. Mon to Fri, 8 a.m. to 1 p.m. Sat (telephone first)
Closed: Sun and bank hols
The Wakefield-Jones' specialize in organic meat, but also supply a range of animal feeds for poultry, pigs, sheep and cattle, produced to Soil Association standards.

BROOKTHORPE
BRENTLANDS COTSWOLD BEEF
Brentlands Farm, Brookthorpe, nr. Gloucester, Gloucestershire
1 mile S of Gloucester on the A4173
Tel: Painswick (0452) 813447
Open: 'anytime'
Jennifer Warner produces naturally reared, hormone-free beef, raised on unsprayed pastures. Beefburgers are one of her specialities. Visitors and parties are always welcome.

GILBERT'S
Gilbert's Lane, Brookthorpe, nr. Gloucester, Gloucestershire
GL4 0UH
1 mile S of Gloucester on the A4173
Tel: Painswick (0452) 812364
Open: 10 a.m. to 5 p.m. all week
Jenny Beer runs this 400-year-old Costwold stone house as a bed and breakfast place with four bedrooms. Outside is an organic small-holding that provides vegetables, fruit, free-range eggs and lamb. Her 50-year-old Aga is the driving force behind her wholefood breakfasts and she says that 'guests often go home with a box of vegetables, eggs or honey, and can see the organic system working'.

BROUGH

R. & P. WOOD
Cedar Lodge, Ninegates Farm, Todds Lane, Ellerker, Brough, Humberside HU15 2DS
Tel: (0430) 423473
Open: 8 a.m. to 5 p.m. ('ring before calling')
The Woods grow and sell organic vegetables produced to Soil Association standards.

BURNHAM MARKET
STUBBINGS
Westgate Nurseries, Market Place, Burnham Market, Norfolk
PE31 8HF
Tel: Fakenham (0328) 738337
Open: 9 a.m. to 1 p.m., 2 p.m. to 5 p.m. Mon to Sat
Closed: Sun
Stubbings can supply some local organic vegetables and apples in season, as well as organic meat, rice and muesli.

BURY ST EDMUNDS
CAROLINE HOLMES HERBS
Denham End Farm, Denham, nr. Bury St Edmunds, Suffolk
IP29 5EE
6 miles W of Bury St Edmunds off the A45 (signposted Barrow)
Tel: Bury St Edmunds (0284) 810653
Open: 10 a.m. to 6 p.m. Sat from Mar. to Oct.; also by
arrangement or booking
Denham End Farm has a wide range of culinary and medicinal
herbs and cottage plants grown organically. Caroline Holmes is
a member of the Herb Society and the Royal Horticultural
Society and gives talks and courses in the subject. Groups and
visitors attending these events are offered aniseed cookies,
rosemary scones and salads as refreshment.

CAMBRIDGE
ARJUNA
12 Mill Road, Cambridge, Cambridgeshire CB1 2AD
Tel: Cambridge (0223) 64845
Open: 9.30 a.m. to 6 p.m. (to 2 p.m. Thur); 9 a.m. to 5.30 p.m. Sat
Closed: Sun, bank hols and 1 week Christmas
A worker's co-operative with over one hundred organic lines,
from fruit and vegetables to dried wholefoods and oils and
pasta. Organic bread is baked each day and fresh produce is
delivered five times each week. On Saturdays (from 9 a.m. to 1
p.m.), local grower Chris Baker sells his own Soil Association
standard vegetables and apples from a stall outside the shop.
There is a cafe attached (see entry).

KARMA FARM
8 Fen Bank, Isleham, Cambridgeshire CB7 5SL
12 miles NE of Cambridge on the B1104
Tel: Newmarket (0638) 721112/780701
Open: 'telephone enquiries and orders only'
Will and Sheila Taylor can supply organic lamb and beef for the
freezer; they will also sell half lambs and one-eighth cuts of
beef for telephone orders. Organic vegetables are also available.

CANTERBURY
A.G. BROCKMAN & CO.
Perry Court Farm, Garlings Green, Petham, Canterbury, Kent
CT4 5RU

4 miles S of Canterbury off the B2068
Tel: Canterbury (0227) 738449
Open: 3 p.m. to 4.30 p.m. Wed and Fri
Closed: Mon, Tue, Thur, Sat and Sun
The farm produces organic vegetables, free-range eggs and flour
(also sold in Canterbury Wholefoods, Northgate, Canterbury).

H. MOUNT & SONS

Woolton Farm, Bekesbourne, nr. Canterbury, Kent CT4 5EA
2 miles SE of Canterbury off the A2
Tel: Canterbury (0227) 830525
Open: 8.30 a.m. to 4.30 p.m. Mon to Fri
Closed: Sat, Sun, bank hols and Christmas
Woolton Farm specializes in growing and supplying top fruit
including apples and pears.

SWEET HEART OF CANTERBURY LTD
47 Whitstable Road, Canterbury, Kent CT2 8DJ
Tel: Canterbury (0227) 450341
Open: 8 a.m. to 8 p.m. all week
Ingrid Eissfeldt has moved from the Old Weavers House to
new premises in the town and is in the process of setting up an
organic wholefood patisserie. She specializes in 'real' breads
and a wide range of Continental cakes made with organic and
wholefood ingredients. She provides a phone-free delivery
service to London and the south-east; orders can be placed by
writing to Freepost 894, Canterbury CT2 7BR. There is a
tearoom/restaurant attached to the shop (see entry).

CARNFORTH
BANK HOUSE FARM
Silverdale, Carnforth, Lancashire LA5 0RE
Tel: Lancaster (0524) 701280
Open: telephone first
This is a small farm without a shop. Free-range eggs and
boiling fowls are sold direct; organic beef and lamb are sold to
branches of E.H. Boorth & Co. Ltd, based in Preston,
Lancashire. Additive-free pork is also available.

CASTLE CARY
CHARLES W. J. DOWDING

Orchard House, Shepton Montague, nr. Castle Cary, BA9 8JW

3 miles E of Castle Cary off the A359
Tel: (0749) 812571
Open: 8.30 a.m. to noon Tue only at Castle Cary Market
Charles Dowding is a well-known grower of organic vegetables
and soft fruit. His only retail outlet is Castle Cary Market.

CAVERSHAM
LITTLE BOTTOM FARM
64 Blenheim Road, Caversham, Berkshire RG4 7RS
Tel: Reading (0734) 473157
Open: 10 a.m. to 4 p.m. Thur to Sun
Closed: Mon, Tue, Wed and Christmas Day
Aidan Carlisle and Peggy Ellis recommend that new customers
telephone first (in the evening) to find out what is available
and to get directions for the farm shop. They specialize in a
wide variety of unusual fruit and vegetables, both home-grown
and bought-in. Wholefoods, wine, bread and bakery products
are also available.

CHALFONT ST PETER
ONLY NATURAL
41 St Peter's Court, Chalfont St.Peter, Buckinghamshire SL9 9QQ
Tel: Gerrards Cross (0753) 889441
Open: 8.30 a.m. to 5.30 p.m. Mon to Sat
Closed: Sun, bank hols and Christmas
Wholefood shop selling organic fruit, vegetables, dairy
produce and wine as well as dried goods.

CHERTSEY
LINTON LODGE
Fancourt Gardens, Longcross Road, Longcross, nr. Chertsey,
Surrey KT16 0DJ
4 miles W of Chertsey on the B386
Tel: Cobham (0932) 872571
Open: Ring first
Catriona and Tony Cattle produce organic vegetables, salad
crops, soft fruit and top fruit, most of which finds its way to
Covent Garden. As a sideline they also grow gladioli organically.

CHINNOR
ICKNIELD NURSERIES
Kingston Stert, Chinnor, Oxfordshire OX9 4NL

Tel: (0844) 52481
Open: 'daylight hours'
Closed: Christmas to New Year
Tanya and Ugo d'Onofrio sell only organic vegetables and soft fruit grown in their nursery.

CHUDLEIGH

FARMBOROUGH HOUSE
Chudleigh, nr. Newton Abbot, Devon TQ13 0DR
Tel: Newton Abbot (0626) 853258
Major and Mrs Edwards are in the process of setting up a vineyard, which will come into commercial production during 1990-91. At present they also have some organic vegetables for sale.

CIRENCESTER
HATHEROP MARKET GARDEN
Hatherop, nr. Cirencester, Gloucestershire GL7 3NA
8 miles E of Cirencester off Akeman Street
Tel: Cirencester (0285) 75326
Open: 9.30 a.m. to 5 p.m. Thur to Sat
Closed: Sun to Wed, and Christmas
The Palmers sell organic fruit and vegetables, dried wholefoods and juices.

CRAVEN ARMS
GUY & JEAN SMITH
The Wain House, Black Hill, Clunton, Craven Arms, Shropshire SY7 0JD
Tel: Clun (05884) 551
Open: 'we are usually available at most times'
From 1990, the Smiths will be in full commercial production, producing and selling their vegetables and goat dairy produce.

CROMER
POPPYLAND ORGANIC PRODUCE
1 Bizewell Cottages, Coast Road, Trimingham, nr. Cromer, Norfolk NR11 8HY
4 miles SE of Cromer on the B1159
Tel: (0263) 78675
Open: 6 a.m. to 9 p.m. all year
David and Jane Barker run a small market-garden and sell

produce from their house. Much of the operation is run on biodynamic lines. You can also buy fresh goat's milk, eggs and honey, as well as organically grown herbs and bedding plants.

CUCKFIELD

LAINES ORGANIC FARM
47 Newbury Lane, Cuckfield, West Sussex RH17 5AA
Tel: Haywards Heath (0444) 452663
Open: 10 a.m. to 6 p.m. all week
Toos Jeuken grows vegetables and soft fruit in season. His self-service farm shop also sells free-range eggs, yoghurt and bread made with organic flour.

CULLOMPTON

LOWER TURLEY FARM
Cullompton, Devon EX15 1NA
Tel: Tiverton (0884) 32234
Open: 'any time'
This is a mixed organic farm producing vegetables and strawberries and rearing sheep for meat and cheese. Devon Dell is a semi-hard oak-smoked cheese made from ewe's milk. Honey is also available.

CULMSTOCK

HUNTERS LODGE
Hunters Hills, Culmstock, nr. Cullompton, Devon
Tel: Tiverton (0884) 40489
Open: any time, telephone first
Mr Harrup supplies a wide range of organic produce including vegetables, dairy produce, additive-free pork and poultry. He is planning to start growing melons in 1990.

DANBY

CAMPHILL VILLAGE TRUST
Botton Village, Danby, nr. Whitby, North Yorkshire YO21 2NJ
Tel: Castleton (0287) 60871 ext 327
Open: 9 a.m. to noon, 2 p.m. to 6 p.m. Mon to Fri
Closed: Sat, Sun
The Trust is a village community where mentally handicapped people live and work with everyone else. The bakery produces breads with organically grown flour; unpasteurized cheeses –

such as Botton and Danbydale – are made with vegetable rennet and sea salt; organic vegetables are grown occasionally and there are supplies of organic and additive-free meat. Products are available at different shops in the village.

DEBENHAM

ASPALL CYDER
Aspall Hall, Debenham, Suffolk IP14 6PD
Tel: Debenham (0728) 860510
Open: 9 a.m. to noon, 2 p.m. to 4 p.m. Mon to Fri
Closed: Sat, Sun, bank hols and Christmas
John Chevallier-Guild was the first cider maker to acquire the Soil Association symbol. In addition to organic 'cyder' (as he calls it), he also produces organic cider vinegar and apple juice from his unsprayed fruit.

DISS
NATURAL FOODSTORE
Norfolk House, St Nicholas Street, Diss, Norfolk IP22 3LB
Tel: Diss (0379) 51832
Open: 9 a.m. to 5.30 p.m. (to 1 p.m. Tue)
Closed: Sun, bank hols and Christmas
Wholefood shop in a converted Victorian warehouse. Supplies of organic vegetables and fruit supplement dried wholefoods, free-range eggs, bread and other staples.

DITCHLING
COOMBE DOWN PUMPING STATION COTTAGE
The Jacketings, Underhill Lane, Clayton, Ditchling, East Sussex BN6 9PL
Tel: Hassocks (07918) 5839/2323
Open: Ring first
Mrs Gasson grows organic vegetables, blackcurrants and gooseberries in her cottage garden.

DORCHESTER
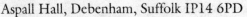
H. & P. CHAPMAN
Longmeadow, Godmanstone, Dorchester, Dorset DT2 7AE
Tel: (03003) 779
Open: 8.30 a.m. to 7 p.m. Mon to Sat ('days and times may alter in winter')
Closed: Sun

The Chapmans grow organic vegetables and operate a self-service stall selling mostly their own produce.

MANOR FARM COTTAGES
Godmanstone, Dorchester, Dorset DT2 7AH
5 miles N of Dorchester on the A352
Tel: (03003) 415
Open: 'telephone orders only, no shop'
Mr Best rears livestock organically and can supply lamb, pork and sausages. Note that there is no retail shop.

TAMARISK FARM
West Bexington, Dorchester, Dorset DT2 9DF
Tel: Dorchester (0308) 897784
Open: 'daylight hours'
Closed: Christmas Day
Arthur and Josephine Pearse grow organic fruit and vegetables to Soil Association standards. Grapes are one of their specialities. They are hoping for a symbol for their meat in 1990.

DORKING
BARN FIELD MARKET GARDEN
Franksfield, Peaslake, nr. Dorking, Surrey GU5 9SR
Tel: Dorking (0306) 731310
Open: 9 a.m. to 2 p.m. Wed and Sat (at Dorking Indoor Market) David Priestley grows organic vegetables, top fruit and soft fruit. He trades at Dorking Indoor Market where he also sells dried wholefoods and juices.

DRIFFIELD
FOSTON GROWERS
Foston on the Wolds, Driffield, Humberside YO25 8BJ
Tel: (026 288) 8843
Open: 8 a.m. to 5 p.m. all week
Closed: Christmas
Foston Growers produce and supply a range of organic vegetables.

DROITWICH
TEMPLE OAK HOUSE
Broughton Green, Hanbury, Droitwich, Hereford and Worcester WR9 7EF

Tel: Himbleton (090569) 683
Open: 9 a.m. to 1 p.m., 2 p.m. to 6 p.m.
Closed: Sun and Christmas
Mr and Mrs Dovey grow organic vegetables and top fruit. They also supply free-range eggs as well as organic pork and lamb.

DURHAM

DURHAM COMMUNITY CO-OP
85A New Elvet, Durham, Co Durham
Tel: Durham (09138) 61183
Open: 10 a.m. to 5.30 p.m. Mon to Sat
Closed: Sun, bank hols and Christmas
The Co-op can supply organic vegetables and top fruit, and there are plans to stock organic wine in the near future.

EAST DEREHAM

MR D.W. SIMMONS
Loke Cottage, 4 Scarning Fen, East Dereham, Norfolk NR19 1LN
Tel: East Dereham (0362) 695947
Open: 9.30 a.m. to 12.15 p.m., 2 p.m. to 6 p.m. Mon, Wed and Thur; 2 p.m. to 6 p.m. Tue and Fri; 9 a.m. to 1 p.m. Sat
Closed: Sun
Dave Simmons grows vegetables and soft fruit to Soil Association standards and supplies additive-free meat as well as dairy produce from his goats.

OLD RECTORY FARM
Great Fransham, nr. East Dereham, Norfolk NR19 2JG
6 miles W of East Dereham on the A47
Open: 8 a.m. to 7 p.m. all week
The Leskanichs are planning to start making cider in the near future, but at present offer vegetables, fruit dairy produce and free-range eggs.

WALNUT FARM
Southburgh, nr. East Dereham, Norfolk IP25 7TE
5 miles S of East Dereham between the A1075 and B1135
Tel: East Dereham (0362) 820218
Open: all week, telephone first
Jock Butler produces organic beef and additive-free meat and

aims to create 'a balanced, non-intensive unit with minimum stress to the animals and the land'. Much of his produce goes to restaurants and retailers.

EAST GRINSTEAD

BUSSES FARM
Harwoods Lane, East Grinstead, West Sussex RH19 4NL
Tel: East Grinstead (0342) 313828
Open: 'telephone first'
Dick Bauer supplies dairy produce under the label of Busses Farm Organic Produce. Yoghurt is his main speciality, but he is planning to start making ice cream in the near future.

OLD PLAW HATCH FARM
Sharpthorne, nr. East Grinstead, West Sussex RH19 4JL
Tel: East Grinstead (0342) 810857
Open: 9 a.m. to 1 p.m., 2 p.m. to 6 p.m. all week
Mr Carnegie runs a mixed organic farm, producing vegetables, milk, yoghurt and cream as well as bacon and sausages from additive-free pork. His beef is purely organic, and he sells beefburgers too.

ELLESMERE
THE ORCHARD NURSERY
Greenhill Bank, Ellesmere, Shropshire
Tel: (069175) 295
Open: 8 a.m. to dusk Thur to Mon
Closed: Tue and Wed
The nursery produces a range of organically grown vegetables and salad crops. Mr Jennings sells direct and also has a stall on Oswestry market (Wed and Sat). In the near future he may also visit Ellesmere and Welshpool markets.

EXETER
CITY WHOLEFOODS
14 South Street, Exeter, Devon EX1 1DZ
Tel: Exeter (0392) 50925
Open: 9 a.m. to 5.30 p.m. Mon to Sat
Closed: Sun and bank hols
Wholefood shop selling vegetables and fruit from symbol growers, as well as dairy produce, dried wholefoods, bread and bakery products. Free-range eggs.

MR R. KERSWELL

11A Thornberry Avenue, Whipton, Exeter, Devon EX1 3HR
Tel: Exeter (0392) 64996
Open: 9 a.m. to 6 p.m. Mon to Sat
Closed: Sun, bank hols and Christmas
Richard Kerswell grows organic vegetables and top fruit, and provides free delivery in the Exeter area. Pumpkins are one of his specialities.

THE KITCHEN GARDEN

Quickes Farm, Newton St Cyres, nr. Exeter, Devon EX5 5AY
4 miles NW of Exeter on the A377
Tel: Exeter (0392) 851681
Open: 10 a.m. to 5 p.m. Tue to Sat
Closed: Sun and Mon
A fully working one-acre walled garden producing organic vegetables and fruit, which are sold through the farm shop. Also free-range eggs, dried wholefoods and fruit juices.

SEASONS

8 Well Street, Exeter, Devon
Tel: Exeter (0392) 436125
Open: 9.30 a.m. to 5.45 p.m.
Closed: Sun
A wide-ranging wholefood shop also selling fruit, vegetables and dairy produce. There is also a good range of oriental products including tempeh and Japanese umeboshi plums.

FALMOUTH

MR B. D. BROADBANK

Brookfield, Constantine, Falmouth, Cornwall TR1 5RR
Tel: Falmouth (0326) 40479
Open: Ring first
Brian Broadbank grows organic vegetables and soft fruit.

MRS E.J. BROWN

Trenance Round Ring, nr. Falmouth, Cornwall TR10 9LA
Tel: Falmouth (0326) 74800
Open: 9 a.m. to 6 p.m.
Closed: Tue, Sun and bank hols
Mrs Brown's farm shop sells a wide range of produce, much of it from symbol holders. Vegetables, fruit, goat produce and

additive-free meat are backed up by dried wholefoods and cereal products.

THE WILD WALNUT
16 High Street, Falmouth, Cornwall
Tel: Falmouth (0326) 311507
Open: 9 a.m. to 5.15 p.m. Mon to Sat
Closed: Sun and bank hols
This used to be Harvest Wholefoods. Organic produce includes vegetables and fruit as well as bread, 'genuine' free-range eggs and dried goods. Organic Christmas puddings are a seasonal speciality.

FORDINGBRIDGE
HOCKEYS-NATURALLY
Newtown Farm, South Gorley, Fordingbridge SP6 2PW
Tel: Fordingbridge (0425) 52542
Open: 9 a.m. to 6 p.m. Mon to Sat
Closed: Sun, bank hols and Christmas
Also mail order
Philip and Carole Hockey have a large area of New Forest grazing land, and rear beef, pork and lamb, as well as geese and chickens without the use of additives or growth promoters. They also grow pot herbs, make preserves, cure their own hams and salt beef, and sell spun wool from their rare breeds of sheep. Farm open-days and a distribution service are other features of the enterprise.

SANDY BALLS ORGANIC GARDENS
Sandy Balls Estate, Godshill, nr. Fordingbridge, Hampshire SP6 2JX
2 miles E of Fordingbridge on the B3078
Tel: Fordingbridge (0425) 54743
Open: 2 p.m. to 6 p.m. all week
Closed: November to Easter
Eden Cormack specializes in vegetables, and also stocks a large selection of organically grown herbs, shrubs and bedding plants.

FOREST ROW
THE SEASONS
10-11 Hartfield Road, Forest Row, nr. East Grinstead, East Sussex RH18 5DN

3 miles SE of East Grinstead on the B2110
Tel: Forest Row (034282) 4673
Open: 8.45 a.m. to 1 p.m., 2 p.m. to 5.30 p.m. (to 1 p.m. Wed and Sat) *Closed*: Sun
An exceptionally well-stocked wholefood shop specializing in organic and biodymically produced foods including vegetables, fruit, dairy produce, beef and pork – not to mention locally-baked bread and baby foods. The shop provides wholesale deliveries to South Sussex.

TABLEHURST FARM
Forest Row, nr. East Grinstead, East Sussex RH18 5DP
3 miles SE of East Grinstead off the B2110
Tel: Forest Row (034282) 3536
Open: 'telephone for orders'
Walter Rudert sells vegetables, free-range eggs and additive-free meat, as well as breads and bakery products.

FROME
THE WHOLEFOOD SHOP
Cork Street, Frome, Somerset
Tel: Frome (0373) 73334
Open: 9.30 a.m. to 5.30 p.m. (to 1 p.m. Thur)
Closed: Sun
This shop sells organic vegetables, fruit, dairy produce and baby foods, as well as dried wholefoods. Organically grown herb plants are also available.

GLASTONBURY

PADDINGTON FARM TRUST
Maidencroft Farm, Wick, Glastonbury, Somerset BA6 8JN
Tel: Glastonbury (0458) 32752
Open: by appointment
The Trust is a wholesale set-up supplying organic vegetables, dairy produce, meat, free-range eggs and poultry. Cider is also available. There is an answerphone for orders.

PHOENIX WHOLEFOODS
4 High Street, Glastonbury, Somerset BA6 9DU
Tel: Glastonbury (0458) 31004
Open: 9.30 a.m. to 6 p.m. Mon to Fri, 11 a.m. to 3 p.m. Sun (in summer)

A wholefood shop specializing in organic fruit and vegetables, wine, cider and breads, as well as serve-yourself mueslis and pulses.

GOXHILL
JOAN & ALAN GOULD
Woodrising, Thorn Lane, Goxhill, South Humberside DN19 7LU
Tel: Goxhill (0469) 30356
Open: 'household hours'
The Goulds are part of the South Humberside Organic Growers Co-operative and are prepared to grow unusual items on request. They normally supply seasonal fruit and vegetables as well as goat's dairy produce.

GREAT MALVERN
ONLY NATURAL
99B Church Street, Great Malvern, Hereford and Worcestershire WR14 2AE
Tel: Great Malvern (0684) 561772
Open: 9 a.m. to 5 p.m. Mon to Sat
Closed: Sun and Christmas
Well-stocked wholefood shop selling organic fruit and vegetables, dairy produce, meat and wine as well as home-made cakes and manna bread. There is a cafe attached (see entry).

GRESHAM
THE STABLES
Gresham, nr. Cromer, Norfolk NR11 8AD
5 miles SW of Cromer
Tel: Matlaske (026377) 468
Open: 'any time, but telephone first'
Anne and Keith Hood's small-holding supports a herd of Jersey cows which supply milk for butter and cheeses. Seasonal vegetables are also part of the enterprise.

GRIMSBY
THE WHOLEFOOD CO-OP
7B East St Mary's Gate, Grimsby, South Humberside
Tel: Grimsby (0472) 251112
Open: 9 a.m. to 5 p.m. Mon to Sat
Closed: Sun, bank hols and Christmas
Carries a similar range to the related shop in Louth (see entry).

GUILDFORD
EARTHBOUND WHOLEFOODS
10 Madrid Road, Guildford, Surrey GU2 5NT
Tel: Guildford (0483) 69611
Open: 9 a.m. to 5.30 p.m. (to 5 p.m. Mon and Sat)
Closed: Sun, bank hols and Christmas
The shop sells dried wholefoods, organic fruit and vegetables, free-range eggs and non-alcoholic drinks. There is a branch at Tudor House, High Street, Cranleigh, Surrey.

LOSELEY PARK FARM SHOP
Loseley Park, nr. Guildford, Surrey GU3 1HS
Tel: Guildford (0483) 571881
Open: noon to 5 p.m. Wed to Sat from June to Sept.; 2 p.m. to 5 p.m. Fri and 10 a.m. to 1 p.m. Sat from Oct. to Mar.
Closed: Mon, Tue, bank hols
The estate and its fine manor house have been in the More family since the sixteenth century. The farm is moving over to organic cereal production and the wheat is stoneground and baked on the premises; a pedigree Jersey herd provides milk for yoghurts, ice creams and other dairy produce. The shop sells the full range, plus organic fruit and vegetables, additive-free meat and free-range eggs.

PICCARDS FARM PRODUCTS
Conduit Farm, Sandy Lane, Guildford, Surrey GU3 1HJ
Tel: Guildford (0483) 63095/35364
Open: by appointment, telephone first
Organic and additive-free meat is the main speciality, but dried wholefoods and bakery products are also available. Piccards operate from Loseley Farm Shop (see entry) from June to September (2 p.m. to 5 p.m. Wed to Sat).

HAILSHAM

GRAEME FISK
The Granary, Prinkle Farm, Bodle Street, Hailsham, East Sussex BN27 4UD
Tel: (0323) 833541
Open: 9 a.m. to 1 p.m., 2 p.m. to 7 p.m. Mon to Sat
Closed: Sun, bank hols and Christmas
Graeme Fisk specializes in soft fruit, especially blackcurrants. He also sells organic wine.

HALESWORTH
POPLAR FARM ORGANIC VEGS
Poplar Farm, Silverleys Green, Cratfield, nr. Halesworth, Suffolk IP19 0QJ
5 miles SW of Halesworth
Tel: (037 986) 241
Open: always open, but telephone first
Anthony Gaze produces a range of organic vegetables on his Suffolk farm. Japanese pumpkins are his most unusual speciality.

HALIFAX
BRACKEN FARM
Priestly Green, Norwood Green, Halifax, West Yorkshire HX3 8RQ
Tel: Halifax (0422) 205578
Open: 9 a.m. to 6 p.m. all week
Closed: Christmas Day and Boxing Day
You can buy organic vegetables, soft fruit, free-range eggs, dried wholefoods and juices from the farm.

HARROGATE
THE NATURAL CHOICE
146 Kings Road, Harrogate, North Yorkshire HG1 5HY
Tel: Harrogate (0423) 508760
Open: 8.30 a.m. to 5.30 p.m. (to 4 p.m. Sat)
Closed: Wed
This used to be Holmes Natural Farming Shop. Hazel Whitaker stocks a wide range of organic foods including dairy produce, meat and bakery products as well as fruit and vegetables.

HARTFIELD
STAIRS FARM PRODUCE
Stairs Farmhouse, High Street, Hartfield, East Sussex TN7 4AB
Tel: Hartfield (089277) 793
Open: 10 a.m. to 6 p.m. (to 1 p.m. Sun)
Closed: Tue
Mrs Pring specializes in additive-free meat, including fully matured beef, free-range pork and lamb. She also sells a wide range of other produce including fruit, vegetables, dairy produce, free-range eggs and poultry, as well as organic wine and cider.

HAY-ON-WYE
HAY WHOLEFOODS & DELICATESSEN
1 Lion Street, Hay-on-Wye, Hereford and Worcester HR3 5AA
Tel: Hay-on-Wye (0497) 820708/820388
Open: 9.30 a.m. to 5.30 p.m. Mon to Sat
Closed: Sun, Christmas Day and Boxing Day
Paul Goldman has been committed to organic produce for more than six years and reports that 'after struggling not to lose money – especially on vegetables – sales are increasing'. He sells a very wide range of produce from fruit and vegetables to cider and wine. Organic meat is available to order.

HEATHFIELD
BARKLYE FARM
Swife Lane, Broad Oak, Heathfield, East Sussex TN21 8UR
Tel: Heathfield (0435) 883536
Open: all weekend, telephone first during the week
Ms Haines produces beef and lamb to Soil Association standards. All joints are available, as well as half or whole lambs butchered and ready for the freezer.

HEREFORD
GREEN ACRES
Dinmore, nr. Hereford, Hereford and Worcester HR4 8ED
Tel: Bodenham (056884) 7045
Open: 9 a.m. to 5.30 p.m. all week
Closed: Christmas Day and Boxing Day
David and Sheila Jenkins can supply a wide range of organic vegetables, top fruit, dairy produce and meat, as well as free-range poultry and eggs.

HENCLOSE COTTAGE
Little Dewchurch, nr. Hereford, Hereford and Worcester HR2 6PP
Tel: Carey (043270) 317
Open: 'any reasonable time, telephone first'
This little cottage enterprise is run by Ms Tibbetts, who can supply organic meat and vegetables at most times.

HERNE
T. & C. DAVIS
3 Broomfield Road, Herne, nr. Canterbury, Kent CT6 7AY

Tel: Canterbury (0227) 372519
Open: 'all times'
The Davis's are renowned for the quality of their organic top fruit, but they also grow organic vegetables and can supply free-range eggs and honey.

HONEYBOURNE
DOMESTIC FOWL TRUST
Honeybourne Pastures, Honeybourne, nr. Evesham, Hereford and Worcester WR11 5QJ
4 miles E of Evesham off the B4035
Tel: Evesham (0386) 833083
Open: 10.30 a.m. to 5 p.m.
Closed: Fri, Christmas Day and Boxing Day
All Mrs Roberts' poultry is raised outdoors without additives. She also supplies free-range eggs and organic meat.

HONITON

ELLIOTS FARM SHOP & NURSERY
Offwell, Honiton, Devon EX14 9RT
2 miles E of Honiton off the A35
Tel: Wilmington (040483) 549
Open: 8.30 a.m. to 6 p.m. all week
The shop sells a wide range of organic produce, including vegetables, fruit, breads, juices and wines, as well as free-range eggs.

HORSHAM
THE COUNTRY BASKET
7 East Street, Horsham, West Sussex RH12 1HH
Tel: Horsham (0403) 65102
Open: 9 a.m. to 5 p.m. Mon to Sat
Closed: Sun and all public hols
The Country Basket is totally vegetarian with a good range of organic fruit and vegetables, grains, pulses, nuts and other wholefoods. There is a takeaway counter and cafe attached (see entry).

HORSMORDEN

J. L. ORBACH
Small's Farm, Horsmorden, Kent TN12 8BW
Tel: (089 272) 2519

Open: 9 a.m. to 5 p.m. Mon to Fri 'by appointment'
Closed: Sat, Sun, bank hols and Christmas
Small's Farm has the Soil Association symbol for its top fruit.
Organically grown vegetables are also available.

HOVINGHAM

S. & D.G. HODGSON
Scackleton, Hovingham, North Yorkshire YO6 4NB
Tel: (065382) 474
Open: 9 a.m. to 8 p.m. all week
The Hodgsons are growers and suppliers of organic vegetables
and soft fruit.

HUDDERSFIELD
THE WHOLEFOOD SHOP
4 Half Moon Street, Huddersfield, West Yorkshire HD1 2JJ
Tel: Huddersfield (0484) 663301
Open: 9.15 a.m. to 5.30 p.m. Mon, Tue, Thur, Fri; 9.15 a.m.
to 5 p.m. Wed; 9 a.m. to 5 p.m. Sat
Closed: Sun, bank hols and Christmas
Adrian Midgeley and Judith Beresford have been in business
for about three years, and have a wide range of organic
produce: fruit and vegetables, dairy produce from Rachel's
Dairy, Borth, wines from Vinceremos, cheese from Botton
Village, flour from The Watermill, Little Salkeld, and much
more. Local delivery service on orders over £5.

HUNGERFORD

DOVES FARM
Salisbury Road, Hungerford, Berkshire RG17 0RF
Tel: Hungerford (0488) 84880
Open: 9 a.m. to 1 p.m., 2 p.m. to 5 p.m. Mon to Fri
Closed: Sat, Sun, bank hols and Christmas
Doves Farm has the widest range of organic flours available in
the UK. It also includes a range of biscuits, breads and cakes
and has recently introduced its own range of breakfast cereals.
Doves Farm products are available direct or from supermarkets
and wholefood shops throughout the country.

ILMINSTER

WIGMORE ORGANICS
Parsonage Cottage, Cudworth, Ilminster, Somerset TA18 0PR

Tel: Ilminster (046 05) 53165
Open: 8 a.m. to 9 p.m. all week
Closed: 3 weeks after Christmas
Mr Wigmore can supply fresh organic vegetables all year round, including outdoor salads through the winter such as corn salad and winter purslane. There is a stall at Cricket St Thomas Wildlife Park every Sunday (noon to 5 p.m.), and occasionally during the week as well (telephone first to check).

IPSWICH
TRICKERS FARM
Kersey, nr. Ipswich, Suffolk IP7 6EW
Tel: Ipswich (0473) 827231
Open: 9 a.m. to dusk Mon to Sat
Closed: Sun
The Partridges sell a wide range of organic vegetables, including tunnel crops, from their roadside stall. Japanese pumpkins are one of their specialities. Telephone first for large orders.

IRONBRIDGE
MR & MRS S. C. BUYS
3 Pool View Park, Buildwas, nr. Ironbridge, Shropshire TF8 7BS
Tel: Ironbridge (095 245) 3400
Open: 'by arrangement only'
Mr and Mrs Buys have no farm shop, but sell most of their produce on the local market. They grow vegetables (including French garlic) and soft fruit, and can also supply dried wholefoods.

ISFIELD
BOAT HOUSE FARM
Isfield, nr. Uckfield, East Sussex TN22 5TY
Tel: (082575) 302
Open: 8 a.m. to 5 p.m. all week
A mixed organic farm producing stoneground wholemeal flour, beef and lamb, as well as free-range eggs.

KINGS LANGLEY
WHOLEFOODS
13A Hempstead Road, Kings Langley, Hertfordshire WD4 8BJ
Tel: Kings Langley (0923) 263195
Open: 9 a.m. to 1 p.m., 2 p.m. to 5.30 p.m. Mon to Sat
Closed: Sun

Clare James sells a wide range of organic wholefoods, plus dairy produce and free-range eggs. Other unusual items include sauerkraut, apple purée and whole grain 'kwasz' (a bread drink). Much of the produce is from symbol holders.

LANCASTER

DR R. D. EVERETT
Middle Wood, Blackbottom Farm, c/o Roeburn Scar, Wray, nr. Lancaster, Lancashire LA2 8QR
Tel: Hornby (05242) 21880
Open: 'telephone first'
Dr Everett produces small quantities of organic vegetables and lamb raised to Soil Association standards. He also runs courses on 'green concepts' at Middle Wood Green College.

S. & G. FOWLER
Ferrocrete Farm, Arkholme, nr. Lancaster, Lancashire LA6 1AV
9 miles NE of Lancaster off the B6254
Tel: Lancaster (0524) 221965
Open: 'any reasonable hour, but telephone first'
The Fowlers have the Soil Association symbol for their vegetables and top fruit, but are best known for their additive-free meat, poultry and goat's dairy produce. The grassland is managed organically and veterinary products are kept to a minimum. The Fowlers also supply wholefood bakery products including those for special diets. They have a stall on Lancaster's Church Street market (Wed and Sat 9.30 a.m. to 5 p.m.).

SINGLE STEP CO-OP LTD
78A Penny Street, Lancaster, Lancashire LA1 1XN
Tel: Lancaster (0524) 63021
Open: 9.30 a.m. to 5 p.m. (to 5.30 p.m. Fri)
Closed: Sun, bank hols and Christmas
Organic vegetables, top fruit, dairy produce and eggs supplement a wide range of wholefoods, from pasta to tofu and soya milk. The shop also sells organic wines.

LANGPORT
A. V. R. CRACKNELL & SON
Free Range Poultry Farm, Huish Episcopi, nr. Langport, Somerset TA10 9EY
1.5 miles E of Langport off B3153

Tel: Langport (0458) 250731
Open: Mon to Sat, 'most daylight hours'
Closed: Sun
Mr Cracknell rears free-range chickens, ducks and geese with no artificial fertilizers used on the pastures and no growth promoters or additives in the feed. Chickens are available throughout the year, ducks in the summer and autumn, and corn-fed geese from Michaelmas to Christmas. Sheep are also reared for meat.

LAUNCESTON
FOOD FOR THOUGHT
4A Market Street, Launceston, Cornwall
Tel: Launceston (0566) 4300
Open: 8.30 a.m. to 5 p.m. Mon to Sat
Closed: Sun
The shop sells vegetables from Soil Association growers, plus dried wholefoods, free-range eggs and cider, as well as breads and juices.

GREENLANDS ORGANIC PRODUCE
Bearah, Bathpool, Launceston, Cornwall PL15 7NW
7 miles S of Launceston off the B3254
Tel: Liskeard (0579) 63060
Open: 10 a.m. to 5 p.m. Fri and Sat
Closed: Sun to Thurs, bank hols and Christmas
Organic fruit and vegetables are supplemented by dairy produce, dried wholefoods, bread and bakery products. Organic wine can be obtained by arrangement. Free deliveries within a 10-mile radius.

MR C. MARSHALL
Coombe Rise, Pipers Pool, Launceston, Cornwall PL15 8QG
Tel: Pipers Pool (0566) 86314
Open: 'any time, but please phone first'
Colin Marshall's enterprising set-up produces organic vegetables, soft fruit, meat and poultry. He also grows trees and shrubs.

LEEDS
BEANO WHOLEFOOD COLLECTIVE
36 New Briggate, Leeds, West Yorkshire LS1 6NU

Tel: Leeds (0532) 435737
Open: 9 a.m. to 5 p.m. (to 5.30 p.m. Thur)
Closed: Sun, bank hols and Christmas
The shop stocks organic fruit and vegetables, dairy produce, dried wholefoods and specialities ranging from pasta to cider vinegar. Delivery service and discount on bulk orders.

MEANWOOD VALLEY URBAN CITY FARM
Sugarwell Road, Meanwood, Leeds 7, West Yorkshire
Tel: Leeds (0532) 629759
Open: 8.30 a.m. to 4.30 p.m. Mon to Fri; 9 a.m. to 4.30 p.m. Sat and Sun (orders can be collected up to 8 p.m.)
The farm produces vegetables and soft fruit including gooseberries and blackcurrants. Everything is freshly picked. Culinary and medicinal herbs are also available.

LEICESTER
WHOLE MEAL
158 Queens Road, Clarendon Park, Leicester, Leicestershire LE2 3FS
Tel: Leicester (0533) 703617
Open: 9 a.m. to 5.30 p.m. Tue to Thur, to 6.30 p.m. Fri, to 5 p.m. Sat
Closed: Sun, Mon, bank hols and Christmas
The shop sells Soil Association vegetables and a good selection of breads, bakery products and dried wholefoods. Free-range eggs too.

LEOMINSTER
BREWER'S BASIC
15A Broad Street, Leominster, Hereford and Worcester HR6 8BT
Tel: Leominster (0568) 2154/5897
Open: 8.30 a.m. to 5 p.m. Mon to Sat
Closed: Sun
Linda Kaye's shop and delicatessen stocks only organic produce: vegetables, fruit, dairy produce, meat, poultry, wholefoods, breads and wine. There are also ready-prepared snacks and vegetarian freezer meals to take away – all prepared with organic ingredients. Other environmental products range from re-cycled paper to mercury-free batteries.

NITTY GRITTY
24 West Street, Leominster, Hereford and Worcester HR6 0HZ
Tel: Leominster (0568) 611600
Open: 9 a.m. to 5.30 p.m. Mon to Sat
Closed: Sun and bank hols
Wholefood shop selling organic vegetables in season, plus an interesting selection of specialities from tofu, seaweed and ewes' milk ice cream to frozen, ready-prepared organic dishes.

RODGERS & LAMBTON
Oak Cottage, The Riddox, Pembridge, nr. Leominster, Hereford and Worcester HR6 9JS
7 miles W of Leominster off the A44
Tel: Kington (0544) 318479
Open: 9 a.m. to 5 p.m. all week
Closed: bank hols and Christmas
This organic enterprise specializes in organic vegetables, winter salads and soft fruit.

LETCHWORTH
FAIRHAVEN WHOLEFOODS
20 Eastcheap, Letchworth, Hertfordshire SG6 3DE
Tel: Letchworth (0462) 677572
Open: 8.45 a.m. to 5.30 p.m. (to 2 p.m. Wed, to 6 p.m. Thur, to 8 p.m. Fri)
Closed: Sun, bank hols and Christmas
A well-stocked wholefood shop that can provide organic vegetables and top fruit in season, as well as other items ranging from organic Italian rice to juices. The office and warehouse is at 27 Jubilee Trade Centre, Letchworth SG6 1SP (Tel: 675300). A twice-monthly delivery operates to surrounding counties for orders over £15.

LEWES
FULL OF BEANS
96-97 High Street, Lewes, East Sussex BN7 1XH
Tel: Lewes (0273) 472627
Open: 9 a.m. to 5.30 p.m. Mon to Fri (to 5 p.m. Sat)
Closed: Sun and bank hols
Also mail order
An enterprising shop with a difference. John Gosling produces

tofu, miso and tempeh (a fermented soya bean cake) from organically grown soya beans, and makes his own ice creams from organic ingredients. Breads, bakery products, organic cheese and wine are also available.

LINCOLN
GREENS HEALTH FOODS
175 High Street, Lincoln, Lincolnshire LN5 7AF
Tel: Lincoln (0522) 24874
Open: 8.30 a.m. to 5.30 p.m. Mon to Sat
Closed: Sun and bank hols
Sells wholefoods, dairy produce and bakery products, some from symbol holders. The shop's own Erica House brand label is used on top quality produce. There is a branch at New Cornhill Market, Lincoln.

F. A. & J. JONES & SON
Red House Farm, Spalford Lane, North Scarle, nr. Lincoln, Lincolnshire LN6 9HB
8 miles SW of Lincoln off the A1133
Tel: Spalford (052277) 224
Open: 9 a.m. to 12.30 p.m., 1.30 p.m. to 5 p.m. Wed, Thur and Sat, to 7 p.m. Fri
Closed: Mon, Tue, Christmas, New Year and 2 weeks summer
The Jones family have been producing additive-free meat and poultry for more than ten years, using traditional feeds and avoiding chemical protein, antibiotics or growth promoters. Their full range of pork pies, pasties and sausage rolls are made with organic wholemeal flour and free-range eggs. They make Lincolnshire sausages and from July to September they also sell organic tomatoes.

T. D. & P. M. ORGAN
East Farm, Normandy by Stow, Gainsborough, nr. Lincoln, Lincolnshire LN21 5LQ
Between Lincoln and Stow off the A1500
Tel: Gainsborough (0427) 788629
Open: most times
Closed: 8 a.m. to 4.30 p.m. Mon to Fri during school terms
Dr Organ grows organic vegetables to strict organic standards and rears additive-free 'real' beef, as he calls it.

LITTLE SALKELD
THE WATERMILL
Little Salkeld, nr. Penrith, Cumbria CA10 1NN
5 miles NE of Penrith, off the A686
Tel: Langwathby (076881) 523
Open: 9.30 a.m. to 12.30 p.m., 2 p.m. to 5 p.m. Mon to Fri
Closed: Sat and Sun
The Jones family produce a range of stoneground flours from organically grown grain in their restored watermill. As well as wholewheat, they produce rye, barley, malted and self-raising, plus mueslis, bran and porridge oats.

LIVERPOOL
ALLERTON HEALTH STORES
77 Allerton Road, Liverpool L18 2DE
Tel: (051) 737 2152
Open: 9 a.m. to 5.30 p.m. (to 6 p.m. Thur and Fri)
Closed: Sun, bank hols and Christmas
Most of the goods are bought direct from growers with up to 3 deliveries each week. The range includes everything from organic fruit and vegetables to dried wholefoods and drug-free skimmed milk. Some items are distributed to other shops under the 'progress and Nature' label.

LONDON
BUSHWACKER WHOLEFOODS
59 Goldhawk Road, London W12 8EG
Tel: (081) 743 2359
Chris Shipton's wholefood shop and delicatessen has a wide range of organic produce from oils and pasta to tomato ketchup, as well as vegetables, fruit and organic wine. Oriental products such as tempeh and umeboshi plums are also available.

CLEARSPRING NATURAL GROCER
196 Old Street, London EC1V 9BP
Tel: (071) 250 1708
Open: 8.30 a.m. to 7 p.m. Mon to Fri; 9.30 a.m. to 5 p.m. Sat
Closed: Sun
Direct imports and macrobiotic foods are the main specialities and the shop is noted for its range of Japanese and other oriental products including seaweeds, pickles, tamari, tea and saké.

CORNUCOPIA WHOLEFOODS
64 St Mary's Road, Ealing, London W5 5EX
Tel: (081) 579 9431
Open: 9 a.m. to 5.30 p.m. Mon to Sat
Closed: Sun, bank hols, Christmas and New Year
Wholefood shop selling organic fruit and vegetables, dairy
produce and wine as well as cider and perry.

CRANKS HEALTH FOODS
8 Marshall Street, London W1V 1LP
Tel: (071) 437 2915
Cranks is the best-known name in wholefoods, with a small
chain of shops and restaurants around London. The Marshall
Street address has an enormous range of organic produce,
from breads, fruit, vegetables and dairy produce to wine.
Other branches are primarily restaurants, although you can buy
quiches, cakes and other cooked items to take away. (See Part
Three for details). Now owned by the Guinness Group.

CRYSTAL PALACE WHOLEFOODS
74 Church Road, Crystal Palace, London SE19
Tel: (081) 771 4605
Open: 10 a.m. to 6 p.m. Tue to Fri; to 5 p.m. Sat
Closed: Sun, Mon, bank hols and Christmas
Wholefood shop selling organic fruit and vegetables, dairy
produce, wine and cider, in addition to specialities such as
mayonnaise and pasta.

NATURAL FOODS LTD
Unit 14, Hainault Road Ind Est, Hainault, London E11 1HD
Tel: (081) 539 1034
Open: 'telephone for orders'
This is a retail delivery service with a wide range of organic
products, taking in everything from vegetables and fruit to
meat, poultry and wine.

NEAL'S YARD
Neal's Yard, Covent Garden, London WC2H 9DP
Tel: (071) 836 5199 (bakery); (071) 379 7646 (dairy)
Open: 9.30 a.m. to 5.30 p.m. (to 6 p.m. Thur and Fri)
Closed: Sun and bank hols
The Neal's Yard complex includes a dairy, bakery and organic

vegetable shop, as well as health and therapy centres. The dairy normally carries up to 50 cheeses, mostly unpasteurized and generally with some organic representatives; the bakery and attached tearoom supplies breads, cakes etc., made with organic flour. There are branches at Chelsea Farmers Market, Sydney Street, London SW3 6NR and Alexandra Palace, Muswell Hill. Outside London, there is an outlet in Oxford (see entry).

NEAL'S YARD WHOLEFOOD WAREHOUSE
21-23 Shorts Gardens, London WC2
Tel: (071) 836 5151
Open: 10 a.m. to 6.30 p.m. (to 8 p.m. Thur, to 5 p.m. Sun)
Part of London's best-known 'real foods' centre. The wholefood warehouse specializes in cereals, grains, dried fruit, nuts and pulses, along with honey, organic cider and wine plus other specialities such as tofu. Organic fruit and vegetables, breads from the Neal's Yard Bakery and some cheeses from the Dairy are also available.

ONLY NATURAL
108 Palmerston Road, Walthamstow, London E17 6PZ
Tel: (071) 520 5898
Open: 9 a.m. to 5.30 p.m. (to 1 p.m. Wed, to 7 p.m. Thur)
Closed: Sun., bank hols and Christmas
Sells a wide range of organic fruit and vegetables as well as eighteen kinds of organic flours from the sack. Free delivery of orders over £10 within a ten-mile radius. There is a wholefood restaurant, Le Soleil, next door (See entry in Part Three).

THE ORGANIC SHOP
120 Ferndale Road, Clapham, London SW4
Tel: (071) 737 1365
Open: 10 a.m. to 6 p.m. Tue to Sat
Closed: Sun, Mon, bank hols and Christmas
As its name suggests, this wholefood shop has plenty of organic produce, from fruit and vegetables to wine and preserves. It also offers an organic catering service.

PEPPERCORN'S WHOLEFOOD & GRANARY
2 Heath Street, Hampstead, London NW3

Tel: (071) 431 1251
Open: 10 a.m. to 6.30 p.m. Mon to Sat; 11 a.m. to 5 p.m. Sun
Organic vegetables and fruit – especially exotic varieties -
appear alongside dried wholefoods, preserves and oils, and
organic wine. There is a branch as 193-195 West End Lane,
London NW6 ((071) 328 6874).

UNIQUE BUTCHERS
217 Holloway Road, London N7 8DL
Tel: (071) 609 7016
Open: 8 a.m. to 5 p.m. (to 6.30 p.m. Fri)
Closed: Sun, bank hols, Christmas Day and Boxing Day
Linda McCrae's shop is one of the few organic butchers in
London. She sells a full range of organic meat, free-range
poultry and additive-free meat products including six kinds of
100 per cent meat sausages, potted meats, paté and lamb
burgers, haggis and black puddings. Fruit, vegetables and eggs
are also available.

WELLBEING FOODS
19 Sydenham Road, London SE26
Tel: (081) 659 2003
Open: 9 a.m. to 6.30 p.m. Mon to Sat
Closed: Sun, bank hols and Christmas
Wholefood shop selling a wide range of dried wholefoods and
Japanese products, plus organic fruit and vegetables from
symbol holders.

WHOLEFOOD
24 Paddington Street, London W1M 4DR
Tel: (071) 935 3924
Open: 8.45 a.m. to 6.30 p.m. (to 6 p.m. Mon, to 1 p.m. Sat)
Closed: Sun
Wholefood opened in 1960 and has one of the most
comprehensive ranges of organic produce in the country –
including fruit and vegetables (home-grown and imported)
grains, pulses, breads, juices, baby foods and much more. The
emphasis is on products with guarantees and preference is
given to the Soil Association and Demeter symbols. The shop
also has an excellent selection of books as well as accessories for
the gardener.

WHOLEFOOD BUTCHERS
31 Paddington Street, London W1M 3RG
Tel: (071) 486 1390
Open: 8.30 a.m. to 6 p.m. (to 6.30 p.m. Fri, to 1 p.m. Sat)
Closed: Sun
Related to Wholefood (see above). This butchers specializes in beef and lamb produced to Soil Association standards as well as pork and bacon from free-range animals.There is also free-range poultry as well as a selection of additive-free meat products such as sausages, haggis and patés.

LOUTH
THE WHOLEFOOD CO-OP
7 Aswell Street, Louth, Lincolnshire
Tel: Louth (0507) 602411
Open: 9 a.m. to 5 p.m. Mon to Sat
Closed: Sun, bank hols
Stocks a wide range of organic wholefoods including flours, grains, pasta, breads and rice cakes, as well as 'cafe organico'. Vegetables and top fruit. There is a branch in Grimsby (see entry).

LUTTERWORTH
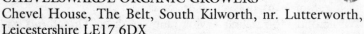
CHEVELSWARDE ORGANIC GROWERS
Chevel House, The Belt, South Kilworth, nr. Lutterworth, Leicestershire LE17 6DX
5 miles SE of Lutterworth on the B5414
Tel: (0858) 575309
Open: 9 a.m. to 6 p.m.
Closed: Christmas Day and Boxing Day
A small organic enterprise producing vegetables, soft fruit and additive-free pork. Free-range eggs, dried wholefoods and organic wine are also available.

MAIDENHEAD
NATURAL LIVING
King Street Market, Maidenhead, Berkshire SL6 1EF
Tel: Maidenhead (0628) 771381/771379
Open: 10 a.m. to 5.30 p.m. Tue to Sat
Closed: Sun, Mon, bank hols and Christmas
This shop aims to stock 'every available organic product', from fruit, vegetables and meat to dairy produce, dried wholefoods

and tofu. They operate a delivery service.

MAIDSTONE
THE POCKET GARDEN
Museum of Kent Rural Life, Lock Lane, Maidstone, Kent
ME14 3AU
Tel: Maidstone (0622) 763936
Open: Apr. – mid-Oct.: 10 a.m. to 5 p.m. Mon, Tue, Thur, Fri;
noon to 5 p.m. Sat; noon to 6 p.m. Sun
Closed: Wed
Orchard fruit, including many old varieties, are the main
specialities here. Organic vegetables are also available. Supplies
may be spasmodic.

MALDON

MILL FARM
Purleigh, nr. Maldon, Essex CM3 6PU
4 miles S of Maldon off the B1010
Tel: Maldon (0621) 828280
Open: 'by appointment please'
Chris and Helen Goldsmith grow organic vegetables to Soil
Association standards.

MALPAS

OAKCROFT GARDENS
Cross o' the' Hill, Malpas, Cheshire SY14 8DH
Tel: (0948) 860213
Open: 8.30 a.m. to 4 p.m. all week, 'prior notice please'
This enterprise has been run organically for more than twenty-
five years. Fruit and vegetables are the main lines, but Mehr
Fardoonji can also supply dairy produce, eggs and bakery
products. There is a stall on Chester Market every Thursday,
10 a.m. to 4.30 p.m..

MANSFIELD
WILD OATS
31A Church Street, Mansfield, Nottinghamshire
Tel: Mansfield (0623) 654121
Open: 9 a.m. to 5.30 p.m. Mon to Sat
Closed: Sun
Organic fruit and vegetables supplement a good range of dried
wholefoods, bakery products and juices in this shop.

MARKET DRAYTON

P. & S. BARTRAM

Hope House, Sandy Lane, Stoke Heath, Market Drayton, Shropshire TF9 2LG

4 miles S of Market Drayton off the A41

Tel: Tern Hill (063083) 348

Open: 'We are very happy to be phoned/visited evenings and weekends'

Peter Bartram's best-known speciality is garlic paste, but he produces a wide range of organic vegetables and herbs as well.

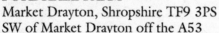

FORDHALL FARM

Market Drayton, Shropshire TF9 3PS

SW of Market Drayton off the A53

Tel: Tern Hill (063083) 255

Open: 'always open, preferably by appointment'

Arthur Hollins has some fifty years' experience of organic farming and developed a machine to assist in cropping. He produces pork, lamb, beef and veal as well as a wide range of poultry – all reared to strict organic standards. Most of his meat is butchered and distributed by Ray Cornmell of Bolton (see entry). Fordhall Farm has a farm walk and nature trail, and afternoon teas are served in the garden.

MARLBOROUGH

MARTIN PITT

Levetts Farm, Clench Common, Marlborough, Wiltshire SN8 4DS

Tel: Marlborough (0672) 54976

Open: 9 a.m. to 5 p.m. Mon to Fri

Closed: Sat, Sun, bank hols and Christmas

Martin Pitt is best known as the country's largest producer of free-range eggs, but he also rears sheep to Soil Association standards. The ewe's milk goes to make a range of vegetarian soft cheeses, under the name of Wiltshire White (natural, with chives, and oak-smoked) and he supplies lamb as well.

MELMERBY

VILLAGE BAKERY

Melmerby, Penrith, Cumbria CA10 1HE

8 miles NE of Penrith

Tel: Langwathby (076881) 515

Open: Easter to Christmas: 8.30 a.m. to 5 p.m. all week (to

12.30 p.m. Mon); Christmas to Easter: 8.30 a.m. to 12.30 p.m. Mon to Sat

Closed: Sun (from Christmas to Easter)

Most of the produce from Andrew and Lis Whitley's remarkable enterprise goes to their restaurant (see entry in Part Three), but they can sometimes supply breads, cakes, vegetables and fruit to visitors, and operate a mail order service. Their produce is also available at the related Village Bakery Food Shop, Angel Lane, Penrith (Tel: 0768 62377).

MORPETH

Mr & MRS A. J. CRERAR

Grasmere House, 56 Station Road, Stannington, nr. Morpeth, Northumberland NE61 6NH

Tel: Stannington (067089) 343

Open: 'open all year for telephone orders; direct sales Fri and Sat'

The Crerars are committed supporters of the organic movement and produce all their fruit, vegetables and salad crops to strict organic standards, although they have discontinued their Soil Association symbol. They are planning to set up a farm shop and seminar room for visiting groups.

MOSSLEY

MOSSLEY WHOLEFOODS

10 Stockport Road, Mossley, nr. Ashton-under-Lyne, Lancashire

Tel: (04575) 67743

Open: 9 a.m. to 5.30 p.m. (to 1 p.m. Tue, to 4.30 p.m. Sat)

Closed: Sun

In addition to a range of wholefood staples such as cereals and juices, this shop also stocks organic fruit vegetables, dairy produce and meat.

MUCH HADHAM

DANE BRIDGE NURSERY

Much Hadham, Hertfordshire SG10 6JG

3 miles W of Bishop's Stortford

Tel: Much Hadham (027984) 3222

Open: 'all times, but telephone to avoid disappointment'

Antony Callegari trained as a chemist, but now specializes in growing organic soft fruit, in particular raspberries (May to November) and tayberries (early June to July). He is also planning to grow Victoria plums and other crops in due course.

NAILSWORTH

BEECHWOOD FARM
Windsor Edge, nr. Nailsworth, Gloucestershire GL6 0NP
Tel: Nailsworth (045383) 3982
Open: 9 a.m. to 1 p.m., 2 p.m. to 5.30 p.m. Mon to Sat
Closed: Sun, bank hols and Christmas
A mixed farm producing organic vegetables, meat and poultry.
The symbol is for vegetables only at present.

NEW COSTESSEY

BRIDGE FARM
Norwich Road, New Costessey, nr. Norwich, Norfolk NR5 0LA
Tel: Norwich (0603) 742822
Open: 9 a.m. to 6 p.m. Tue to Sat
Closed: Sun and Mon
Betty Green grows organic vegetables and can also supply a
range of dried wholefoods and baby foods.

NEW YORK

HERMITAGE FARM
Havenbank Road, New York, nr. Lincoln, Lincolnshire LN4 4XJ
2.5 miles S of New York on the B1192
Tel: (020573) 286
Open: Mon to Fri, telephone first
Closed: Sat and Sun
Organically grown potatoes, swede and Dutch cabbage are the
main products, but the Lawsons can also supply home-bred
additive-free beef.

NEWARK

BUMBLEBEE HALL
Westbrook Lane, South Collingham, Newark, Nottingham-
shire NG23 7RE
Tel: Newark (0636) 892638
Open: 'any time'
Organic vegetables grown to Soil Association standards.

NEWCASTLE-UNDER-LYME
M. & B. DEAVILLE
New House Farm, Acton, Whitmore, Staffordshire ST5 4EE

4 miles SW of Newcastle-under-Lyme on A53
Tel: Whitmore (0782) 680366
Open: 9 a.m. to 6 p.m. Mon to Sat
Closed: Sun
Michael and Betty Deaville have been farming organically for almost twelve years. Their main product is Staffordshire Organic Cheese -a hard cheese made with vegetable rennet and unpasteurized milk from their own cows. They also produce ice cream and yoghurt. The Deavilles grow vegetables and can supply organic beef and lamb as well as additive-free pork and poultry.

NEWCASTLE-UPON-TYNE
CITY FARM BYKER
Stepney Bank, Newcastle-upon-Tyne, Tyne & Wear NE1 2PF
Tel: (091) 232 3698
Open: 10 a.m. to 5.30 p.m. Tue to Sun
Closed: Mon
Dairy produce from the farm's goats, free-range eggs and poultry and additive-free meat are offered for sale.

MANDALA WHOLEFOODS
43 Manor House Road, Jesmond, Newcastle-upon-Tyne, Tyne & Wear
Tel: (091) 281 0045
Open: 9.30 a.m. to 6 p.m. Mon to Sat
Closed: Sun
This shop averages twenty-five types of organic vegetable and ten different fruits every week, in addition to dairy produce, eggs and assorted wholefoods. There is also a good stock of macrobiotic and oriental foods, and organic wines can be supplied wholesale. There is a branch – The Fenham Real Food Store – at 299 Two Ball Lonnen, Fenham, Newcastle-upon-Tyne (Tel: (091) 274 0329).

ONLY NATURAL
290 Chillingham Road, Heaton, Newcastle-upon-Tyne, Tyne & Wear NE6 5LQ
Tel: (091) 265 0070
Open: 9.30 a.m. to 6 p.m. (to 5.30 p.m. Sat)
Closed: Sun
Stocks a wide range of organic products, from fruit and

vegetables to pasta and sunflower oil.

NEWNHAM
CAMPHILL VILLAGE TRUST
Oaklands Park, Newnham, Gloucestershire GL14 1EF
Tel: (0594) 516230
The Trust, which is a community for handicapped people, can
supply organic vegetables and soft fruit to consumer groups
and shops, but not to individual customers.

NEWQUAY
MITCHELL FARM
Mitchell, Newquay, Cornwall TR8 5AX
6 miles SE of Newquay off the A30
Tel: Mitchell (0872) 510657
Open: 'orders taken by telephone and by arrangement'
Mr Sessions grows organic vegetables and strawberries, which
can be collected by individual customers who telephone their
orders.

NEWTON ABBOT
MOORFOOT ORGANIC GARDEN
Denbury, nr. Newton Abbot, Devon
3 miles SW of Newton Abbot between A38 and A381
Tel: Ipplepen (0803) 813161
Open: 10 a.m. to 6 p.m. Wed
Closed: Sun, Mon, Tue, Thur, Fri, Sat, Christmas and New
Year
Linda Phelps and Gordon Strutt grow a wide range of organic
fruit and vegetables; they can also supply imported fruit when
avalaible, as well as wholefoods and juices. Their mobile shops
operate a delivery service to local customers each week, and
they accept telephone orders.

NORTHAMPTON
DAILY BREAD CO-OPERATIVE
The Old Laundry, Bedford Road, Northampton,
Northamptonshire NN4 0AD
Tel: Northampton (0604) 21531
Open: 9 a.m. to 5.30 p.m. (to 4 p.m. Sat)
Closed: Sun
This co-operative specializes in wholefoods, with a large

number of organic lines, from tofu to cider vinegar. There is a wholesale outlet, too.

NORTHWOOD
MOORPARK FRUITERERS
Moorpark, Northwood, Middlesex
Tel: (09274) 21707
Open: 8 a.m. to 5.45 p.m. (to 1 p.m. Wed)
Closed: Sun
An enterprising greengrocers with a good range of organic vegetables and top fruit from the UK and abroad.

NORWICH
CHURCH BARN FARM
Arminghall Lane, Norwich, Norfolk
Tel: 'leave a message with Mrs Warns on (0603) 627307'
Open: 8 a.m. to 'dark'
Jeremy Kent's farm operates mainly on a Pick-your-own basis. In the summer there are blackcurrants, broad beans and peas; from autumn onwards, the emphasis is on potatoes, root crops and cabbages. He says that he can supply quarters of organic beef packed ready for the freezer, 'if I can can get four customers lined up'.

MANGREEN GARDEN
Mangreen, Swardeston, Norwich, Norfolk NR14 8DD
4 miles S of Norwich off the B1113
Tel: Mulbarton (0508) 70444
Open: 8 a.m. to 10.30 p.m. 'every day'
The Duffields grow organic vegetables and seasonal fruit to Soil Association standards. They can also supply free-range eggs and juices.

RAINBOW WHOLEFOODS
16 Dove Street, Norwich, Norfolk NR2 1DE
Tel: Norwich (0603) 630484
Open: 9 a.m. to 5.30 p.m. Mon to Sat
Closed: Sun
Organic fruit and vegetables supplement a wide range of wholefoods, with the emphasis on nuts, grains and pulses. There is a wholesale outlet at 12 St Mary's Works, Duke Street, Norwich.

NOTTINGHAM
PHIL CORBETT
5 Colville Villas, Nottingham, Nottinghamshire NG1 4HN
Tel: Nottingham (0602) 474977
Open: 'please telephone first'
As well as organic fruit and vegetables, Phil Corbett can supply
herb plants, cut herbs and wild flowers.

HIZIKI WHOLEFOOD COLLECTIVE LTD
15 Goosegate, Hockley, Nottingham, Nottinghamshire
NG1 1FE
Tel: Nottingham (0602) 505523
Open: 10 a.m. to 5.30 p.m. Mon and Thur (to 6 p.m. Tue,
Wed and Fri); 9.30 a.m. to 5 p.m. Sat
Closed: Sun, bank hols and Christmas
Sells an extensive range of vegetarian and organic wholefoods,
ranging from seasonal fruit and vegetables, to cheese, pasta,
oils and muesli. Organic wines and cider are also available.
There is a cafe on the premises.

OUROBOROS WHOLEFOOD COLLECTIVE
37A Mansfield Road, Nottingham, Nottinghamshire
NG1 3FB
Tel: Nottingham (0602) 419016
Open: 10 a.m. to to 5.30 p.m. (to 8 p.m. Wed)
Closed: Sun
Set up in 1977 as an outlet for wholefoods with the emphasis
on organic produce. As well as vegetables, fruit, herb plants
and bread, the range includes everything from marmalade to
oils and cider vinegar.

NUNEATON

R.M. ELGIN & SONS LTD
Bramcote Mains, Wolvrey Road, Bulkington, nr. Nuneaton,
Warwickshire CV12 9JX
Tel: (0455) 220441
Open: 'during coarse fishing season 16th June to 16th March'
David Elgin grows vegetables and soft fruit to Soil Association
standards and can supply additive-free pork and lamb. He is
planning to set up a farm shop tied to his coarse fishing
enterprise.

ORMSKIRK

MR A. GIELTY

Lyncroft, Butchers Lane, Aughton Green, Ormskirk, Lancashire L39 6SY

Tel: Ormskirk (0695) 421712

Open: 'anytime'

Alf Gielty produces organic vegetables; he also supplies free-range eggs and poultry – in particular, turkeys.

OSBASTON

OSBASTON HALL ESTATE

Osbaston, nr. Nuneaton, Warwickshire CV13 0DR

Tel: Market Bosworth (0455) 290737

Open: Ring first

The estate is currently producing a range of organically grown vegetables and fruit. It should receive the Soil Association symbol in September 1990.

OSWESTRY

HONEYSUCKLE WHOLEFOODS CO-OPERATIVE

53 Church Street, Oswestry, Shropshire SY11 1BD

Tel: Oswestry (0691) 653125

Open: 9 a.m. to 5 p.m. Mon to Sat

Closed: Sun and bank hols

This co-operative stocks organic vegetables and seasonal fruit, in addition to a good range of organic wholefoods, bread and bakery products.

OTTERY ST MARY

FOOD ON THE HILL

5A Mill Street, Ottery St Mary, Devon EX11 1AB

Tel: Ottery St Mary (0404) 812109

Open: 9 a.m. to 1 p.m., 2 p.m. to 5 p.m. (to 1 p.m. Wed, to 4 p.m. Sat)

Closed: Sun

The range of organic products includes vegetables, top fruit, Staffordshire Farm Cheese, tofu, dried wholefoods and wine.

OXBOROUGH

FERRY FARM

Oxborough, nr. Kings Lynn, Norfolk PE33 9PT

Tel: Gooderstone (036621) 287

12 miles S of Kings Lynn off the A134
Open: 8 a.m. to 4 p.m.
Mrs Wilson grows organic vegetables and soft fruit, but recommends that customers visit her stalls on Mildenhall market (Friday) and Thetford market (Saturday) for the best choice of her own and bought-in produce.

OXFORD
NEAL'S YARD (OXFORD)
Golden Cross (off Cornmarket), Oxford, Oxfordshire
Tel: Oxford (0865) 792102
A branch of the Covent Garden-based organic/wholefood enterprise. (For details see London.)

PAR
STONEY BRIDGE ORGANIC NURSERY
Tywardreath, Par, Cornwall PL24 2TY
Tel: Par (072681) 3858
Open: Mar. to Oct.: 9 a.m. to dusk all week; Nov. to Feb.: Fri only, or by arrangement
Closed: Sun
David Pascoe's nursery is part of the Cornish Organic Farm Shops Co-operative. He can supply vegetables, fruit, meat and poultry.

PEMBRIDGE

DUNKERTONS CIDER COMPANY
Luntley, Pembridge, nr. Leominster, Hereford & Worcester HR6 9ED
1 mile from Pembridge off the A44
Tel: Pembridge (05447) 653
Open: 10 a.m. to 6 p.m. Mon to Sat; noon to 3 p.m. Sun (Easter and May to Sept. only)
Ivor and Susie Dunkerton produce a fine range of ciders and perries from traditional apple and pear varieties. The Soil Association symbol applies to two brews at present, but all fruit is unsprayed and no additives are used on their products.

PENZANCE
GRANARY TRADITIONAL FOODS
15D Causeway Head, Penzance, Cornwall
Tel: Penzance (0736) 61869
Open: 9 a.m. to 5.30 p.m. Mon to Sat

Closed: Sun
A food shop selling organic vegetables, cheese, dried
wholefoods and juices.

HEWAS FIELD FARM

Trenerth Bridge, Leedstown, Hayle, Penzance, Cornwall TR27 5ER
4 miles SE of Hayle off the B3302
Tel: Penzance (0736) 850637
Open: 8 a.m. to 1 p.m., 2 p.m. to 7 p.m.
Closed: Sun, Mon, bank hols and Christmas
Snails are an unlikely speciality at Squadron Leader Jones'
farm. He also grows unusual vegetables and soft fruit, and can
supply organic meat and poultry.

MR & MRS H. LUCAS

Sunshine Cottage, 2 Lelant Gardens, Hayle, Penzance,
Cornwall TR27 6LL
Tel: Penzance (0736) 756509
Open: 'anytime by arrangement'
Closed: Christmas
Because of their geographical location, Hugh and Claire Lucas
specialize in early crops such as winter cauliflowers and winter
squash.

PERRANPORTH

ROBERT BURNS
Lovely Vale, Higher Penwartha, Perranporth, Cornwall TR6 0BA
Tel: Truro (0872) 573863
Open: 9 a.m. to 5 p.m. Mon to Sat
Closed: Sun
Visitors can purchase organic vegetables and soft fruit from
Robert Burns' farm.

PERSHORE
PERSHORE COLLEGE OF AGRICULTURE
Avonbank, Pershore, Hereford & Worcester WR10 3JP
Tel: Pershore (0386) 552443
Open: 9 a.m. to 1 p.m., 2 p.m. to 5 p.m.
Closed: Wed, Thur, Fri
Supplies of organically grown vegetables can be purchased
from the College – which also runs courses on organic
agriculture (see Appendix).

PETERBOROUGH
NOTHING BUT WHOLEFOODS LTD
26 Leighton, Orton Malborne, Peterborough, Cambridgeshire
PE2 0QB
Tel: Peterborough (0733) 238239
Open: 8 a.m. to 4 p.m.
Closed: Sun, Mon, Thur
A registered co-operative selling organic fruit and vegetables as
well as dried wholefoods. There is also a stall at Peterborough
market.

PETERSFIELD

CUMBERS FARM
Rogate, Petersfield, Hampshire GU31 5DB
Tel: Rogate (073080) 840
Open: 'any time by appointment, but usually Saturday
morning; please telephone first'
Organic vegetables are available wholesale in season (i.e. by the
sack). Mr Ballard and Ms Rogers can also supply butchered,
packed and frozen lamb.

PICKERING

STANDFIELD HALL FARM
Westgate Carr Road, Pickering, North Yorkshire YO18 8LX
Tel: Pickering (0751) 72249
Open: 2 p.m. to 6 p.m. Wed and Thur; 9 a.m. to noon Sat
Closed: Sun, Mon, Tue, Fri
Supplies of organic vegetables, top fruit, wholefoods and juices
can be obtained on certain days from the farm shop. The owners
also have a stall at Helmsley market (9 a.m. to 5 p.m. Fri).

PILLING

BRADSHAW LANE NURSERY
Pilling, nr. Preston, Lancashire PR3 6AX
Tel: Poulton-le-Fylde (0253) 790046
Open: 'most of the time'
Alan Schofield can supply a range of organic vegetables grown
to Soil Association standards.

PLYMOUTH
BARBICAN WHOLEFOODS
Citadel Ope (off Southside Street), The Barbican, Plymouth,
Devon PL1 2JY

Tel: Plymouth (0752) 660499
Open: 9.30 a.m. to 6 p.m. Mon to Sat
Closed: Sun, bank hols and Christmas
A broadly based shop selling organic fruit and vegetables, plus a range of dried wholefoods, breads, soya products and the like.

PRESTON
AMBER WHOLEFOOD CO-OPERATIVE LTD
31 Cannon Street, Preston, Lancashire PR1 3NS
Tel: Preston (0772) 53712
Open: 9.30 a.m. to 5 p.m. Mon to Sat
Closed: Sun
This shop's organic range includes vegetables, some top fruit, cheese, yoghurt and dried wholefoods, as well as bakery products, juices and baby foods.

LOW CARR NURSERY
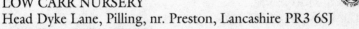
Head Dyke Lane, Pilling, nr. Preston, Lancashire PR3 6SJ
Tel: Pilling (0253) 790471
Open: 8 a.m. to noon, 1 p.m. to 5 p.m. Mon to Fri
Closed: Sat, Sun, bank hols and Christmas
The Blairs are well known within the organic movement, and are the leading growers of organic glasshouse crops in the country. Their tomatoes, cucumbers and peppers are available from April until October. They are primarily wholesalers, but will supply bulk orders to individuals or groups if given two days' notice.

MANOR FARM
Shore Road, Hesketh Bank, Preston, Lancashire PR4 6XQ
Tel: Preston (0772) 812530
Open: May to Dec. 'every day until dusk, best to telephone first'
Keith Dickinson grows and can supply a range of organic vegetables and herbs to callers.

PULBOROUGH
CATTLESTONE FARM
Harbolets Road, West Chiltington, nr. Pulborough, West Sussex RH20 2LG
3 miles E of Pulborough off the B2133

Tel: West Chiltington (07983) 3156
Open: 9 a.m. to 'dusk' every day
Visitors can purchase supplies of organically grown vegetables and top fruit from the farm, as well as free-range eggs.

RAINHAM
RAINHAM HEALTH FOOD CENTRE
28 Rainham Shopping Precinct, Rainham, Kent ME8 7HW
Tel: Medway (0634) 362267
Open: 9 a.m. to 5.30 p.m. Mon to Sat
Closed: Sun
Sells a range of organic vegetables, top fruit, dried wholefoods and bakery products, as well as free-range eggs.

READING

GARLANDS ORGANIC FARM SHOP
Garlands Farm, Gardeners Lane, Upper Basildon, Reading, Berkshire RG8 8NP
Tel: Upper Basildon (0491) 671556
Open: 9 a.m. to 4 p.m. Tue to Sat
Closed: Sun, Mon, bank hols and Christmas
The farm sells its own organic produce, as well as many items from outside. The range takes in everything from fruit and vegetables to dairy produce, meat, wholefoods and wine. There are plans to open new shops at Springhill Centre, Cuddington, near Aylesbury and in Sunningwell, Oxfordshire in the near future.

HARDWICK ESTATE ORGANIC FARM PRODUCE
Path Hill Farm, Whitchurch, Reading RG8 7RE
Tel: Reading (0734) 842955
Open: 8.30 a.m. to 5.30 p.m. Mon to Fri
Closed: Sat and Sun
Sir Julian Rose sits on the Council of the Soil Association and was instrumental in the campaign for 'green milk'. His farm specializes in dairy produce, organic meat and poultry, as well as eggs. Telephone orders can be accepted between 9 a.m. and 12.30 p.m..

HARDWICK ORGANIC GARDENS
Path Hill Farm, Whitchurch, Reading RG8 7RE
Tel: Reading (0734) 845224

Open: 10 a.m. to 7 p.m. Tue to Sun (May to Aug. only);
'other times by appointment
Closed: Mon
Iain Tolhurst operates this farm on a share basis with Julian Rose
(see above). Like his nursery near Bodmin in Cornwall (see
entry), this enterprise concentrates on vegetables and fruit.

RINGWOOD

MR S. WEIR
Turcroft, Burley, Ringwood, Hampshire BH24 4DF
E of Ringwood between A31 and A35
Tel: Burley (04253) 3502
Open: 'all times'
Simon Weir grows organic vegetables and soft fruit to Soil
Association standards.

ROBERTSBRIDGE

SCRAGOAK FARM
Brightling Road, Robertsbridge, East Sussex TN32 5HB
Tel: Brightling (042482) 364
Open: 9.30 a.m. to 5 p.m. Tue to Sun
Closed: Mon
The shop sells up to fifty different fruits and vegetables, many
grown on the farm to Soil Association standards. Other
products include organic cheese, ewes' milk yoghurt, bread
and wine. Books and gardening accessories are also available.

SEDLESCOMBE VINEYARD

Robertsbridge, East Sussex TN32 5SA
1.5 miles N of Sedlescombe
Tel: Staplecross (058083) 715
Open: 10 a.m. to 6 p.m. daily from Easter to Christmas
Closed: Christmas to Easter
This is one of the very few commercial organic vineyards in
Britain. It also produces apple juice, cider and apple wine, and
has a stock of around fifty wines from abroad. Organic
vegetables and strawberries are also available.

RUGBY
THE WHOLEFOOD SHOP
St Andrews Church House, Church Street, Rugby, Warwick-
shire CV21

Open: 8.30 a.m. to 5 p.m. Thur and Fri
Closed: Sat to Wed
Dave Kerruish's little retail outlet can supply organic
vegetables and fruit, as well as dried wholefoods, bakery
products and eggs. He also sells home-made pasties. Free
delivery in Rugby and reductions for bulk purchases.

RYE
LADY DAPHNE RUSSELL
Oak Cottage, Beckley, Rye, East Sussex TN31 6TL
5 miles NE of Rye off the A28
Tel: (079726) 265
Open: 'please telephone'
Lady Russell grows a range of organic vegetables, apples and
soft fruit, including raspberries and currants.

RYTON-ON-DUNSMORE
RYTON GARDENS
National Centre for Organic Gardening, Ryton-on-Dunsmore,
nr. Coventry CV8 3LG
5 miles SE of Coventry off the A45
Open: 10 a.m. to 5 p.m. all week (to 4 p.m. in winter)
Closed: Christmas
Ryton Gardens shop has a very wide selection of organic
produce and wholefoods, from fruit and vegetables supplied
by Soil Association growers to organic dairy produce, meat
and additive-free poultry. Ryton Gardens now has its own
range of organic breads and stocks one of the most
comprehensive selections of organic wines in the country.
Gardening accessories, books and gifts are also available from
the shop.

SAFFRON WALDEN
NEWHOUSE FARM
Radwinter, nr. Saffron Walden, Essex CB10 2SP
4 miles E of Saffron Walden off the B1054
Tel: (079987) 211
Open: 9 a.m. to 5 p.m. 'when produce is available'
Organically grown potatoes are available from September to
February; lamb from June to September and beef from
November onwards.

SANDY

ROSEHAVEN ORGANICS
110 Cinques Road, Gamlingay, Sandy, Bedfordshire SG19 3NR
Tel: Biggleswade (0767) 50142
Open: Fri and Sat, 'please telephone first'
Closed: Sun to Thur
This is a mixed enterprise producing organically grown vegetables (including garlic), seasonal fruit, meat and poultry. The new farm shop is due to open in 1990.

SARRATT

CHERRY TREES FARM
Olleberrie Lane, Belsize, Sarratt, Hertfordshire WD3 4NU
Tel: Sarratt (09277) 68289
Open: 10 a.m. to 5.30 p.m. Wed to Sat; 2 p.m. to 6 p.m. Sun
Closed: Mon and Tue
Michael and Mary Bell run a very enterprising organic farm and shop, with an extensive range of produce. As well as organic vegetables and fruit, they can supply dairy produce, meat, poultry, wine and all kinds of wholefoods. They have recently begun to do their own oak-smoking, and are setting up a tearoom/restaurant on the premises as well as an information centre.

SAUL

PRIDING FARM
Framilode, Saul, Gloucestershire GL2 7LB
Tel: Gloucester (0452) 741272
Open: 10 a.m. to 6 p.m. all week
In addition to organic vegetables and soft fruit, Peter Smithies supplies additive-free meat, including sausages and bacon. He also sells cider.

SAXMUNDHAM

SWALLOW ORGANICS
High March Farm, Darsham, nr. Saxmundham, Suffolk IP17 3RN
6 miles N of Saxmundham off the A12
Tel: Yoxford (072877) 201
Open: 8 a.m. to 'dusk' all week
Closed: Christmas Day and Boxing Day
Has a wide range of organic fruit and vegetables, as well as

wholefoods. Herbs and seaweed feeds are sold under the Swallow Organics label.

SCARBOROUGH
GREATFRUITS
1A North Marine Road, Scarborough, North Yorkshire YO12 7EY
Tel: Scarborough (0723) 374633
Open: 9 a.m. to 5.30 p.m. Mon to Sat
Closed: Sun
A wholefood/vegetarian shop with a range of organic produce including fruit, vegetables, dairy produce and other specialities such as tofu, biscuits and muesli.

SETTLE
T. LORD & SONS
Cheapside, Settle, North Yorkshire BD24 9EW
Tel: Settle (07292) 3772
Open: 9 a.m. to 5 p.m. Mon and Sat; to 5.30 p.m. Tue and Thur; to 12.30 p.m. Wed; to 6 p.m. Fri
Closed: Sun
Established in 1860, this family greengrocers is now run by the Hodgsons. The range of organic fruit and vegetables is increasing and the shop also sells free-range eggs.

SHAFTESBURY

HAYGROVE HONEY FARM
Twyford, Shaftesbury, Dorset SP7 0JF
2.5 miles S of Shaftesbury off the A350
Tel: Shaftesbury (0747) 811855
Open: 9 a.m. to 5 p.m. 'most days'
Although this is essentially a honey farm, there is a 1.5 acre plot for organic vegetables and soft fruit (for which the symbol is given). The range includes globe artichokes, asparagus and garlic, among others. Organic gardening demonstrations by prior arrangement.

SHEFFIELD

ALDERMANS HEAD FARM
Langsett, Stocksbridge, Sheffield, South Yorkshire S30 59Y
10 miles NW of Sheffield off the A616
Tel: Barnsley (0226) 767616

Open: 8 a.m. to 1 p.m. Sat only
Closed: Sun to Fri
Visitors can buy organically grown vegetables, soft fruit and additive-free goat meat direct from the farm.

HEELEY CITY FARM
Richards Road, Heeley, Sheffield, South Yorkshire S2 3DT
Tel: Sheffield (0742) 580482
Open: 9 a.m. to 4 p.m. all week
The farm offers organic vegetables and special herbs such as coriander and fenugreek for sale. Dairy produce from the goats is also available.

RIDGEWAY ORGANIC FARM CO-OP LTD
Kent House Farm, Main Road, Ridgeway, Sheffield, South Yorkshire S12 3XR
5 miles SE of Sheffield on the B6054
Tel: Sheffield (0742) 474258
Open: 'Fri evening to Sun evening only'
Closed: Mon to Thur
An organic market garden run by a workers' co-operative. The aim is to create an enterprise that will benefit the community by providing work and supplies of organic food. Vegetables and top fruit are the main crops. Bulk orders can be arranged by telephone on Monday mornings.

SHEPTON MALLET
AVALON VINEYARD
The Drove, East Pennard, Shepton Mallet, Somerset BA4 6UA
5 miles SW of Shepton Mallet off the A37
Tel: Ditcheat (074986) 393
Open: 2 p.m. to 6 p.m. all week (June and July only); 'other times telephone first'
Dr Howard Tripp planted his vineyard in 1981 and produces commercial quantities of wine organically. He also makes cider and grows a limited range of organic vegetables and soft fruit.

SHERBORNE
BOOKHAM STUD
Bishopsdown, Sherborne, Dorset DT9 5PL
Tel:(096321) 248

Open: 8 a.m. to 8 p.m. all week
Mr Loftus rears his livestock entirely on grass, and supplies of
his organic meat are available direct from the farm.

FOOD FOR THOUGHT
64 Cheap Street, Sherborne, Dorset DT9 3BJ
Tel: Sherborne (0935) 814262
Open: 9 a.m. to 5.30 p.m. Mon to Sat
Closed: Sun, bank hols and Christmas
A wholefood shop with a range of organic produce including
fruit, vegetables, dairy produce, baby foods and juices. Organic
breads and bakery products are made on the premises.

SHIPSTON ON STOUR
HAWKINS & SON
Market Place, Shipston on Stour, Warwickshire CV36 4AG
Tel: Shipston on Stour (0608) 61207
Open: 8 a.m. to 5.30 p.m. Mon to Sat
Closed: Sun
The Hawkins family began by selling fish, but now have
supplies of organic fruit and vegetables in addition to free-
range poultry and eggs.

SHREWSBURY
CRABAPPLE WHOLEFOODS
1-2 Castle Gates, Shrewsbury, Shropshire
Tel: Shrewsbury (0743) 64559
Open: 9.30 a.m. to 5.45 p.m. Mon to Sat
Closed: Sun, bank hols and Christmas
Stocks a range of organic produce including fruit, vegetables,
dairy produce, bread and juices, as well as staple wholefoods.
Manna bread (made with sprouted organic wheat grain) is a
speciality.

PIMHILL PRODUCE
Lea Hall, Harmer Hill, Shrewsbury, Shropshire SY4 3DY
5 miles N of Shrewsbury on the A528
Tel: Bomere Heath (0939) 290342
Open: 8 a.m. to 5 p.m. (from 9 a.m. Sat)
Closed: Sun, bank hols and Christmas
The Mayall family celebrated 40 years of organic farming in
1989. Pimhill now produces its own range of stoneground

flours and other cereal-based products. Vegetables are grown organically and the Mayalls also sell their own sausages, pork pies, home-cured hams, cakes and quiches, as well as other wholefoods and wine. There is a picnic site on the farm.

THE VILLA FARM SHOP

Plealey Villa, Pontesbury, nr. Shrewsbury, Shropshire SY5 0XT
8 miles SW of Shrewsbury on the A488
Tel: Shrewsbury (0743) 860304
Open: 10 a.m. to 1 p.m., 2 p.m. to 6 p.m. Mon to Sat
Closed: Sun and Christmas
Ben Hamer grows and supplies organic vegetables and fruit produced to Soil Association standards.

SIBSEY

MR J. E. DUNCAN
South View, Trader Bank, Sibsey, nr. Boston, Lincolnshire PE22 0UJ
5 miles N of Boston on the A16
Tel: Boston (0205) 750470
Open: 'all hours within reason'
Mr Duncan grows organic vegetables and fruit to Soil Association standards. He also supplies dried wholefoods.

SITTINGBOURNE

MR M. J. BELL
Pett Lane, Stockbury, Sittingbourne, Kent
4 miles E of Sittingbourne off the A249
Tel: Wormshill (062784) 318 (temporary number)
Open: 9 a.m. to 7 p.m.
Closed: Thur and Christmas
Michael Bell's organic produce includes vegetables and fruit. He also sells free-range eggs.

SOHAM

DOWNFIELD WINDMILL
Fordham Road, Soham, Cambridgeshire
Tel: Peterborough (0533) 707625 (home); Ely (0353) 720333 (mill)
Open: 11 a.m. to 5 p.m. Sun and bank hol Mons
Closed: Christmas and New Year week

Nigel Moon runs this classic East Anglian windmill, and produces a range of organic stoneground flours, including wholemeal, rye, barley and oatmeal. He is planning to supply a new bakery in Leicester with his produce.

SOLIHULL
THE HEALTH FOOD CENTRE
20 High Street, Solihull, West Midlands B91 3TB
Tel: (021) 705 0134
Open: 9 a.m. to 5.30 p.m. Mon to Sat
Closed: Sun
This wholefood shop sells organic vegetables, fruit and dried goods as well as organic meat, free-range poultry and wine.

SOUTH BRENT
MR V. H. COKER & SON
Home Park, Rattery, South Brent, Devon TQ10 9LL
4 miles NE of South Brent between the A38 and A385
Tel: Ashburton (0364) 73208
Open: 'always open'
A mixed enterprise producing vegetables as well as organic and additive-free meat.

SOUTHAMPTON
NATURALLY BEST FOODS
78 Ewell Way, Totton, Southampton, Hampshire SO4 3PP
Tel: Southampton (0703) 868384
Open: 'open all hours, but please telephone'
This is not a shop, but a home delivery service specializing in organic produce, much of it from local growers. The range includes vegetables, fruit, wholefoods, juices and wines.

SOUTHAMPTON COMMUNITY CO-OPERATIVE LTD
The Veg Co-Op, 92 St Mary's Road, Southampton, Hampshire SO2 0AH
Tel: Southampton (0703) 632583
Open: 8.30 a.m. to 5.30 p.m. (to 5 p.m. Sat)
Closed: Sun
Stocks a wide range of organic items, from vegetables and fruit to dairy produce and juices. Wholesale and distribution of fresh produce to neighbouring counties.

SOUTHBOURNE
EARTH FOODS LTD
75 Southbourne Grove, Southbourne, nr. Bournemouth, Dorset
Tel: Bournemouth (0202) 422465
Open: 9 a.m. to 6 p.m. Mon to Sat
Closed: Sun
Wholefood shop selling organic fruit and vegetables, dairy produce and dried goods.

SOUTHPORT
CORNUCOPIA
71 Everton Road, Southport, Merseyside PR8 4BT
Tel: Southport (0704) 69020
Open: 8.30 a.m. to 5.30 p.m. Mon to Sat
Closed: Sun, bank hols and Christmas
The shop sells wholefoods as well as organic dairy produce, bakery products, juices and wines. There is a mobile van which covers Formby, Hightown, Crosby and Hesketh Bank/Tarlton.

SPALDING

BIRCHWOOD FARM
Draw Dyke, Sutton St James, Spalding, Lincolnshire PE12 0HP
10 miles E of Spalding off the B1165
Tel: (094585) 388
Open: Ring first
Mr Sadd grows organic fruit and vegetables to Soil Association standards.

STALYBRIDGE
THE GOOD FOOD SHOP
2 Melbourne Street, Stalybridge, Greater Manchester
Tel: (04574) 65278
Open: 9.30 a.m. to 5.30 p.m. Mon to Sat
Closed: Sun, bank hols and Christmas
The shop's range of organic produce includes vegetables, fruit, dairy produce, wholefoods and bakery products.

STICKFORD

PAM & RICK BOWERS
Strawberry Fields, Scarborough Bank, Stickford, Lincolnshire PE22 8DR

10 miles N of Boston off the A16
Tel: Boston (0205) 480490
Open: 'please telephone first'
Rick Bowers is chairman of Eastern Counties Organic
Producers, an expanding group of farmers drawing members
from the East of Scotland to Suffolk. He produces organically
grown vegetables.

STOCKBRIDGE

S. L. & J D. TIDY
The Anchorage, Salisbury Road, Broughton, nr. Stockbridge,
Hampshire
1 mile S of the A30 on the B3084
Tel: (0794) 301234
Open: 10 a.m. to 6 p.m. Mon to Sat
Closed: Sun, bank hols and Christmas
Visitors can purchase organic vegetables, poultry and dried
wholefoods as well as free-range eggs from the Tidy's
premises.

STOW-ON-THE-WOLD
WYE ORGANIC FOODS
The Square, Stow-on-the-Wold, Gloucestershire GL54 1AB
Tel: Cotswold (0451) 31004
Open: 9 a.m. to 5.30 p.m. Mon to Sat
Closed: Sun
Charles Wye's shop stocks everything organic, from vegetables
and dairy produce to meat and wine. Flour is ground on the
premises and he also produces ready-made vegetarian and non-
vegetarian dishes with organic ingredients, as well chutneys
and marmalades. He plans to open a tearoom in the near
future.

STRATFORD-UPON-AVON
THE CREATIVE BEING CENTRE
30 Albany Road, Stratford-upon-Avon, Warwickshire CV37
6PG
Tel: Stratford-upon-Avon (0789) 292052
Open: 9 a.m. to 5 p.m. 'telephone to check'
Choyous Choy is a student of The Country College Organic
Food Studies Department. He sells organic vegetables, fruit
and juices, as well as ready-made vegetarian meals.

SUDBURY
PLAIN & SIMPLE
8 Acton Square, Sudbury, Suffolk CO10 6HQ
Tel: Sudbury (0787) 73315
Open: 8.45 a.m. to 5 p.m. (to 1.30 p.m. Wed)
Closed: Sun, bank hols and Christmas
Anne Mauldon's shop sells organic fruit and vegetables in season, wholefoods, dairy produce and free-range eggs. Bread is baked locally with organic flour; quiches, pizzas and cakes are made on the premises.

SWINDON
HOBSLEYS ORGANIC FOODS
Eastbrook Farm, Bishopstone, nr. Swindon, Wiltshire SN6 8PW
4 miles E of Swindon off the B4000
Tel: Swindon (0793) 790460/790078
Open: 9 a.m. to 5 p.m. Tue to Fri (to 1 p.m. Sat)
Closed: Sun, Mon and bank hols
Hobsleys is a member of the Wiltshire Larder group of local producers. They supply organic vegetables, free-range poultry, eggs and- from time to time – organic meat as well. They have recently opened a shop at 50 High Street, Shrivenham, Oxfordshire.

TAUNTON
OAKE BRIDGE FARM
Oake, Taunton, Somerset TA4 1AY
Tel: Taunton (0823) 461317
Open: 'all hours'
Closed: Christmas Day
This is essentially a wholesale enterprise, but Mr Martin is prepared to serve retail customers. Main crops are limited to a small range of vegetables: leeks, Brussels sprouts, celery and so on.

TAVISTOCK
KILWORTHY KAPERS
11 King Street, Tavistock, Devon PL19 0DS
Tel: Tavistock (0822) 615039
Open: 9 a.m. to 1 p.m., 2 p.m. to 5.30 p.m. Mon to Thur; 9 a.m. to 5.30 p.m. Fri (to 5 p.m. Sat)
Closed: Sun

Kilworthy Kapers is attached to a children's charity. It can supply organic vegetables, fruit, dairy produce and staple wholefoods. There is a stall on Tavistock Pannier Market (9 a.m. to 4 p.m. Fri).

TEIGNMOUTH
J. REDDAWAY
Lower Rixdale, Luton, Ideford, nr. Teignmouth, Devon TQ13 0BN
5 miles NE of Newton Abbot off the A380
Tel: Teignmouth (06267) 775218
Open: 'most days, but telephone to avoid disappointment'
John Reddaway produces organic cider as a sideline on his farm. Fruit is pressed on the premises and the scrumpy can be bought and sampled from the farm

THATCHAM
GARLANDS HEALTH FOODS & COFFEE SHOP
Shop 3, 16 High Street, Thatcham, Berkshire RG13 4JD
Tel: Thatcham (0635) 61017
Open: 9 a.m. to 5.30 p.m. Mon to Fri; 8.30 a.m. to 5 p.m. Sat
Closed: Sun and bank hols
Stocks some organic produce, including dried wholefoods, bakery products, tofu and herbs. Free-range eggs are also available.

TIVERTON
ANGEL FOOD
1 Angel Terrace, Tiverton, Devon
Tel: Tiverton (0884) 254778
Open: 8.30 a.m. to 5.30 p.m. (to 2.30 p.m. Thur)
Closed: Sun, bank hols and Christmas
Wholefood shop with a cafe attached (see entry in Part Three). The range of organic produce includes vegetables, soft fruit, dried wholefoods and breads. Cakes, pies and other savouries are made on the premises.

BARTON FARM
Bickleigh, Tiverton, Devon EX16 8HD
5 miles S of Tiverton on the A396
Tel: Tiverton (0884) 5471
Open: 'telephone first'

Mr Coney grows organic vegetables and rears livestock to Soil Association standards.

COOMBE FARM

Cove, Tiverton, Devon EX16 7RU
Tel: Bampton (0398) 31808
Open: 'by appointment'
Michael Cole's main crops are organic vegetables and soft fruit, but he also produces 'leaf curd' (a high quality protein food ingredient made from green herbage).

REAPERS WHOLEFOODS
23 Gold Street, Tiverton, Devon EX16 6QD
Tel: Tiverton (0884) 255310
Open: 9 a.m. to 5 p.m. (to 4 p.m. Sat)
Closed: Sun, bank hols and Christmas
Stocks organic vegetables and fruit, dried wholefoods and other basic goods. Free-range eggs are also available. There is a cafe in the shop (open 10 a.m. to 3 p.m. Mon to Sat).

TOPSHAM
TOPCROPS
Highfield Farm, Clyst Road, Topsham, Devon EX3 0BY
Tel: Exeter (0392) 432103
Open: 8 a.m. to 7 p.m. Tue to Sun
Closed: Mon, bank hols and Christmas
Ian Shears is in the process of setting up an 'organic food and farming centre', with the help of government diversification grants. This will incorporate a butchery and bakery (making use of his own organic wheat). Other produce currently available includes vegetables, fruit, dairy produce, meat and dried wholefoods.

TORPOINT
THE GRANARY
Sheviock Barton, Sheviock, Torpoint, Cornwall PL11 3EH
Tel: (0503) 30793/30909
Open: 10 a.m. to 5 p.m. (to noon Sat)
Closed: Sun
Mr Bersey grows vegetables to Soil Association standards. He also rears sheep and produces Sheviock ewe's milk cheese.

TOTNES
LIPTON FARM

East Allington, Totnes, Devon TQ9 7RN
10 miles S of Totnes off the A381
Tel: (054852) 252
Open: 'telephone first'
Organic beef and lamb are the specialities on Roger Jones'
farm. Freezer packs of beef are always available; fresh supplies
can be ordered at the middle of each month.

RIVERFORD FARM VEGETABLES
Riverford Farm, Staverton, Totnes, Devon TQ9 6AF
2 miles N of Totnes off the A384
Tel: Staverton (080426) 513
Open: 9.30 a.m. to 6 p.m. Mon to Sat; 11 a.m. to 4 p.m. Sun
Closed: Christmas Day to 2nd Jan
Riverford Farm is best known for naturally reared pork and
lamb, which is turned into hams and sausages. Guy Watson
also grows organic vegetables to Soil Association standards and
sells organic wine.

SACKS WHOLEFOODS
High Street, Totnes, Devon
Tel: Totnes (0803) 863263
Open: 9 a.m. to 5.30 p.m. Mon to Sat
Closed: Sun and bank hols
Wholefood shop selling organic vegetables and fruit, as well as
dried goods, bakery products and juices.

TRURO
R. & F. B. H. BOWCOCK
Polsue Cottage, Ruan High Lanes, Truro, Cornwall TR2 5LU
Tel: Truro (0872) 501596
Open: 'telephone first'
Closed: Sun
The Bowcocks can supply organically grown vegetables by
arrangement.

CARLEY & CO.
34-36 St Austell Street, Truro, Cornwall TR1 1SE
Tel: Truro (0872) 77686

Open: 8.45 a.m. to 5.30 p.m. (to 6.30 p.m. Fri)
Closed: Sun
The best-known organic/wholefood shop in Cornwall. John Carley stocks a vast range of items, all carefully selected, from organic fruit and vegetables to dairy produce, dried goods and wine. Bread and cakes are baked on the premises.

P. J. & J. CURD

Lanhay, Portscatho, Truro, Cornwall TR2 5ER
10 miles S of Truro off the A3078
Tel: Portscatho (087258) 282
Open: 8 a.m. to 8 p.m. all week
The Curds have 25 acres of fully organic land with the rest in transition. They can supply vegetables, fruit, additive-free meat and dairy produce.

DEEPDALE NATURAL GROWERS

Wheal Frances, Goonhavern, nr. Truro, Cornwall TR4 9NR
Tel: Zelah (087254) 370
Open: Ring first
This enterprise produces organic vegetables grown to Soil Association standards.

PENAIR ORGANIC PRODUCERS

St Clement, Truro, Cornwall TR1 1TD
Tel: Truro (0872) 71937
Open: 2 p.m. to 5 p.m. Mon; 9 a.m. to 6 p.m. Thur and Fri; 10 a.m. to 4 p.m. Sat
Closed: Tue, Wed, Sun and bank hols
At present Mr Leonard produces organic vegetables and fruit, and also sells dried wholefoods and juices. He is hoping to extend his range with dairy produce and meat.

TUNBRIDGE WELLS
NATURAL LIFE
66 Grosvenor Road, Tunbridge Wells, Kent TN1 2AS
Tel: Tunbridge Wells (0892) 543834
Open: 9 a.m. to 5.30 p.m. Mon to Sat
Closed: Sun
A wholefood shop selling organic vegetables and fruit, dairy produce, dried goods and bakery products.

TWICKENHAM
GAIA
123 St Margaret's Road, Twickenham TW1 2LH
Tel: (081) 892 2262
Open: 9.30 a.m. to 7 p.m. (to 5 p.m. Sat)
Closed: Sun and bank hols
Wholefood shop specializing in organic produce and
macrobiotic foods. The range includes up to thirty different
types of vegetables and fruit, wholefoods and oriental foods.

UPAVON

RUSHALL FARMS
The Manor, Upavon, Pewsey, Wiltshire
Tel: (0980) 630264
Open: 7.30 a.m. to 12.30 p.m., 1.30 p.m. to 4.30 p.m. Mon
to Sat *Closed*: Sun, bank hols and Christmas
Barry Wookey runs one of the best-known organic cereal farms
in the UK. He produces wholemeal flour from his own wheat
and has a bakery producing bread, scones and rolls twice a
week.

UTTOXETER

CROWTREE ORGANIC FARM
Loxley, Uttoxeter, Staffordshire ST14 8RX
3 miles SW of Uttoxeter on the A518
Tel: Uttoxeter (0889) 565806
Open: 10 a.m. to 6 p.m. Wed to Sat
Closed: Sun, Mon, Tue
Mike Moore sells and distributes organic produce from his
own farm and from other growers. He has a wide range of fruit
and vegetables plus Staffordshire Farm cheese, apple juice and
bread. Organic wine is available wholesale. He also operates a
delivery sevice to retail customers throughout Staffordshire.

WADHURST
WEALDEN WHOLEFOODS
High Street, Wadhurst, East Sussex
Tel: (089288) 3065
Open: 9.15 a.m. to 5.15 p.m. (to 1 p.m. Wed and Sat)
Closed: Sun
Stocks a full range of wholefoods and many organic items,
from fruit, vegetables, dairy produce and wine to Aspall cider

vinegar, and tofu from Full of Beans in Lewes.

WARMINSTER

WHITBOURNE FARM
Corsley, Warminster, Wiltshire BA12 7QJ
Tel: Chapmanslade (037338) 495
Open: 9 a.m. to 6 p.m. (to noon Sun)
Michael Forward grows organic fruit and vegetables, rears
sheep and can supply dairy produce and eggs as well.

WARWICK
WARWICK HEALTH FOODS
40A Brook Street, Warwick, Warwickshire CV34 4BL
Tel: Warwick (0926) 494311
Open: 9 a.m. to 5.30 p.m.
Closed: Sun and bank hols
This wholefood shop sells as much organic produce as it can
obtain, from vegetables and fruit to dried goods, bread, juices
and marmalade.

WASHINGTON
BARNARD'S NURSERY
Rock Road, Washington, West Sussex RH20 3BH
Tel: Arundel (0903) 892320
Open: 'by orders in advance only'
The nursery specializes in organically grown vegetables and
salad crops.

WELLINGTON
SUNSEED
12 South Street, Wellington, Somerset TA21 8NS
Tel: Taunton (0823) 662313
Open: 9 a.m. to 5.30 p.m. Mon to Sat
Closed: Sun, bank hols and Christmas
Tony Bourne's shop stocks organic fruit and vegetables, dried
wholefoods, juices and specialities such as cider vinegar and
rice cakes.

WELLS
GOOD EARTH RESTAURANT & WHOLEFOOD STORE
4 Priory Road, Wells, Somerset BA5 1SY
Tel: Wells (0749) 78600

Open: 9 a.m. to 5.30 p.m. Mon to Sat
Closed: Sun and bank hols
The shop sells dried wholefoods, plus organic dairy produce and wine, free-range eggs and baby foods. The restaurant follows the same theme.

WEST WICKHAM
FARRINGTONS
7-9 Beckenham Road, West Wickham, Kent BR4 0QR
Tel: 01 777 8721
Open: 9 a.m. to 5.30 p.m. (to 1 p.m. Wed)
Closed: Sun and bank hols
Stocks organic fruit and vegetables as well as FREGG-approved free-range eggs, dairy produce and dried goods.

WHITBY
BANK HOUSE FARM
Glaisdale, Whitby, North Yorkshire
6 miles SW of Whitby off the A171
Tel: Whitby (0947) 87297
Open: 'by telephone appointment only'
Giles and Mary Heron can supply organic and additive-free meat as well as poultry.

WHITCHURCH
JACKIE & JOHN GUNTON
Green Gorse Wood, Whitchurch Road, Prees, Whitchurch, Shropshire SY13 3JZ
Open: 8 a.m. to 11.30 a.m. Fri (Whitchurch market)
Jackie and John Gunton grow a comprehensive range of organic vegetables including spinach, Swiss chard, celeriac and ridge cucumbers. The stall in Whitchurch market is their only retail outlet.

WHITE WALTHAM

WALTHAM PLACE FARM
Church Hill, White Waltham, Berkshire SL6 3JH
Tel: Littlewick Green (062882) 5517
Open: 2 p.m. to 5.30 p.m. Fri only
Closed: Sat to Thur
The farm produces organic vegetables and meat and can supply dairy produce, free-range eggs, bread and preserves.

WIMBORNE
RIVERSIDE ORGANIC GROWERS
Riverside Farm, Slough Lane, Horton Heath, Wimborne, Dorset
Tel: Bournemouth (0202) 826509
Open: 2 p.m. to 6 p.m. Thur only
Closed: Fri to Wed
Riverside Farm produces organic fruit and vegetables to Soil Association standards. There is a stall every Friday at Wimborne market.

SPILL THE BEANS
7 West Street, Wimborne, Dorset
Tel: Bournemouth (0202) 888989
Open: 9 a.m. to 5 p.m. (to 1 p.m. Wed)
Closed: Sun
As the name suggests, this shop stocks staple wholefoods as well as organic fruit and vegetables, bread and dairy produce.

WINDERMERE
E. H. BOOTH & CO. LTD
The Old Station, Victoria Street, Windermere, Cumbria LA23 1QA
Tel: Windermere (09662) 6114
Open: 9 a.m. to 5.30 p.m. (to 7 p.m. Thur, to 8 p.m. Fri)
Closed: Sun
Booths is the largest food retailer in the Lake District with a rapidly expanding organic section, including fruit, vegetables, dairy produce, wholefoods, wine and meat cut to customers' requirements.

WINDSOR
OASIS WHOLEFOODS
96 Peascod Street, Windsor, Berkshire SL4 1DH
Tel: Windsor (0753) 860618
Open: 9 a.m. to 5.30 p.m. (from 8.30 a.m. Sat)
Closed: Sun and bank hols
Stocks a wide range of organic grains, pulses, dried fruit and nuts, as well as organic wines. There is a branch at 112 High Street, Rickmansworth, Hertfordshire (Tel: (0923) 896600).

WISBECH
M. J. FEENEY
Sayers Field, Garden Lane, Wisbech St Mary, Cambridgeshire
PE13 4RZ
Tel: Wisbech (0945) 81335
Open: 'telephone first'
The Feeneys grow organic soft fruit and can supply additive-free lamb, pork and poultry.

WOKING
MIZEN'S FARM SHOP
Mizen's Farm, Chertsey Road, Woking, Surrey
Tel: Woking (0483) 30754
Open: 9 a.m. to 5.30 p.m. all week
Organic produce includes fruit, vegetables, wholefoods and juices, as well as additive-free meat.

WOLVERHAMPTON
GRANGE FARM
Hollies Lane, Pattingham, nr. Wolverhampton WV6 7HJ
3 miles W of Wolverhampton
Tel: Wolverhampton (0902) 700248
Open: 'telephone first'
Chris McLean produces organic fruit, vegetables and lamb, and can also supply wholefoods, dairy produce and juices.

WOODBRIDGE
LOAVES & FISHES
52 Thoroughfare, Woodbridge, Suffolk IP12 1AL
Tel: Woodbridge (03943) 85650
Open: 8 a.m. to 5.30 p.m. (to 2 p.m. Wed)
Closed: Sun
An enterprising shop combining fresh fish with organic produce and wholefoods. The organic range takes in everything from vegetables to wines, with specialities such as soya products and cider as well.

YELVERTON
N. & M. WILLCOCKS
Higher Birch, Bere Alston, Yelverton, Devon PL20 7BY
9 miles N of Plymouth off the A386
Tel: Tavistock (0822) 840257

Open: 'any time subject to prior telephone appointment'
Norman and Mary Willcocks run their farm on strict organic
lines. They specialize in beef and lamb, and will supply
butchered cuts as requested.

YORK
ALLIGATOR
104 Fishergate, York, North Yorkshire YO1 4BB
Tel: York (0904) 654525
Open: 9 a.m. to 6 p.m. (from 10 a.m. Mon)
Closed: Sun, bank hols and Christmas
This food shop sells organic fruit and vegetables, dried
wholefoods, bread and juices. Organic wines are available from
the York Beer Shop 50 yards away.

GILLYGATE WHOLEFOOD BAKERY
Millers Yard, Gillygate, York, North Yorkshire YO3 7EB
Tel: York (0904) 610676
Open: 9 a.m. to 6 p.m. Mon to Sat
Closed: Sun, bank hols, Christmas and New Year
All the baking is done with Soil Association grade flour, and
the bakery also stocks dried wholefoods, dairy produce and
juices. The attached cafe is open from 10 a.m. to 4 p.m. (see
entry in Part Three).

SCOTLAND

ABERDEEN
AMBROSIA WHOLEFOODS LTD
160 King Street, Aberdeen, Grampian AB2 3BD
Tel: Aberdeen (0224) 639096
Open: 9.30 a.m. to 5.30 p.m. (to 7 p.m. Thur)
Closed: Sun, bank hols and Christmas
This wholefood shop specializes in organic grains, and pulses,
herbs and spices as well as oriental and macrobiotic foods. It
also stocks organic fruit and vegetables from symbol holders.

AUCHTERARDER
DRUMMAWHANCE FARM

Auchterarder, Perthshire, Tayside PH3 1NP
Tel: (0764) 81267

Open: Ring first
Mr Cepok's farm can supply organic vegetables, meat, poultry
and free-range eggs.

AUCHTERMUCHTY
FLETCHERS FINE FOODS
Reediehill Deer Farm, Auchtermuchty, Fife KY14 7HS
Tel: Auchtermuchty (0337) 28369
Open: 9 a.m. to 4.30 p.m.
Closed: 25th Dec to 3rd Jan, except by arrangement
Set up in 1973 by John and Nichola Fletcher as Britain's
first commercial deer farm. It is not fully organic as yet,
but animals are naturally raised on grass with minimum
use of drugs or artificial fertilizers. As well as different
cuts and joints of venison, the Fletchers can supply
venison burgers and sausages, haggis and pâté. They also
sell unpasteurized cheese and clotted cream. They will
supply by mail order.

CUPAR
MR BENNETT'S ORGANIC FARM PRODUCE
Pillars of Hercules, Falkland, Cupar, Fife KY7 7AD
l0 miles W of Cupar off the A91
Tel: Auchtermuchty (0337) 57749
Open: 10.30 a.m. to 6.30 p.m. all week
Mr Bennett's small farm shop stocks fruit and vegetables
grown to Soil Association standards, as well as herb plants,
free-range eggs and dried flowers.

DUMFRIES

CAMPHILL VILLAGE TRUST
Loch Arthur Village Community, Beeswing, Dumfries,
Dumfries & Galloway DG2 8JQ
6 miles SW of Dumfries off the A711
Tel: (038776) 621
Open: 9 a.m. to noon, 2.30 p.m. to 5 p.m. Mon to Fri
Closed: Sat, Sun
A community including mentally handicapped adults, Camphill
has a farm and garden producing organic vegetables – mainly
potatoes – as well as dairy produce and beef. At present the
symbol applies to vegetables only, but approval of the beef is
imminent.

EDINBURGH
THE EDINBURGH ORGANIC SHOP
132 Lauriston Place, Edinburgh, Lothian EH3 9HX
Tel: (031) 228 3405
Open: 10 a.m. to 5.30 p.m. Tue to Sat
Closed: Sun, Mon, Christmas to New Year
The shop is part of SAMH (Day Services) Ltd, a registered charity providing supported work/training experience. The range of produce includes fruit, vegetables and dairy produce as well as dried wholefoods, breads, juices and oriental foods.

KIRKHILL GARDENS

Arniston, nr. Gorebridge, Lothian EH23 4LJ
S of Edinburgh off the A7
Tel: (0875) 20230
Open: 'telephone to arrange time'
This is a working market garden rather than a retail outlet, but Mr Scarlett will supply callers with organic fruit and vegetables.

REAL FOODS
37 Broughton Street, Edinburgh, Lothian EH1 3JU
Tel: (031) 557 1911
Open: 9 a.m. to 6 p.m. (5.30 p.m. Wed)
Closed: Sun
One of the most comprehensive wholefood/organic shops in the country. It sells a vast range, from cereals, grains and pulses in open sacks to dairy produce, macrobiotics and organic wines. It also operates a mail order service and a wholesale outlet. There is a branch at 8 Brougham Street, Tollcross, Edinburgh EH3 9JH (Tel: (031) 228 1651).

ELLON

C. M. LEITH & SON
Meikle Tillyeve, Udny, Ellon, Grampian AB4 0SJ
Tel: Udny (06513) 2223
Open: 9 a.m. to noon, 1 p.m. to 5 p.m. Mon to Sat
Closed: Sun, Christmas Day, New Year's Day
The Leiths can supply vegetables grown to Soil Association standards from August to April.

GIRVAN
DR G. EGGINGTON
8 Back Road, Dailly, Girvan, Strathclyde KA26 9SH
Tel: (046581) 247
Open: 'any time, but telephone first'
Dr Eggington grows organic vegetables to Soil Association standards.

MEIGLE
MR D. E. CLERK
South West Fullarton, Meigle, Tayside PH12 8SN
Tel: (08284) 391
Open: 'seasonally during July and August'
Closed: Sept. to June
Donald Clerk specializes in organically grown soft fruit – mainly strawberries, raspberries and black-and redcurrants. Visitors can order or pick-their-own (details of opening times are advertised in the *Dundee Courier*). Some organic vegetables are on sale along with the fruit.

NEWBURGH
IAN MILLER'S ORGANIC MEAT
James Field Farm, Newburgh, Fife KY14 6EW
Tel: Newburgh (0738) 85498
Open: 'telephone any time of day'
Ian Miller operates a mail order service for organic meat, including Aberdeen Angus beef, haggis and black pudding. James Field is the site of the new Safeway Organic Farming Centre.

STIRLING
I. & A. LAMBIE
Tigh Voulin, Thornhill, Stirling, Central
Tel: Thornhill (078685) 367
8 miles W of Stirling off the A84
Open: 'telephone first'
Ian and Alison Lambie grow organic soft fruit, vegetables and culinary herbs. Customers should telephone first so that orders can be made up ready for collection. The Lambies will deliver free to wholesale customers within a ten-mile radius.

TROON

MR J. DE VRIES
Auchenkyle, Southwoods Road, Troon, Strathclyde KA10 7EL
Tel: Prestwick (0292) 311414/317785
Open: 8.15 a.m. to 10 p.m. Mon to Sat
Closed: Wed, Fri and Sat evenings, Sun, Christmas and New Year
Growers and suppliers of organic vegetables in season.

TURRIFF
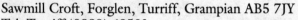

L. & M. ALLISON
Sawmill Croft, Forglen, Turriff, Grampian AB5 7JY
Tel: Turriff (0888) 68501
Open: 'most times, advisable to ring first'
The Allisons run a small farm rather than a retail outlet, but
will usually be able to supply organic vegetables to callers.
They also produce organic beef.

J. & P. BENNETT
Blakeshouse, Crudie, Turriff, Grampian AB5 7FS
Tel: Turiff (0888) 5276
Open: 'telephone before calling'
This is a farm shop selling butchered organic beef, vegetables,
a range of organic wholefoods and environmental products.

WALES

ABERYSTWYTH

FROST'S
Market Hall, Great Darkgate Street, Aberystwyth, Dyfed
SY23 1DW
Tel: Aberystwyth (0970) 615980
Open: 9 a.m. to 5.30 p.m. (to 5 p.m. Tue, to 6 p.m. Wed and Fri)
Closed: Sun
David Frost's market garden at Llanrhystyd, Dyfed SY23 1DW
(Tel: 097 46 364) provides much of the organic fruit,
vegetables and goat's dairy produce for his stall at Aberystwyth
market and the salad shop opposite. Salads are his speciality.

BORTH

G. & R. A. ROWLANDS
Brynllys, Borth, Dyfed SY24 2LZ

Tel: Aberystwyth (0970) 871489
Open: 9 a.m. to 5.30 p.m. all week from May to end of Sept.;
9 a.m. to 3 p.m. Thur, Fri and Sat from Oct. to end Apr.
Closed: Sun to Wed from Oct. to end Apr.
Brynllys Farm has been run organically for three generations.
Gareth and Rachel Rowlands are best known for the Rachel's
Dairy range of yoghurts, butter, cream and cheese which are
now widely available in shops and some supermarkets. They
also grow organic vegetables. Afternoon teas are served during
the summer.

BUILTH WELLS

MR & MRS P. DAVIES
Riandi, Erwood, Builth Wells, Powys LD2 3AJ
Tel: Erwood (09823) 230
Open: 'please telephone'
Philip Davies and his wife run an organic small-holding and
can supply vegetables (potatoes, swedes and carrots in season)
as well as lamb.

CARDIFF
WHOLEFOOD SHOP
1A Fitzroy Street, Cathays, Cardiff, South Glamorgan CF2 4BL
Tel: Cardiff (0222) 395388
Open: 9 a.m. to 6 p.m. Tue to Sat
Closed: Sun and Mon
Stocks a range of dried wholefood, bakery products and free-
range eggs as well as organic fruit and vegetables.

CARDIGAN

NEILL HARRIS
Trewidwal Farm, Moylegrove, Cardigan, Dyfed SA43 3BY
Tel: Moylegrove (023986) 211
Open: 8 a.m. to 8 p.m. all year, 'but telephone first'
The farm produces organic vegetables to Soil Association
standards. Neill Harris turns some of these into pickles.

M. J. RAY
Pencrugiau, Velindre, Crymych, nr. Cardigan, Dyfed SA41 3XH
Tel: Moylegrove (023986) 265
Open: 9 a.m. to 7 p.m. Mon, Tue, Thur, Fri, Sat from mid-
June to mid-Oct.

Closed: Wed and Sun
Mike Ray grows organic vegetables and soft fruit to Soil Association standards. He sells from his roadside farm shop during the season.

CARMARTHEN

CLEANGROW
Gellicoedgain, Capel Dewi, Carmarthen, Dyfed SA32 8AF
Tel: Llanddarog (026786) 625
Open: 'daily for door sales'
Closed: Wed and Sun
At present the Kings can supply organically grown vegetables and additive-free meat. They are planning to extend their range to include herbs.

CHEPSTOW

MEDHOPE ORGANIC GROWERS
The Nurtons, Tintern, Chepstow, Gwent
Tel: Chepstow (0291) 689797
Open: 9 a.m. to 5 p.m. all week
This enterprise can supply a range of organically grown vegetables as well as soft and top fruit.

CORWEN
SIMON'S
4 Edyrnion Terrace, Corwen, Clwyd
Tel: Corwen (0490) 2297
Open: 9 a.m. to 5.30 p.m. (to 1 p.m. Wed, to 5 p.m. Sat)
Closed: Sun, bank hols and Christmas
Simon Jones specializes in organic bread and bakery products, as well as dried wholefoods and juices.

FISHGUARD

LLANGLOFFAN FARMHOUSE CHEESE
Castle Morris, nr. Haverfordwest, Dyfed SA62 5ET
Tel: (03485) 241
Open: 9 a.m. to 6 p.m. Mon to Sat
Closed: Sun
One-time professional viola player Leon Downey now produces excellent organic cheeses from his fifteen-acre small-holding, using milk from his herd of Jersey cows. The range includes a naturally coloured red version flavoured with home

grown chives and garlic. Visitors can watch the cheese-making, and traditional Welsh teas are provided.

GLASBURY-ON-WYE
MRS SHEILA LEITCH
Wye View, Glasbury-on-Wye, Powys HR3 5NU
Tel: (04974) 354
Open: 'any time, please telephone first'
Sheila Leitch operates a small organic garden and orchard, producing vegetables and fruit. Most supplies are fresh, but frozen soft fruit is available out of season. She also grows sorrel and sells wine and juices.

HAVERFORDWEST

GREG NUTTGENS
Carnachenwen, Mathry, Haverfordwest, Dyfed SA62 5HL
Tel: Fishguard (0348) 3636
Open: 'no particular opening times'
Most of Greg Nuttgens' produce is sold direct off the farm and there are farm gate sales when supplies are available. The range includes organic vegetables as well as organic and additive-free meat.

HEBRON

C A. CHALONER & H. E. VESSEY
Pengelli, Hebron, nr. Whitland, Dyfed SA34 0JX
Tel: Hebron (09947) 600
Open: 8 a.m. to 8 p.m. Wed only
Closed: Thur to Tue
Most of the produce from this enterprise is sold wholesale to local shops and restaurants, but the retail farm shop is open to callers every Wednesday. Produce includes organic vegetables, top fruit and soft fruit in season.

KILGETTY
HEATHER HUGHES
Carew Mountain, Carew Lane, Cresselly, nr. Kilgetty, Dyfed SA68 0TR
Tel: Carew (0646) 651465
Open: 'any time we are there'
Heather Hughes can supply organic vegetables and free-range eggs. She recommends that customers telephone their orders

and collect at their convenience.

LAMPETER

D. & A. CAMPBELL
Goetre Isaf, Betwys Bledrws, Lampeter, Dyfed SA48 8NP
Tel: Lampeter (0570) 45237
Open: 'retail customers advised to telephone first'
The Campbells produce hard cheeses from their own herd and
are hoping for a Soil Association symbol in 1990. They are
best known for Tyn Grug – an unpasteurized Welsh version of
farmhouse Cheddar. Most of their trade is wholesale, but
callers are welcome.

MULBERRY BUSH WHOLEFOODS
2 Bridge Street, Lampeter, Dyfed
Tel: Lampeter (0570) 423317
Open: 9 a.m. to 5.30 p.m. (to 1 p.m. Wed)
Closed: Sun
An expanding wholefood shop with a good range of organics,
including dried wholefoods, breads, juices, cider vinegar and
soya milk.

LLANDRINDOD WELLS

VAN'S FRUIT AND VEG SHOP & GOOD FOOD SHOP
Laburnum House, Middleton Street, Llandrindod Wells,
Powys
Tel: Llandrindod Wells (0597) 3074
Open: 9 a.m. to 5.30 p.m. (to 4 p.m. Wed, to 6 p.m. Fri, to 5
p.m. Sat)
Closed: Wed lunch, Sun and bank hols
Organic vegetables, seasonal soft fruit, cheeses and dried
wholefoods are the main lines in this shop. Wine and cider are
also available.

LLANDYBIE

CAEGU NEWYDD FARM
Milo, Llandybie, Ammanford, Dyfed SA18 3LZ
Tel: Cross Hands (0269) 842698
Open: 'telephone first'
The Mitchells are basically distributors of Soil Association
symbol meat and poultry, and their refrigerated van covers
outlets throughout Wales and southern England. However,

they are happy to deliver freezer orders to private customers who telephone their requirements.

LLANDYSSUL

BRYN SARON FARM
Saron, Llandyssul, Dyfed SA44 5HB
Tel: Velindre (0559) 370405
Open: 'any reasonable time, with notice'
Chas and Anne Griffin grow organic vegetables and can also supply comfrey.

LLANWRDA

E. O. JONES
Briwnant, Pumpsaint, Llanwrda, Dyfed SA19 8UT
Tel: Pumpsaint (05585) 410
Open: 'telephone orders only'
This is essentially a wholesale business, but Evan Owen Jones will take freezer orders from individual customers who telephone first. He supplies organic meat and poultry to many retail outlets.

LLWYNGWRIL
NICK & MARGARET SMYTH
Pentre Bach, Llwyngwril, Gwynedd LL37 2JU
Tel: (0341) 250294
Open: 'we never close'
Organic fruit and vegetables, plus free-range eggs are the main lines here. The Smyths also make chutneys, jams and other preserves.

NEWPORT

P. M. COOPER
The Old Rectory, Llanvaches, Newport, Gwent NP6 3AY
Tel: Newport (0633) 400406
Open: Ring first
Mr Cooper grows and supplies organic vegetables and soft fruit grown to Soil Association standards.

NEWTOWN
BETA FRUIT
9 Market Street, Newtown, Powys
Tel: Newtown (0686) 628447
Open: 9 a.m. to 6 p.m. Mon to Sat

Closed: Sun
Beta Fruit claims to sell the largest selection of organic fruit and vegetables in mid-Wales. In addition, the shop stocks dairy produce and juices.

MACBEAN WHOLEFOODS
13 High Street, Newtown, Powys SY16 2NX
Tel: Newtown (0686) 627002
Open: 9 a.m. to 5.30 p.m. (from 9.30 a.m. Mon, to 5 p.m. Sat)
Closed: Sun, bank hols and Christmas
In addition to a full range of wholefoods, this shop sells organic fruit and vegetables, dairy produce, breads, juices and locally produced organic tofu. They can put customers in touch with local sources of organic meat and poultry too.

PENCOED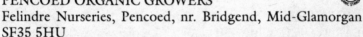
PENCOED ORGANIC GROWERS
Felindre Nurseries, Pencoed, nr. Bridgend, Mid-Glamorgan SF35 5HU
4 miles E of Bridgend on the A473
Tel: Bridgend (0656) 861956
Open: 'by arrangement, preferably Saturday morning'
Organically grown vegetables and additive-free meat are the principal supplies, but the nursery also produces 'fancy' lettuces and winter salads.

PONTARDULAIS
LLWYN IFAN DDU FARM
Garnswllt Road, Pontardulais, West Glamorgan SA4 1QJ
Tel: Ammanford (0269) 2090
Open: 10 a.m. to 5 p.m. Mon to Sat
Closed: Sun and Christmas
Jean Flintan used to operate from Clayton Farmhouse in Mayfield, Sussex, but moved to Wales in 1987, and is concentrating on supplies of additive-free beef and lamb, as well as free-range chickens and turkeys. She is awaiting a Soil Association symbol for the land so that she can begin to market fully organic meat.

PWLLHELI
RHOSFAWR NURSERIES
Rhosfawr, Y-Ffor, Pwllheli, Gwynedd LL53 6YA

Tel: Porthmadog (0766) 810545
Open: 9 a.m. to 7 p.m.
Closed: Tue
Janet and Peter Gomme specialize in organic vegetables, top fruit and gooseberries; they also supply free-range eggs and honey. A touring van/caravan site is open on site all year round.

REYNOLDSTON

L. J. TUCKER & SONS LTD
Knelston Hall Farm, Knelston, Reynoldston, Swansea, West Glamorgan SA3 1AR
Tel: Gower (0972) 390062
Open: Ring first
Knelston Hall Farm produces organically grown vegetables and top fruit grown to Soil Association standards.

SWANSEA
EAR TO THE GROUND
68A Bryn-y-Mor Road, Swansea, West Glamorgan SA1 4JJ
Tel: Swansea (0792) 463505
Open: 9 a.m. to 6 p.m. (to 4.30 p.m. Tue)
Closed: Sun, bank hols and Christmas
An enthusiastic workers' co-operative stocking a wide range of organic wholefoods, plus fruit and vegetables, herbs and dairy produce.

TALGARTH

MR R. T. PRICE
Neuadd Fach, Talgarth, Brecon, Powys LD3 0HA
Tel: Brecon (0874) 711307
Open: 'all day, everyday'
Vegetables and meat are produced to Soil Association standards on Mr Price's holding.

TENBY
FRESHFIELD FARM
Manorbier Station, nr. Tenby, Dyfed SA70 9VV
5 miles SW of Tenby off the B4585
Tel: Tenby (0834) 871823
Open: 10 a.m. to 6 p.m. Mon to Sat
Closed: Sun

Mr Rees-Thomas grows organic vegetables to Soil Association standards.

RED HOUSE FARM
New Hedges, Tenby, Dyfed SA69 9DP
Tel: Tenby (0834) 813918
Open: 'we never close'
Visitors can call at the farm to purchase supplies of organic vegetables and free-range eggs.

WELSHPOOL
P. J. MORRIS
Little Wern, Pool Quay, Welshpool, Powys SY21 9LQ
Tel: (0938) 75555
Open: 'any reasonable hours'
Mrs Morris can offer supplies of organically grown vegetables, including garlic. She also sells honey.

WHITLAND
PENRHIW FARM
Cefn-y-Pant, Llanboidy, Whitland, Dyfed SA34 0TR
5 miles N of Whitland
Tel: Hebron (09947) 657
Open: 2 p.m. to 8 p.m. all week (provisional)
The farm has recently been taken over by Philip Webb who has applied to re-register with the Soil Association and is looking at the UKROFS scheme. He produces organic vegetables, herbs and soft fruit, additive-free meat and poultry and eggs. He also runs a nursery of native trees and shrubs.

REPUBLIC OF IRELAND AND NORTHERN IRELAND

There is a good deal of interest in organic food and farming throughout Ireland, but information is hard to come by. The Irish Organic Farmers & Growers Association (IOFGA) sets organic standards in the Republic and has its own logo.

We have not been able to obtain specific details about organic growers and outlets in Ireland, but have received some general recommendations. We should point out that these have not been verified.

DUBLIN
Branches of Superquin Superstores and Tony Quin Health Centres in the city (there is also a branch in Dundalk). Also Dunnes Stores and Nature's Way in the city.

MANORHAMILTON
The Co-op Shop, Main Street, Manorhamilton, Co. Leitrim

ROSSINVER
Eden Plants, Eden, Rossinver, Co. Leitrim

SLIGO
Tir na Nog, Gratton Street, Sligo

BELFAST
Branches of Stewarts Supermarkets

We would especially welcome comments and recommendations from Irish readers so that we can extend our coverage. Please use the form at the back of the book.

WHOLESALERS AND DISTRIBUTORS

There are many wholesalers and distributors of organic food in various parts of the country. Some are wholefood specialists who include some organic items among their list of products; others are solely concerned with fresh produce. A few deal in both camps.

Although they supply retailers and members of the trade, some also have their own shops or retail outlets. If you have difficulty in locating organic produce in your area, they may be able to advise you.

Wholesalers are listed alphabetically by town.

BRIGHTON
INFINITY FOODS CO-OPERATIVE
67B Norway Street, Portslade, Brighton, East Sussex BN4 1AE
Tel: (0273) 424060
(For details of retail outlet, see p.143)

BRISTOL
NOVA WHOLEFOODS
Unit 1, Barton Hill Industrial Estate, Bristol, Avon
Tel: (0272) 583550

HALIFAX
SUMA WHOLEFOODS
Unit AX1, Dean Clough Industrial Park, Halifax, West Yorkshire HX3 5AN
Tel: (0422) 45513

ILMINSTER
SOMERSET ORGANIC PRODUCERS LTD
Wyvern Farms, Seavington St Michael, Ilminster, Somerset TA19 0PZ
Tel: (0460) 42149

LETCHWORTH
FAIRHAVEN WHOLEFOODS LTD
27 Jubilee Trade Centre, Letchworth, Hertfordshire SG6 1SP
Tel: (0462) 675300
(For details of retail outlet see p.170)

MALVERN
GLOBAL ORGANICS
c/o 99B Church Street, Great Malvern, Hereford & Worcester WR14 2AE
Tel: (0684) 565922

NEEDHAM MARKET
ORGANIC FARMERS & GROWERS LTD (OFG LTD)
Abacus House, Station Yard, Needham Market, Suffolk IP6 8AT
Tel: (0449) 720838
An organic growers' marketing co-operative specializing in cereals.

NORTHAMPTON
DAILY BREAD CO-OPERATIVE
The Old Laundry, Bedford Road, Northampton, Northamptonshire NN4 0AD
Tel: (0604) 21531
(For details of retail outlet see p.182)

NOTTINGHAM
BLOOMSGORSE/AGRICOLA
Unit 29, Salisbury Square, Radford, Nottingham NG7 2AB
Tel: (0602) 785696

PRESTON
BLAIRS ORGANIC GROWERS
Low Carr Nursery, Head Dyke Lane, Pilling, nr. Preston,
Lancashire PR3 6JS
Tel: (039130) 471

BATHGATE
ORGANIC FARM FOODS (SCOTLAND) LTD
Block 9, Whiteside Industrial Estate, Bathgate EH48 2RX
Tel: (0506) 632911

EDINBURGH
GREENWAY ORGANIC FARMS
FREEPOST, Edinburgh, Lothian EH1 0AQ
Tel: (031) 557 8111
Distributors of organic meat and poultry

REAL FOODS
Ashley Place, Edinburgh, Lothian EH6 5PX
Tel: (031) 554 4321
(For details of retail outlets see p.213)

LAMPETER
ORGANIC FARM FOODS (WALES) LTD
Units 23 – 27, Lampeter Industrial Estate, Lampeter, Dyfed
Tel: (0570) 423099/423130

PART THREE

Chapter 11

GOING FREE-RANGE

For twelve years, Alison and Andrew Johnson ran Scarista House, a remote hotel on the Isle of Harris – a miraculous landscape overlooking the Atlantic. From here they waged a passionate campaign against factory farming and processed food, and championed the cause of wild and organic produce long before it became the fashion. In 1989 they retired. Alison Johnson looks back and gives a personal view of the issues and problems involved, the humane arguments and some disquieting comments on intensive farming – not only of livestock, but of fish as well.

'Asparagus!' cried our English friends. 'Of *course* it will grow!' They stood in the midsummer sunshine, inhaling the scent of flowery meadows, admiring the test bore of deep sandy soil inside our rather collapsing garden walls. At the time, I believed them. We had plenty of other things to do – indeed there was very little that didn't have to be done to turn our ruinous purchase into the hotel of repute we intended it to be; but I had special ambitions for the food. I spent weeks clearing and digging the enormous gardens, applying tons of hen muck, cow muck, seaweed. But force ten gales, fifty inches of rain and a mean – very mean – summer temperature of 13°C don't suit asparagus, or courgettes, or tomatoes, or sweetcorn; or anything, really. Potatoes, carrots and lettuces could just about survive in our garden, and one or two dour old crofters would sell surplus cabbages, though they considered it an outrage to part with them before they tipped the scales at a couple of kilos. But as for those little, local growers who pirouette into the kitchens of reputable restaurants in more southerly parts, dispensing chanterelles and baby okra from wicker baskets – they would get blown into the sea here. So much for our organic vegetables; as for the rest, we had to be content with whatever glossy, pesticide-bloated horrors were sent up from Glasgow.

Nevertheless, Scarista House gained a reputation for fresh, natural food cooked with proper attention. By our fifth season we had received outstanding write-ups in most of the major hotel and restaurant guides. Our rise to fame had interesting personal results. We had the usual influx of 'foodies', who turn up at any newly-starred establishment with their favourite guide under one arm and indigestion tablets in their sponge-bags. We didn't like them, especially *I* didn't like them. We live on a beautiful island teeming with wildlife; and I have always prided myself on providing the kind of wholesome food which renders indigestion a thing of the past. It was a double insult to serve customers who didn't even notice the view *and* who destroyed the balance of their food by leaving all the fibre-rich bits so that they could stuff down more animal protein. I very quickly went off cooking.

Ethical questions that we had put at the back of our minds for years reasserted themselves. We had used free-range meat and eggs when available, as we used organic vegetables, because the quality was obviously better. If our hens were off-lay or the pork was flabby, we didn't enquire too closely. But exposure to the gourmet mentality brought it suddenly home. Hens were crammed in wire cages, pigs lived all their desperate lives in concrete pens, to feed *those* people; people who ate strangled Rouennais duck and foie gras; people whose belly was god. I have quite a belly myself, and spend a lot of time thinking about the next meal – perhaps I should have sympathized, but I didn't.

We almost gave up the business there and then, but reflection during an incomeless winter suggested a compromise. We would ban all factory-farmed products and make it clear to our customers that we did so on humane grounds. We would make the plan succeed, so that no-one could turn round and say that it was an impossible, uneconomic thing for restaurants to do. And instead of turning a blind eye to the abuse of farm animals, we found out more about it, and what we could do about it, so that the facts would prevent us from backtracking.

Once we had taken all that on board, we had to change our style. Eggs were no problem – we and many of our neighbours kept laying-hens. Pork presented more of a problem, as the great majority of Britain's pigs are reared in confined systems (although free-range pig farming is reviving and becoming profitable at last). We also knew the horror stories about veal. Yes, humane rearing is possible, but any veal which is 'white' rather than pinky red – and that includes almost all restaurant veal – still comes from the iniquitous crate system.

We also learned about Scottish salmon and how it is 'farmed'. The fish are intensively reared, crammed ten to a cubic metre in a net prison, rubbing their tail fins away in ceaseless circling. And there is more. Farmed salmon can only be kept free of lethal parasitic infestation by application of a chemical that is carcinogenic to humans and causes extreme genetic damage in shellfish. Shetland's huge sea-bird colonies are suffering massive breeding failure because their main source of food – sandeels – is going to manufacture feedstuffs for poultry and fish farms. We wouldn't touch farmed salmon – and neither would most of the locals on the island.

We had access to excellent venison, mutton, fish and shellfish, and as we always operated a set dinner menu, there were no real problems in providing sufficient variety. Many customers were pleased with our stance, read the propaganda leaflets and later bought my recipe book. Others said nothing, and a few sulked. We did have the occasional person who asked for chicken because red meat caused a squeamish shudder or health worries. They got a short answer from me. If 'health' requires a finicky choice between one creature's flesh and another's, the obvious solution is not to eat meat at all. Nutritionally it is a luxury, and not an innocent one.

I still find it worth pointing out to people what else they might be eating when they eat factory-farmed meat: drug and pesticide residues, unpublicized substances to make animals yield more muscle, more milk, tenderer meat, less fat. There is an official conspiracy to keep it quiet, but the fact that free-range producers can now do well enough to attract establishment fury is encouraging in itself.

As long as consumers continue to buy free-range and organic products whenever they are available, and ask for them when they are not, things will improve. That's why restaurateurs have to wake up and realize that there *is* a demand, and there is money in it. Ten years ago, remember, it was almost impossible to get a vegetarian meal except in specialist restaurants; now even the ferry to the Isle of Harris serves a vegetarian salad. In ten years' time it could be the same with organic food. Restaurateurs should try putting one or two organic items into long menus between the tournedos Rossini and the chicken Kiev, just to see what happens. I bet they would be hot sellers.

We certainly didn't find our policy anything but a help to custom. We could count on running over 90 per cent full for both rooms and meals although we never advertised. Of course, it was not simply due to our free-range philosophy, but that helped. How could it not, in a rural location where many visitors stayed with us because of an existing interest in the countryside? If their experience was all of a piece, they would go away saying 'That was magic' – and they would come again. Almost any eating-place in a country setting could profit by this psychology. If we could do it on the Isle of Harris, where supplies are invariably difficult and expensive, how easy it would be in Gloucestershire or Kent!

Our own decision to 'go free-range' was not made on grounds of quality or taste, although everything *does* taste better. Although that consideration ought to be of prime importance to everyone who is interested in food – consumer or caterer – for us, the humane aspect was paramount. No one, least of all a cook, can always keep clean hands; but we once had a honeymoon couple to stay, so young and shy that they hardly uttered a word. Eventually they got up the courage to speak when they paid their bill: 'We're really impressed. We're never going to buy battery-farmed produce again.' That was the best compliment we received in twelve years of hotel-keeping.

Chapter 12

EAT OUT – EAT ORGANIC

A GUIDE TO RESTAURANTS

Some of the first to realize that there was a virtue in using unprocessed – and in many cases organic – ingredients in their kitchens, were the wholefood annd vegetarian restaurants which started to appear during the 1970s and spread like a green swath across the land in the 1980s. Organic produce fitted their concern for health, natural foods and unrefined quality. Of course, it was often no more than sporadic supplies of basic organic vegetables and free-range eggs, but it was a start.

Now other restaurants are beginning to catch up. This is partly because organic produce is easier to obtain and more reliable in quality than it was a few years ago. Also it is now possible to find producers and suppliers of organic and additive-free meat and free-range poultry and dairy produce, as well as fruit and vegetables. The 'search for flavour' is the logical next step from the quest for so-called 'real foods'. Organic produce generally comes from small-scale, local enterprises – farmers, growers, millers, cheesemakers – which need support from restaurants if they are to survive.

Many regional producers are now banding together to form collectives. Devon was the first county to spearhead this trend, and Devon Harvest is one of the best organized groups in the country. Others have followed suit: Taste of Somerset, Wiltshire Larder, Herefordshire Hamper – and more are sure to follow. Most of these groups have organic growers and producers among their ranks – which is an enormous help for restaurants wanting to obtain reliable supplies.

Increasingly, the kitchen and the garden are starting to go hand-in-hand. Hope End Hotel was one of the first to pioneer this idea. John and Patricia Hegarty started growing organically in 1979 and transformed their beautiful eighteenth-century walled garden into one of the showpieces of organic horticulture in Britain. It was started because the Hegartys recognized the disastrous effects that a purely technological and commercial approach to agriculture was likely to have on our environment and our health. Their enterprise isn't a return to the Dark Ages or a new version of medievalism; modern glasshouses and complex irrigation systems are used alongside old pottery cloches and mulches. The whole enterprise is sustained by sheer hard work and a belief in the rightness of organic methods.

The same is true of Andrew and Lis Whitley's Village Bakery in Melmerby, Cumbria, also started in the late seventies. Behind their remarkable bakery is a five-acre small-holding which they have farmed organically from the start, and which now holds the Soil Association symbol. They have two large polytunnels, and make clever use of a small glasshouse which sits on top of the baking oven and provides an excellent, warm propagating house right through the year. Their flock of 120 free-range hens, two sows, and nine ewes produce eggs and meat for the restaurant. The Whitleys' dedication is to the cause of better, natural, wholesome food; it is healthy rather than virtuous.

As the momentum builds up, more restaurants are making an effort; places such as the Old Vicarage at Ridgeway, Oakes, in Stroud, and the Ceilidh Place in Ullapool are starting to grow at least some fruit, vegetables and herbs organically in their own kitchen gardens. Not so long ago, the standard comment from most restaurateurs was 'I'd like to use organic produce, but I can't get hold of it.' That is changing fast. So fast, in fact, that there's little excuse for restaurants which have nailed their colours to the mast in other areas, not to use organic ingredients in their kitchens.

ABOUT THE ENTRIES

The restaurants listed on the following pages are making a conscious effort to use organic, free-range and additive-free produce in their kitchens. Entries are listed alphabetically by town or location in England, Scotland and Wales.

Opening times listed indicate when food is available. Hotels and pubs are likely to be open at other times as well. Some places offer a single sitting at a specific time, e.g. dinner at 8 p.m.

Specialities listed at the end of entries are typical of each restaurant's menu. All of them include organic ingredients. Because these restaurants use fresh, seasonal produce and often change their menus from day to day, the listed specialities may not be available all the time.

Further details of specific growers, producers and suppliers mentioned in the entries can be found in the Directory in Part Two.

TEN OF THE BEST
(listed in alphabetical order)

* Brookdale House, North Huish, Devon

* Dining Room, London SE1

* Granary, Cardigan, Dyfed

* Hope End Hotel, Hope End, Ledbury, Hereford & Worcester

* Moorings Restaurant, Wells-next-the-Sea, Norfolk

* Poppies Restaurant at The Roebuck, Brimfield, Hereford & Worcester

* Stones Restaurant, Avebury, Wiltshire

* Sunflower Country Kitchen, Edinburgh, Lothian

* Village Bakery, Melmerby, Cumbria

* Village Restaurant, Ramsbottom, Lancashire

ENGLAND

AVEBURY
STONES RESTAURANT
High Street, Avebury, nr. Marlborough, Wiltshire SN8 1RF
Tel: Avebury (06723) 514
Open: 10 a.m. to 6 p.m.
Closed: Nov. to Easter, except weekends up to Christmas
Hilary Howard and Michael Pitts have made a great success of
their imaginative vegetarian restaurant not far from Avebury's
legendary standing stones. Their list of local organic suppliers
is impeccable: 100 per cent wholemeal flour from Rushall
Farms, Pewsey; vegetables from Hobsleys Organics at
Bishopstone; free-range eggs from Martin Pitt at Levetts Farm,
near Marlborough. Other staples come from Nova Wholefoods
in Bristol. West Heath supply organic wines and Dunkertons
provide the cider. This translates into a menu of soups (often
flavoured with herbs from the garden), pizzas, 'Megalith' main
dishes, 'Stonewiches', home-baked scones and cakes, backed
up by herb teas, apple juice and real ale.
Specialities: *cream of the garden soup; mushroom and runner
bean cacciatore; 'egghogs'.*

BARNSTAPLE
HEAVENS ABOVE
4 Bear Street, Barnstaple, Devon EX32 7BU
Tel: Barnstaple (0271) 77960
Open: 10 a.m. to 3 p.m.
Closed: Sun, bank hols, Christmas to New Year
Straightforward, home-cooked vegetarian food is served in this
upstairs restaurant decorated with paintings and flowers.
Pizzas, quiches and cakes are made with organic wholemeal
flour supplied by the Granary, Truro, and cashewnut rissoles
are coated with organic sesame seeds. Locally-based growers,
including Smith's Organics and Marshford Organic Nurseries,
Northam, supply fruit and vegetables as available. The house
wine is organic too.
Specialities: *leek and pepper quiche; cider loaf; date flapjacks.*

BARWICK
LITTLE BARWICK HOUSE
Barwick, nr. Yeovil, Somerset BA22 9TD

Tel: Yeovil (0935) 23902
Open: dinner 7 p.m. to 9 p.m.
Closed: Sun, Christmas and New Year
This converted dower house is run by Christopher and
Veronica Colley with old-fashioned family hospitality. They put
their faith in fine seasonal ingredients: naturally-reared spring
lamb, organic fruit and vegetables during the summer, game in
the winter, backed up by good cheese and bakery. As well as
traditional items such as roast poussin or pigeon pie, there
might be iced cucumber and yoghurt soup or pancakes stuffed
with spinach, cheese and herbs.
Specialities: *hot leek and tarragon tartlet; roast rack of lamb
with mint and cucumber sauce; home-made sorbets.*

BERKHAMSTED
COOK'S DELIGHT OF BERKHAMSTED
360-364 High Street, Berkhamsted, Hertfordshire HP4 1HU
Tel: Berkhamsted (0442) 863584
Open: 10 a.m. to 9.30 p.m. Thur and Fri; 10.30 a.m. to 3.30
p.m., 8 p.m. to 'late' Sat; 10.30 a.m. to 5.30 p.m. Sun
Closed: Mon, Tue, Wed and Christmas Day
Since 1981, Rex Tyler has been putting his organic principles
into practice – and into poems as well. This remarkable 'natural
grocer's' is part wholefood shop and delicatessen (see entry),
alternative bookstore and tearoom-cum-restaurant. During the
day you can get scones, cakes, buckwheat quiches and casseroles
all prepared from organic ingredients. Rex's wife is from South-
East Asia and evening meals centre on Indonesian and Malaysian
dishes including satays, gado-gado, curries and rice rolls. Cook's
Delight is also one of the few places to offer a macrobiotic
Sunday lunch. To drink there are teas, coffees, organic beers and
ciders, as well as a stock of over 90 organic wines.
Specialities: *organic vegetable terrine; sweet and sour tempeh;
pear flan.*

BRIGHTON
FOOD FOR FRIENDS
17-18 Prince Albert Street, The Lanes, Brighton, East Sussex
BN1 1HF
Tel: Brighton (0273) 202310
Open: 9 a.m. to 10 p.m. Mon to Sat; 10 a.m. to 10 p.m. Sun
Closed: Christmas Day and Boxing Day

Brighton is full of vegetarian restaurants, but Food for Friends stands out because it offers genuine ingredients cooked with plenty of flair and few compromises. Organic vegetables come from the town's municipal vegetable market, flour is from Doves Farm, Hungerford and dairy produce from Loseley Park Farms, Guildford. Simon Hope and his cooks also use free-range eggs and organic grains and pulses for soups, salads, stir-fries and pizzas. The food is incredibly cheap, and to drink there's apple juice, cidre bouche and organic wines from The Organic Wine Company. The atmosphere is rather chaotic and cramped, but the room is ionized.

Specialities: *tandoori kebabs with organic rice and cucumber raita; mushroom and kidney-bean bourguignonne pie; tijuana tortillas with salsa and guacamole.*

BRIMFIELD
POPPIES RESTAURANT AT THE ROEBUCK
Brimfield, nr. Ludlow, Hereford & Worcester SY8 4WE
Tel: Brimfield (058472) 230/654
Open: noon to 2 p.m., 6 p.m. to 10 p.m.
Closed: Sun, Mon, 2 weeks in Feb., 1 week in Oct., Christmas Day and Boxing Day

Carole and John Evans' four-square black and white hostelry is just off the A49 between Ludlow and Leominster. The village has been by-passed but there are plenty of signs. Locals use this place as the village pub; visitors drive up to a hundred miles for a meal in its modern, airy restaurant. This is bistro cooking at its best, based on sound ingredients: eggs from hens that range freely in the garden; some herbs and vegetables grown by John; organic meat and free-range poultry from reliable suppliers. Look for the impressive cheese menu which has a dozen interesting British specialities, including organic Pencarreg, Llangloffan and Llanboidy. The Evans also stock organic wines, as well as Dunkerton's cider made a few miles away at Luntley.

Specialities: *deep-fried Pencarreg cheese with bramble chutney; rack of Welsh lamb with rosemary and herb crust; honey wafers with a chestnut, walnut and hazelnut cream and coffee sauce.*

CAMBRIDGE
ARJUNA
12 Mill Road, Cambridge, Cambridgeshire CB1 2AD

Tel: Cambridge (0223) 64845
Open: 9.30 a.m. to 6 p.m. (to 2 p.m. Thur); 9 a.m. to 5.30
p.m. Sat
Closed: Sun, bank hols, 1 week Christmas
In-store cafe attached to a wholefood shop with more than one
hundred organic lines. Food is simple: soups, pizzas, flans and
cakes made with organic ingredients wherever possible.

CANTERBURY
SWEET HEART OF CANTERBURY
47 Whitstable Road, Canterbury, Kent CT2 8DJ
Tel: Canterbury (0227) 450341
Open: 8 a.m. to 8 p.m.
Closed: Christmas and New Year
Canterbury's best-known coffee-house has moved from the
Old Weaver's House to a new site on Whitstable Road. Ingrid
Eissfeldt specializes in Swiss and German cakes and breads, and
is currently setting up a wholefood patisserie using classic
European recipes and organic ingredients. There is a phone-
free delivery service to most parts of the south-east.
*Specialities: diplomat torte; 'Romantic Gourmet Wedding
Cake'; savoury croissants.*

CASTLE CARY
OLD BAKEHOUSE
High Street, Castle Cary, Somerset BA7 7AW
Tel: Castle Cary (0963) 50067
Open: 9 a.m. to 5 p.m. Tue to Sat
Closed: Sun, Mon and bank hols
A good-value daytime restaurant with a bias towards vegetarian
and wholefood dishes. As well as fresh soups such as tomato
and orange, there might be pizzas, vegetable curry with brown
rice, or mushroom and cashewnut roast with mushroom and
sherry sauce. Vegetables and herbs come from Charles
Dowding of Shepton Montague Organics.
*Specialities: leek and potato soup; vegetable bake; tomato and
mushroom lasagne.*

CHELMSFORD
MELISSA WHOLEFOOD RESTAURANT
21 Broomfield Road, Chelmsford, Essex CM1 1SY
Tel: Chelmsford (0245) 353009

Open: 8 a.m. to 4 p.m. Mon to Sat
Closed: Sun and bank hols
Chelmsford's first vegetarian restaurant is still going strong. Dishes are exclusively wholefood, everything is made on the premises and many ingredients – including most fruit, vegetables and herbs – are organically grown. The place is well known for its wholemeal pizzas and a big choice of up to eighteen different salads, but it also offers interesting three-course lunches featuring dishes such as pea and mint soup or chick pea and mushroom Stroganoff with noodles.
Specialities: *cheese and vegetable charlotte; lentil and fresh herb loaf with coconut cream sauce; home-made ice creams.*

CHESTER
ABBEY GREEN RESTAURANT
2 Abbey Green, Northgate Street, Chester, Cheshire CH1 2JH
Tel: Chester (0244) 313251
Open: noon to 2.30 p.m., 6.30 p.m. to 10.15 p.m.
Closed: all Sun and Mon dinner
Abbey Green was was voted National Vegetarian Restaurant of 1988/89. It is noticeably civilized, with a new, landscaped garden and elegant décor that has echoes of a country drawing-room. The cooking is exotic, colourful and international, roaming far and wide for dishes such as gougère dijonnais and courgette kofta. Organic fruit and vegetables are used wherever possible, eggs are free-range and the organic wines are the stars of the cellar.
Specialities: *pasta polenesia; nut roast with whisky, apple and tarragon sauce; stuffed vegetables with coconut and vermouth.*

CORSE LAWN
CORSE LAWN HOUSE HOTEL
Corse Lawn, nr. Tewkesbury, Gloucestershire GL19 4LZ
Tel: Tirley (045278) 479
Open: 12.30 p.m. to 2 p.m., 7 p.m. to 10 p.m. all year
Built in 1745, this fine Queen Anne house set back from the B4211 is now the setting for Baba Hine's distinctive cooking, which combines modern trends with classical ideas. Game and wild foods feature prominently – as in saddle of hare with port, cinnamon and mushroom mousse. There's also a full and very enterprising vegetarian menu including dishes such as baby sweetcorn in puff pastry or brochette of mixed vegetables with

wild rice and tomato coulis. Some fruit, vegetables and herbs are organic, bread is made with organic flour and there are supplies of free-range poultry and organic cheese.

Specialities: *terrine of wild mushrooms with soy and Madeira sauce; roast duckling with apple confit and orange sauce; raspberry shortcake.*

CROMER
LAZYBONES
2 Brook Street, Cromer, Norfolk NR27 9EY
Tel: Cromer (0263) 515185
Open: 10 a.m. to 4 p.m. Tue to Sun, from 7.30 p.m. Fri and Sat (from Mon to Sat in summer)
Closed: Mon (exc. bank hols) in winter
Sally Morphew and Barbara Vanlint use organic produce as a matter of course, changing their menus every day and offering a mix of innovative vegetarian, meat and fish dishes, ranging from bean, courgette and olive casserole with Feta cheese to plaice stuffed with Parmesan cheese, roasted almonds and parsley. Fruit and vegetables are from Poppyland Organic Produce and there are supplies of milk and yoghurt from hormone-free herds. The commitment to additive-free produce extends to undyed smoked fish, and sausages made without preservatives.

Specialities: *Scandinavian apple soup; lamb in walnut and orange sauce; baked fruit cheesecake.*

CROYDON
HOCKNEYS VEGETARIAN RESTAURANT
96-98 High Street, Croydon, Surrey CR0 1ND
Tel: (081) 688 2899
Open: noon to 10 p.m. Tue to Sat
Closed, Sun, Mon, 2 weeks Christmas, 1 week Easter, 2 weeks Aug.
Simon Beckett's restaurant is linked to Croydon's Buddhist Centre (with courses on Buddhist cookery as well as yoga) and the Independent Arts Centre. The cooking is vivid with some original ideas and a commitment to sound ingredients. Organic flour, vegetables and free-range eggs are used for dishes ranging from broccoli pie with Camembert to mushroom brioche with red wine sauce and cranberry compote. There's no licence, but there are non-alcoholic

wines, juices and a range of infusions and herb teas.
Specialities: potato and watercress soup; aubergine and tomato quiche; banana and yoghurt pie.

CUCKFIELD
JEREMY'S RESTAURANT
King's Head Hotel, South Street, Cuckfield, West Sussex
RH17 5VY
Tel: Haywards Heath (0444) 440386
Open: 12.30 p.m. to 2 p.m., 7.30 p.m. to 10 p.m.
Closed: Mon dinner, Sat, Sun, bank hols and 2 weeks Aug.
Jeremy Ashpool worked for a while with John Kenward (see Lewes) before taking a franchise on this restaurant in an unremarkable village pub. Like Kenward, his cooking is potent and uncompromising, with vivid flavours and a liking for fish, game and wild foods. He has reliable supplies of vegetables from nearby Laines Organic Farm, and makes interesting use of free-range poultry and naturally-reared meat – including home-cured bacon from Old Spot Farm, Newick. This translates into dishes such as grilled leg of lamb with runner bean purée and rosemary sauce, or pheasant with herb dumplings, apple and rhubarb. He makes everything in-house, including breads with organic flour.
Specialities: pumpkin soup with toasted seeds; free-range chicken with lemon risotto and sorrel sauce; local smoked bacon with stir-fried leeks and ginger.

GREAT MALVERN
ONLY NATURAL
99B Church Street, Great Malvern, Hereford & Worcester
WR14 2AE
Tel: Great Malvern (0684) 561772
Open: 9 a.m. to 5 p.m. Mon to Sat
Closed: Sun and Christmas
Vegetarian cafe attached to a wholefood shop (see entry) specializing in organic produce. The kitchen makes use of fruit and vegetables from Global Organics and wholefoods from Harvest Natural Foods of Bath, as well as dairy produce and free-range eggs.
Specialities: vegetable soup; quiche and mixed salad; lentil shepherd's pie.

HEREFORD
RESTAURANT NINETY-SIX
96 East Street, Hereford, Hereford & Worcester HR1 2LW
Tel: Hereford (0432) 59754
Open: dinner from 7 p.m.
Closed: Sun, Mon and bank hols
This used to be Effy's – an odd little crooked cottage, painted in pink and green in the old cobbled streets near the cathedral. New owners, the Chichesters, have redecorated and updated its image, but are maintaining supplies of organic produce. Among the starters might be locally-grown organic melon filled with grapes and peach schnapps or cream of chervil soup with hazelnuts. Main courses feature fish, seasonal game and free-range poultry, and to drink there is Dunkerton's cider.
Specialities: *cheese soufflé with salad and sesame dressing; goat's cheese with mushrooms and peanuts en croûte with chervil sauce; paupiette of chicken breast with spinach and tarragon sauce.*

HOLT
YETMAN'S
37 Norwich Road, Holt, Norfolk NR25 6SA
Tel: Holt (0263) 713320
Open: 12.30 p.m. to 2 p.m., 7.30 p.m. to 9 p.m. Wed to Sun
Closed: Mon, Tue
A pretty little restaurant in a row of old cottages not far from the church. Alison and Peter Yetman slant their menus towards fresh fish and local organic produce, with vegetarian options and some fine British cheeses to match.
Specialities: *crab salad with avocado and basil mayonnaise; stuffed courgettes with Parmesan sauce; peach Melba with raspberry purée.*

HORSHAM
COUNTRY BASKET
7 East Street, Horsham, West Sussex RH12 1HH
Tel: Horsham (0403) 65102
Open: 9 a.m. to 5 p.m. Mon to Sat
Closed: Sun and public hols
Vegetarian cafe and takeaway attached to a wholefood shop (see entry). As much organic produce as possible is used in the cooking.

LANCASTER
LIBRA
19 Brock Street, Lancaster, Lancashire LA1 1UU
Tel: Lancaster (0524) 61551
Open: 9 a.m. to 5 p.m. Mon to Sat
Closed: Sun, bank hols and 1 week Christmas
A useful vegetarian restaurant with smart décor and a
wholesome daytime menu of soups, quiches, pizzas and pies.
Organic flours and porridge oats come from The Watermill,
Little Salkeld, free-range eggs are from a nearby farm.
Specialities: *samosas; broccoli and cheese pie; three-layer bake
with rice salad.*

LEDBURY
HOPE END HOTEL
Hope End, Ledbury, Hereford & Worcester HR8 1JQ
Tel: Ledbury (0531) 3613
Open: 7.30 p.m. to 8.30 p.m. Wed to Sun (dinner only)
Closed: Mon, Tue and Jan. to March
John and Patricia Hegarty founded Hope End in 1979,
believing that 'good wholesome, seasonal, local British food
was the best recipe for a small country hotel at a time when
"French cuisine" ruled'. The first task was to restore their
eighteenth-century walled garden and move over to organic
production. Now they grow a hundred different kinds of herbs
and vegetables, forty kinds of apples and other soft and top
fruits – including many unfashionable and old-fashioned
varieties that have been rescued from extinction. The Hegartys
defend the British garden and the British kitchen; their
solutions are constructive and successful. Their own produce is
backed up by first-rate supplies of organic flour, dairy produce
(including cheeses such as Pencarreg and Llanboidy), organic
meat and free-range poultry. Patricia uses organic cider and
cider vinegar in the kitchen, while John has some organic
wines in his magnificent cellar. Their rebuilt mansion was the
childhood home of Elizabeth Barrett Browning, a sanctuary
nestling in a glacial hollow, and in keeping with the philosophy
of the place, the grounds are protected by up-to-date
conservation principles.
Specialities: *carrot and thyme soup; best end of Ledbury lamb
stuffed with apricots and walnuts; baked custard with loganberry
sauce.*

LEWES
KENWARDS
Pipe Passage, 151A High Street, Lewes, Sussex BN7 1XY
Tel: Lewes (0273) 472343
Open: noon to 2.15 p.m., 7.30 p.m. to 9.30 p.m.
Closed: Mon dinner, Sat lunch, all Sun and bank holiday Mons
Potent natural flavours are the hallmarks of John Kenward's
cooking, and he puts the emphasis firmly on fresh fish and
game. He only serves beef, lamb and pork if he can obtain
reputable supplies of organic or additive-free meat. His menus
change regularly, but typically there might be duck salad with
fruit preserves alongside bass and monkfish steamed with
basil, along with vegetarian dishes such as Bonchester cheese
baked with leeks. His sauces are powerful reductions of stock
and pan juices, pointed up with alcohol but seldom with
cream. As well as organic vegetables, herbs, free-range eggs
and poultry, there is home-baked bread made with Doves
Farm flour.
Specialities: squash with goat's cheese and sage; artichoke and
leeks with ginger and parsley; guinea fowl with vine leaves, thyme
and oloroso sherry.

LONDON
ALASTAIR LITTLE
49 Frith Street, London W1V 5TE
Tel: (071) 734 5183
Open: 12.30 p.m. to 2.30 p.m., 7.30 p.m. to 11.15 p.m.
Closed: Sat lunch, Sun, bank hols and 2 weeks Christmas
Alastair Little has turned this modish, monochromatic
restaurant into one of the finest eating places in London. The
décor is minimal, the food is everything. He builds his ideas
around the best quality fresh ingredients, changes his menus
twice a day and has a seemingly endless capacity for invention.
This is the new cooking at its best, pulling together influences
from around the world: sashimi and pot-roasts, couscous and
Chinese-style sea bass steak with soy. Flour, breads and cheeses
come from Neals Yard; the All Organic Company provides
fruit, vegetables and herbs. Free-range poultry is used where
possible and there are occasional supplies of additive-free meat.
Organic wines.
Specialities: bruschetta; risotto with courgette flowers; mirabelle
and greengage tart.

CHERRY ORCHARD

241-245 Globe Road, London E2 0JD
Tel: (071) 980 6678
Open: noon to 3 p.m., 6 p.m. to 10.30 p.m. Tue to Fri; noon
to 10.30 p.m. Sat
Closed: Sun, Mon, Christmas
A peaceable vegetarian restaurant run by the women of The
Pure Land Co-operative. Meals are served in the light,
sophisticated dining-room or in the pleasant garden outside.
The quality is high, prices are low. Organic flour and cakes,
free-range eggs from Martin Pitt and dairy produce from Neals
Yard are used for a menu that takes in soups, quiches, fresh
pasta and some good sweets. Unlicensed, but take your own
wine or choose from the range of juices and teas.
Specialities: *leek croustade; mushroom moussaka; salads with
home-made mayonnaise.*

CLARKE'S

124 Kensington Church Street, London W8 4BH
Tel: (071) 221 9225
Open: 12.30 p.m. to 2 p.m., 7.30 p.m. to 11 p.m.
Closed: Sat, Sun, bank hols, 4 days Easter, 3 weeks Aug., 10
days Christmas
Sally Clarke draws her inspiration from trips to Paris,
California and Japan, and has established a distinctive style all
her own. The emphasis is on fresh fish, seasonal game and
salad ingredients, with lots of marinating and char-grilling
pointed up with relishes: pineapple for monkfish, tomato and
coriander with grilled pork and pork kidney sausage. A new
bakery produces not only brilliant breads often made with
organic flour, but incomparable pizzas topped with organic
vegetables and herbs. Cheeses from Neals Yard often include
some organics. There is a retail shop and delicatessen next
door.
Specialities: *clear vegetable soup with anchovy and olive toasts;
baby sweetcorn steamed with chilli and coriander; pizzas.*

CRANKS

8 Marshall Street, London W1
Tel: (071) 437 9431
Open: 8 a.m. to 10.30 p.m. (from 10 a.m. Sat)
Closed: Sun and bank hols

17-18 Great Newport Street, London WC2
Tel: (071) 836 5226
Open: 8 a.m. to 8.30 p.m. Mon to Sat
Closed: Sun and bank hols

11 The Market, Covent Garden, London WC2
Tel: (071) 379 6508
Open: 10 a.m. to 8 p.m. (to 7 p.m. Sun)
Closed: bank hols

9-11 Tottenham Street, London W1
Tel: (071) 631 3912
Open: 8 a.m. to 8 p.m. (from 9 a.m. Sat)
Closed: Sun

Unit 13, 10 Adelaide Street, London WC2
Tel: (071) 379 5919
Open: 10.30 a.m. to 10.30 p.m. Mon to Sat
Closed: Sun and bank hols

Since the first branch opened in Carnaby Street in 1961,
Cranks has been synonymous with a particular style of
wholesome vegetarian cooking. The mini-chain is still reliable
and immensely popular, largely because dishes are cooked fresh
each day, there is always plenty of variety and proper care is
taken with ingredients. Organic flour is used for their excellent
range of breads and cakes (including their famous version of
the Doris Grant loaf); organic fruit and vegetables appear in
salads, casseroles and pies, and to drink there are organic
wines, cider and juices.
Specialities: *parsnip and apple soup; vegetarian goulash;
banana yoghurt flan.*

DINING ROOM
1 Cathedral Street, London SE1 9DE
Tel: (071) 407 0337
Open: 12.30 p.m. to 2.30 p.m., 7 p.m. to 10 p.m.
Closed: Sat, Sun and Mon
In a curious basement in the shadow of Southwark Cathedral is
this functional vegetarian restaurant with almost bare walls and
a handful of tables. The menu spans the globe, taking in cream
of coconut soup, bean curd and peanut sauce, mushroom

risotto and piperade with lentil purée and steamed lettuce. To finish there are wholefood sweets and rare unpasteurized cheeses. Almost all the produce is organic, from the wholewheat flour, brown rice and cold-pressed oils to some of the wines.

Specialities: seaweed and chestnut fritters with dill mayonnaise; okra and chick pea stew; buckwheat noodles with broccoli and pine nuts.

EAST WEST RESTAURANT
188 Old Street, London EC1V 9BP
Tel: (071) 608 0300
Open: 11 a.m. to 9.30 p.m. (to 3 p.m. Sat and Sun)
Closed: bank hols, Christmas to New Year
This is one of the few restaurants run on purely macrobiotic lines, with a balance between grains, vegetables and protein; no meat, no animal fats, no sugar and no dairy produce are used in the cooking. It is part of the Community Health Foundation, with a bookshop and grocery attached (see entry). All dishes include organic produce from soups and salads to desserts. There is also a balanced set meal that changes each day, with a grain such as brown rice or millet, a protein dish (perhaps haricot bean stew with almonds), pickles, sea vegetables, greens and the like. To drink there are organic wines, as well as juices and teas.

Specialities: miso soup; pan-fried noodles with tempeh; rice balls with seaweed.

NEALS YARD BAKERY & TEA ROOM
6 Neals Yard, Covent Garden, London WC2
Tel: (071) 836 5199
Open: 10.30 a.m. to 6.30 p.m. (to 5 p.m. Sat)
Closed: Sun, bank hols
Set up as a bakery and wholefood co-operative in 1978, Neals Yard is now London's leading centre for 'real foods'. Ten kinds of bread are made from organically grown cereal ground in their own mill, and the little upstairs tearoom also sells pizzas, quiches, beanburgers and a range of cakes and pastries produced with organic flour, free-range eggs and vegetarian cheese. (For details of the bakery and other Neals Yard outlets, see Directory).

Specialities: breads; cakes; pizzas.

LE SOLEIL
110-112 Palmerston Road, Walthamstow, London E17 6PZ
Tel: (071) 520 5898
Open: 7 a.m. to 5 p.m. Mon to Sat; also 7 p.m. to 10 p.m.
Thur to Sat
Closed: Sun, bank hols and Christmas
Next door to Only Natural – a committed organic wholefoods
shop (see entry). Additive-free and organic produce is used for
a wide range of vegetarian dishes. Snacks are served during the
day; more formal meals appear in the evening. Unlicensed, but
you are welcome to bring your own drinks.
Specialities: *melon and grapefruit cocktail; lentil and vegetable
lasagne; apricot and almond crumble.*

MANCHESTER
BILLIES
115 Manchester Road, Chorlton, Manchester
Tel: (061) 881 9338
Open: noon to 2.30 p.m., 6 p.m. to 11 p.m.
Closed: Christmas
A principled vegetarian restaurant run by a women's co-
operative. The ideology of the enterprise takes in everything
from the careful choice of organic ingredients to the nappy-
changing facilities in the men's as well as the ladies' toilets. The
menu is international and eclectic, and to drink there are
organic wines as well as additive-free beers and lagers.
Specialities: *watercress soup; stuffed choux buns; Korean pancake
with peanut sauce.*

GREENHOUSE VEGETARIAN RESTAURANT
331 Great Western Street, Rusholme, Manchester M14 4AQ
Tel: (061) 224 0730
Open: 10 a.m. to 11.30 p.m. Mon to Fri (from 1 p.m. Sat and
Sun)
Closed: 24th Dec. to 1st Jan.
This family-run vegetarian restaurant is in a converted corner
house with window boxes and pot plants. Rose and Mark
Baxter make imaginative use of seasonal ingredients for dishes
with a pronounced oriental flavour, ranging from spring rolls
and vegetable roast with satay sauce to strudels filled with
mushrooms or spinach. Their loyalty to organic produce
extends to some of the wines.

Specialities: *sweet potato goulash with organic Basmati rice; Greenhouse strudel; thali.*

ON THE EIGHTH DAY
109 Oxford Road, All Saints, Manchester, M1 7DU
Tel: (061) 273 1850
Open: 10 a.m. to 7 p.m. (to 4.30 p.m. Sat)
Closed: Sun
An admirably run workers' co-operative, with cooks taking turns in the kitchen. The menu is short, prices are low and dishes are cooked fresh each day. These usually include one soup, one stew and one bake, with assorted salads and sweets prepared using organic flour and rice, free-range eggs and organic vegetables whenever possible. Unlicensed, but there's barley cup, a good choice of herb teas and hot spiced apple juice.
Specialities: *pinto bean and vegetable stew with rice; pasta and fagioli bake; cheesecake.*

MELMERBY
VILLAGE BAKERY
Melmerby, nr. Penrith, Cumbria CA10 1HE
Tel: Langwathby (076881) 515
Open: 8.30 a.m. to 5 p.m. Tue to Sun
Closed: Mon, Christmas to Easter
Since 1977 Lis and Andrew Whitley have been have running this converted pig-sty and chicken loft as a remarkable bakery-cum-restaurant. Organic ideas are at the heart of their enterprise and their use of resources is brilliant. Stoneground flour comes from The Watermill, Little Salkeld, and the Whitleys run a five-acre small-holding behind the bakery. The baking is done in a wood-fired brick oven that works through the day: fierce heat for the breads and pies; cakes and biscuits later; pizzas on the brick sole – even grilled meat and fish over the embers. The Whitleys prefer butter to margarine and aren't averse to serving kippers or Cumberland sausages. They stock organic wines, cider from Aspall and Avalon, as well as organic Pinkus lager from Germany.
Specialities: *tomato tart; cream of cauliflower soup; home-raised lamb baked with vegetables.*

MONTACUTE
MILK HOUSE
17 The Borough, Montacute, Somerset TA15 6XB

Tel: Martock (0935) 823823
Open: 7.30 p.m. to 9.15 p.m. Wed to Sat; also 12.30 p.m. to 2 p.m. Sun
Closed: lunch Mon to Sat; dinner Sun to Tue
Lee and Bill Dufton have restored this beautiful fifteenth-century stone house and have regenerated the kitchen garden. Inside it is all beams, rough stone walls and log fires. The emphasis is on good quality ingredients – mostly organic – for a menu that features fish, game and vegetarian dishes such as nut fricadelles. Everything is made in-house and the Duftons sensibly limit the numbers of people they will serve in an evening. Petit fours are often filled with organic fruit pastes and the wine list has a few organic representatives.
Specialities: *salad with smoked quail's eggs and apple vinaigrette; smoked salmon roule with celery and walnut stuffing; venison braised in red wine.*

NAILSEA
WRAXALL HOUSE HOTEL
Nailsea, nr. Bristol, Avon BS19 1BU
2 miles E of Nailsea on the B3130
Tel: Bristol (0272) 810363
Open: noon to 2 p.m., 7 p.m. to 10.30 p.m. all week
Closed: Christmas Day
Sue and Philip Prideaux run this seventeenth-century country house in spacious grounds within striking distance of junction 20 of the M5. Their Victorian walled garden is run organically and provides vegetables, herbs and fruit for the kitchen. Meals are prepared from purely organic and wholefood ingredients, including flour, dairy produce, meat and poultry. There are organic wines too.
Specialities: *leek and potato soup; baked pork chop with apple and tomato sauce; peach custard.*

NEWARK
GANNETS
35 Castlegate, Newark, Nottinghamshire
Tel: Newark (0636) 702066
Open: 10 a.m. to 4.30 p.m. Mon to Sat
Closed: Sun, bank hols and 1 week Christmas
Hilary Bower's enterprising restaurant is in a listed Georgian building overlooking the River Trent and the castle. Self-

service lunches have strong vegetarian leanings, with seaweed roulade and walnut, mushroom and basil pâté alongside pasta and beef bake, and meatballs with tomato and celery sauce. Imaginative salads, good cakes and indulgent sweets. Wine by the glass.

NORTH HUISH
BROOKDALE HOUSE
North Huish, South Brent, Devon TQ10 9NR
Tel: Gara Bridge (054882) 402
Open: dinner 7.30 p.m. to 9 p.m.
Closed: 3 weeks Jan.
The Trevor-Ropers moved from Knights Farm in Burghfield, Berkshire to this lovely Tudor mansion set in four acres of wooded gardens. High-class cooking with a healthy bias makes use of as much organic and additive-free produce as possible. Devon is well served by small producers and the fly-leaf on their menu tells all: 'Ben Watson at Riverford Farm rears pigs on natural diets and also provides us with chickens, again fed on a natural diet, well-hung Devon beef and lamb reared on organic pastures. Peter Hayford from Lower Bearscombe provides us with free-range quail, guinea fowl, Aylesbury and cross-bred ducks as well as quail eggs...Charles Staniland from Buckland-in-the-Moor grows us herbs, specialist vegetables and delicious strawberries in his organic garden...This buying policy ensures the highest quality of ingredients as well as a diet free from all chemical food additives.' The Trevor-Ropers are planning to stock organic wines too.
Specialities: *carrot, mushroom and tarragon gâteau with white wine sauce; roast best end of lamb with herb crust and port sauce; summer fruits bound in yoghurt served in filo pastry with raspberry sauce.*

NORWICH
LLOYD'S OF LONDON STREET
66 London Street, Norwich, Norfolk NR2 1JT
Tel: Norwich (0603) 624978
Open: noon to 2 p.m., 6.30 p.m. to 9.30 p.m.
Closed: Mon dinner, Sun and most public hols
A co-operative venture that reflects the history of Norwich and the surrounding countryside, providing displays of local

interest as well as a seasonal menu of local dishes. Organic vegetables, fruit and salads come from Mangreen Gardens, and the kitchen uses free-range poultry and eggs. Organic wines. During the summer, there are tables outside at Lloyd's Street Cafe.

Specialities: *chestnut and brazil nut roast with fresh tomato sauce; breast of free-range chicken stuffed with julienne of vegetables and served with chicken mousse and saffron and tarragon sauce.*

TREEHOUSE
16 Dove Street, Norwich, Norfolk NR2 1DE
Open: 11.30 a.m. to 3 p.m. Mon to Sat
Closed: Sun
Vegetarian restaurant above Rainbow Wholefoods shop (see entry), and only fifty yards from Norwich market. Dishes are cooked fresh each day, and good use is made of organic flour, vegetables and free-range eggs for a varied menu that ranges from potato and cauliflower curry with dhal and chutney, to salads.
Specialities: *pumpkin and cashewnut bake; cheese, leek and mushroom pie; apricot, apple and hazelnut millet cake.*

RAMSBOTTOM
VILLAGE RESTAURANT
16 Market Place, Ramsbottom, Greater Manchester BL0 9HT
Tel: Ramsbottom (070682) 5070
Open: dinner at 8 p.m. Wed to Sat
Closed: Sun, Mon and Tue
Ros Hunter and Chris Johnson take their cue from the Englishness of their setting – a village of cobbled streets on the edge of the moors. Dinner is a six-course feast that can last up to four hours. Vegetables and salads are provided by Coopers Organic Growers in Chorley; organic meat and free-range poultry from Arthur Hollins at Fordhall Farm, Market Drayton. Meals always feature half a dozen vegetables: perhaps potatoes, carrots, beetroot with lemon, broad beans with summer savory, spinach with dried fruit and sour cream, sweetcorn with green peppers. The cheeseboard includes some organics, such as Staffordshire Farm Cheese and Llanboidy, while the astonishing 800-strong wine list has around thirty from organic growers.

Specialities: courgette and ginger soup; chicken with apricot and Meaux purée and cider and tarragon; summer pudding.

RIDGEWAY
OLD VICARAGE
Ridgeway Moor, Ridgeway, Derbyshire S12 3XW
Tel: Sheffield (0742) 475814
Open: 7 p.m. to 9.30 p.m. Tue to Sat; noon to 2.30 p.m. Sun
Closed: Mon, 1 week Aug., 1 week Christmas
The handsome Victorian house is set in well-tended grounds and Tessa Bramley's cooking is dictated by the garden, the seasons and the countryside. Dishes are immaculate, nouvelle English, often decorated with flowers, and salads are a course in their own right. Tessa makes good use of game and wild foods for dishes such as roast guinea fowl with sage and apple stuffing, while free-range poussin might be stuffed with tarragon and served with saffron sauce and lemon compote. Much of the produce is grown organically in the family's own kitchen garden; they have two greenhouses and polytunnels to keep their herbs and edible flowers going through the year. Ridgeway Organic Farm Co-operative is next door, free-range eggs come from a farm two fields away and unpasteurized farmhouse cheeses are from reliable suppliers.
Specialities: hotch-potch of game birds with wild mushroom sauce and a compote of gooseberries and elderflowers; fillet of fallow deer with spiced red cabbage and chestnuts; courgette flowers stuffed with girolles on tomato and basil coulis.

ROCKLEY
LOAVES AND FISHES
Rockley Chapel, Rockley, Wiltshire SN8 1RT
Tel: Marlborough (0672) 53737
Open: 7.30 p.m. to 8.30 p.m. Wed to Sat, also 12.30 p.m. to 1 p.m. Sun
Closed: Mon and Tue
As the address suggests, this is a quaint and unusual restaurant in a small grey chapel set in a hollow surrounded on three sides by hills. Nikki Kedge and Angela Rawson include a good deal of local and organic produce in their short set menus, which are dominated by classic cream-based sauces. Herbs are used imaginatively, chicken is free-range and meat is from naturally-reared livestock. Eggs and goat's cheese are delivered from a

farm up the road. The restaurant is unlicensed, but your can bring your own wine.

Specialities: *roast rib of beef with peppered brandy and cream sauce; supreme of chicken with champagne cream sauce; gâteau Diane.*

RYTON-ON-DUNSMORE
RYTON GARDENS

The National Centre for Organic Gardening, Ryton-on-Dunsmore, nr. Coventry, Warwickshire CV8 3LG
Tel: Coventry (0203) 303517
Open: 10 a.m. to 5 p.m. in summer (to 4 p.m. in winter)
Closed: Christmas Day and Boxing Day

Ryton Gardens is the home of The Henry Doubleday Research Association, the country's leading charitable organization devoted to 'researching, demonstrating and promoting environmentally safe growing techniques'. The twenty-two acre site lays out the evidence for organic horticulture and there is an open-plan daytime cafe serving vegetarian and wholefood dishes made exclusively with organic ingredients. The style includes excellent soups, casseroles, quiches and dishes such as mushroom Stroganoff, backed up by salads (with unusual leaves and herbs), cakes and organic bread. Ryton Gardens also have a very comprehensive stock of organic wines (as well as cognac and cider) supplied by Vinceremos Wines.

Specialities: *pumpkin soup; broad bean cutlets with onion sauce; upside-down apple pudding.*

ST IVES
WOODCOTE HOTEL

The Saltings, Lelant, St Ives, Cornwall TR26 3DL
Tel: Hayle (0736) 753147
Open: dinner 6 p.m. to 10.30 p.m.
Closed: Nov. to Feb.

Woodcote Hotel has two great attractions; its unique setting overlooking the tidal estuary of the Hayle, and the fact that it caters exclusively for vegetarians. John and Pamela Barrett use organic flour, fruit, vegetables and herbs for their fixed-price dinner menus, and include organic cider in their cooking too. The hotel is unlicensed, but guests can bring their own wine. It is important to pre-book tables at least one day in advance.

Specialities: *stuffed marrow; savoury pancakes; tomato and mushroom curry.*

ST NEOTS
POPEYE'S FLOATING VEGETARIAN RESTAURANT
Hardwick Road, Eynesbury, nr. St Neots, Cambridgeshire PE19 2UD
Tel: St Neots (0480) 406948
Open: 7.30 p.m. to 11 p.m. (from 7 p.m. Sat and Sun); also noon to 2.30 p.m. Sun
Closed: Mon
As you might expect, this vegetarian restaurant is on a boat permanently moored on the River Ouse just south of St Neots (take the B1043 out of the town). The short, enterprising menu ranges far and wide for onion bhajias, braised celery with yoghurt and Roquefort cheese sauce, and walnut and thyme loaf with parsley sauce. Fruit and vegetables are supplied by Rosehaven Organics, dairy products are from Loseley Farm; wines and organic cognac are from The Organic Wine Company.
Specialities: *pears with fromage frais dressing; leek pancakes mornay; apple turnovers.*

SHREWSBURY
DELANY'S
St Julians Craft Centre, St Alkmonds Square, Shrewsbury, Shropshire SY1 1UH
Tel: Shrewsbury (0743) 60602
Open: 10 a.m. to 3.30 p.m. Mon to Sat; also 7 p.m. to 10 p.m. Thur to Sat
Closed: Sun
The panelled dining-room in the old church vestry is now a colourful and committed vegetarian restaurant with green tablecloths and bright blue chairs. During the day it is exclusively vegetarian, but meat dishes appear on the evening menu. Breads are made with Pimhill organic flour; vegetables, herbs and salads are largely organic too. The philosophy extends to the fruit juices and wines, and to the filtered water used for teas and coffees. There is a branch in an oak-panelled pub at Wyle Cop, Shrewsbury (0743 66890).
Specialities: *cauliflower paprika; celery and lentil burgers; chick pea and vegetable casserole.*

SOUTHWOLD
CROWN HOTEL
90 High Street, Southwold, Suffolk IP18 6DP
Tel: Southwold (0502) 722275
Open: 12.30 p.m. to 2 p.m., 7.30 p.m. to 9.45 p.m. all year
Although it is called a hotel, The Crown is more like a town pub, bistro-restaurant and up-market inn, all rolled into one. It is also the showcase for Adnams' extraordinary wine list – which now includes some organics. Dishes served in the bar and the dining room are modern, light and healthy, with the emphasis on local fish and game. The kitchen makes use of organically grown herbs, free-range poultry and eggs, some organic cheese and dairy produce as well as cider.
Specialities: *salade niçoise; hot goat's cheese with seasonal salads; roast duck breast with saffron and olives.*

STOCKPORT
COCONUT WILLY'S
37 St Petersgate, Stockport, Greater Manchester SK1 1DH
Tel: (061) 480 7013
Open: 11.30 a.m. to 11 p.m. Tue to Sat
Closed: Sun, Mon and bank hols
Martin Rooney trained as a chef and ran a health food shop before opening this colourful vegetarian restaurant. At lunchtime it's self-service, with more ambitious dishes and table service in the evening. All the baking is done with organic stoneground flour and free-range eggs, and organic fruit and vegetables are used when they are available. A feature of the place is the list of drinks, which takes in not only organic wines and ciders, but a range of naturally brewed, unpasteurized beers, including Flag porter brewed in London.
Specialities: *quiche; brazilnut Wellington; zyldyke casserole.*

STROUD
OAKES
169 Slad Road, Stroud, Gloucestershire GL5 1RG
Tel: Stroud (0453) 759950
Open: 12.30 p.m. to 1.45 p.m. Tue to Sun, 7.30 p.m. to 9.30 p.m. Tue to Sat
Closed: Sun dinner, Mon, Jan. and 2 weeks Aug.

Chris and Caroline Oakes have turned this nineteenth century girl's school built of Cotswold stone into one of the finest restaurants in the west of England. Chris offers high-powered modern cooking from set menus that are strong on fish – baked sea bass with lime vinaigrette; monkfish braised in red wine with chives and parsley. Herbs, fruit and vegetables are grown organically in their own garden, and they get supplies of free-range poultry and eggs as well as organic flour from local producers.

Specialities: breast of chicken filled with mushroom mousse served with madeira sauce; ragout of seafood served in pastry case with tarragon sauce; summer pudding.

TIDEFORD
HESKYN MILL
Tideford, nr. Saltash, Cornwall PL12 5JS
Tel: Landrake (0752) 851481
Open: noon to 2 p.m., 7 p.m. to 10 p.m. Tue to Sat
Closed: Sun, Mon and Christmas
This converted mill is just outside the village of Tideford on the way to St Germans. The Edens concentrate their efforts on local produce, especially fish and game; like many restaurateurs they still have difficulty obtaining guaranteed supplies of organic fruit and vegetables out of season, but report that the situation is getting better. Even so the quality shows in the rack of lamb and the beef. They are hoping to sell organic wine in the near future.

Specialities: vegetable crudités with yoghurt and watercress dip; escalope of salmon with tarragon and cream; rack of Cornish lamb with redcurrants and oranges.

TIVERTON
ANGEL FOOD
1 Angel Terrace, Tiverton, Devon
Tel: Tiverton (0884) 254778
Open: 8.30 a.m. to 5.30 p.m. (to 2.30 p.m. Thur)
Closed: Sun, bank hols and Christmas
Tiny cafe behind a wholefood shop (see entry) specializing in organic produce. Through the day you can get pies and savouries dishes, Greek salad with hummus, Feta cheese and olives, quiches, cakes and ice creams.

Specialities: vegetable pasty; bean burgers; carrot cake.

TORQUAY
MULBERRY ROOM
1 Scarborough Road, Torquay, Devon TQ2 5UJ
Tel: Torquay (0803) 213639
Open: 10 a.m. to 5 p.m. Wed to Sun, also 7.30 p.m. to 9 p.m.
(Sat only)
Closed: Mon and Tue
At first glance this seems like just another old-fashioned
dining-room attached to a seaside guest house. But owner,
cook and Jill-of-all-trades, Lesley Cooper, offers excellent value
lunches, and proper home-cooking with proper ingredients.
She produces her own honey, herbs and ice cream, bakes bread
with flour from Crowdy Mill, Harbertonford, and makes use
of local cheeses and ewes' milk yoghurt. Her meat and poultry
is of superb quality, likewise the vegetables.
Specialities: *roast chicken with honey and herbs; breast of lamb
with haricot beans and garlic; nut roast with tomato, mushroom
and mixed fresh herbs.*

TOTNES
WILLOW VEGETARIAN RESTAURANT
87 High Street, Totnes, Devon TQ9 5PB
Tel: Totnes (0803) 862605
Open: 10 a.m. to 5 p.m. Mon to Sat; also 6.30 p.m. to 10 p.m.
Tue to Sat July-Sept. (Wed, Fri and Sat Oct.-June)
Closed: Sun, bank hols and 1 week Christmas
An easy-going vegetarian restaurant bedecked with paintings,
tapestries and fresh flowers. The menu spells out exactly which
ingredients are organic, from the carrots in the carrot and
coriander soup, and the brown rice that comes with the
butterbean and cider casserole, to the fruit for the strawberry
ice cream sundae. Wednesday night is devoted to Indian
vegetarian thalis (set meals). A useful list of a dozen organic
wines as well as Pinkus organic lager.
Specialities: *fresh herb and tofu dip; spinach lasagne; strawberry
cheesecake.*

TUNBRIDGE WELLS
THACKERAY'S HOUSE
85 London Road, Tunbridge Wells, Kent TN1 1EA
Tel: Tunbridge Wells (0892) 37558
Open: 12.30 p.m. to 2.30 p.m., 7 p.m. to 10 p.m. Tue to Sat

Closed: Sun, Mon, 1 week Easter

Bruce Wass has transformed the second oldest house in Tunbridge Wells into a high-flying modern restaurant. This used to be the home of novelist William Makepeace Thackeray, and now it's a showcase for sophisticated cooking with lots of fish, game, herbs and exotic salads. Meals are expensive, but Bruce Wass makes no compromises with ingredients: he never serves farmed salmon or any fish that has been frozen; he is always seeking local supplies of organic vegetables and herbs; his bread is made with organic flour and he buys additive-free pork, Shetland lamb and sausages from Anne Petch at Heals Farm.

Specialities : *chicken boudin with hot onion marmalade; mutton with port, juniper and orange; coconut parfait with exotic fruit.*

WELLS-NEXT-THE-SEA
MOORINGS RESTAURANT
6 Freeman Street, Wells-next-the-Sea, Norfolk NR23 1BA
Tel: Fakenham (0328) 710949
Open: 12.30 p.m. to 2 p.m. Fri to Tue, 7.30 p.m. to 9 p.m. Thur to Mon
Closed: Tue dinner, Wed, Thur lunch, late Nov. to mid-Dec., Christmas Eve to Boxing Day, 2 weeks mid-June

Bernard and Carla Phillips have turned this one-time quayside cafe into a remarkable little restaurant dedicated to local food – from organic vegetables to goat's cheese. Carla points out that some so-called free-range eggs are suspect, but hers come from a farmer who makes up his own meal and feeds. Local organic beef appears in the form of meatballs, although the emphasis is really on fish, game and vegetarian dishes, from pigeon breasts with port and cream to poached sea trout with white wine and orange. Carla makes a feature of food from the wild – for instance, casserole of giant puffball with tomatoes and herbs. Some organic wines.

Specialities: *meatballs with tomato, cumin and cinnamon sauce; lamb with garlic, parsley and olive oil; olive and almond cream with eggs and tomatoes.*

WESTON-SUPER-MARE
LA PETITE AUBERGE
37 Upper Church Road, Weston-super-Mare, Avon BS23 2DX
Tel: Weston-super-Mare (0934) 622351

Open: 12.30 p.m. to 4 p.m., 7.30 p.m. to 11 p.m.
Closed: Sun and some bank hols
This cosy bistro is not far from the harbour, and the owners make a feature of fresh local fish on their menus. Dart salmon might be served with mint and lime sauce (herbs are grown organically in the garden). They also take care in obtaining other supplies, including free-range eggs, organic vegetables and locally baked bread.
Specialities: *fresh tomato, cream and chive soup; deep-fried mixed cheese wrapped in fresh herbs and breadcrumbs; skate with hollandaise sauce.*

WHITBY
SHEPHERD'S PURSE
Sanders Yard, 95 Church Street, Whitby, North Yorkshire
Tel: Whitby (0947) 604725
Open: 10 a.m. to 9.30 p.m.
Closed: end Sept. to Easter
The old mill in a cobbled courtyard is now a vegetarian restaurant decorated with folksy bric-à-brac. Fresh ingredients and organic produce are used for curries, stuffed pancakes, nut loaf and salads. To drink there are unusual teas and organic wines.

WORCESTER
BROWN'S
24 Quay Street, Worcester, Hereford & Worcester WR1 2JN
Tel: Worcester (0905) 26263
Open: 12.30 p.m. to 1.45 p.m. (to 2 p.m. Sun), 7.30 p.m. to 9.30 p.m.
Closed: lunch Sat, dinner Sun, bank hols and 1 week Christmas
A romantic converted cornmill on the banks of the Severn, with an arched window overlooking the water. The short menu of modern dishes makes extensive use of organic herbs and vegetables, while salads might consist of some fifteen different organic ingredients on the plate.
Specialities: *warm duck salad; crab with radicchio, endive and oak-leaf lettuce; strawberry ice cream with raspberry coulis.*

YORK
MILLER'S YARD CAFE
Miller's Yard, Gillygate, York, North Yorkshire YO3 7EB

Tel: York (0904) 610676
Open: 10 a.m. to 4 p.m. Mon to Sat
Closed: Sun, Christmas Day, Boxing Day, New Year's Day
Part of the Gillygate Wholefood Bakery, which mills its own organic flour and carries the Soil Association symbol. The cafe is in a collection of converted buildings near the City Art Gallery. Organic fruit, vegetables, herbs and free-range eggs are used for daily-changing soups, hot dishes, salads and snacks from pizzas to pastries. Unlicensed, but there are herb teas and juices to drink.
Specialities: *carrot and coriander soup; stir-fried vegetables with tofu and rice; courgette and tomato quiche.*

SCOTLAND

ABERDEEN
JAWS WHOLEFOOD CAFE
St Katherines, 5 West North Street, Aberdeen, Grampian
Tel: Aberdeen (0224) 645676
Open: noon to 3 p.m. (to 9 p.m. Thur and Fri)
Closed: Sun and Christmas
A useful vegetarian/wholefood cafe next to the Arts Centre. The menu has a wide choice of international dishes, from pizzas and pies to couscous and casseroles. Vegetables, flour and dairy produce are organic, poultry and eggs are free-range.
Specialities: *beancurd curry with cauliflower pakhoras; spinach roulade; fritatta parmigiana.*

EDINBURGH
HELIOS FOUNTAIN
7 Grassmarket, Edinburgh, Lothian EH1 2HY
Tel: (031) 229 7884
Open: 10 a.m. to 6 p.m. Mon to Sat (to 8 p.m., also 11 a.m. to 5 p.m. Sun during Aug.)
Closed: Sun (except during Aug.), Christmas and New Year
Part of the Rudolf Steiner centre with a bookshop and craft shop attached. The menu changes each day and dishes are attractively prepared from organic ingredients: wholesome soups, hot dishes such as pinto bean and pimento pie, and salads dressed with virgin olive oil are the high points. There are also quiches, scones and wholefood cakes. No wines, but there is organic apple juice to drink.

Specialities: *leek and spinach soup; tofu and vegetable stir-fry; pasta in wine and cream sauce.*

HENDERSON'S SALAD TABLE
94 Hanover Street, Edinburgh, Lothian EH2 1DR
Tel: (031) 225 2131
Open: 8 a.m. to 9 p.m. Mon to Sat (8 a.m. to 11 p.m. Mon to Sat, 9 a.m. to 9 p.m. Sun during Festival)
Closed: Christmas and New Year
'Healthy living is our aim,' says Janet Henderson, who opened this basement, self-service vegetarian restaurant in 1962 as an outlet for her farm produce. Organic ingredients are still the basis of her wide-ranging cosmopolitan menu, in which salads and sweets are the highlights. Organic wines, herb teas and freshly squeezed juices to drink. Next door is the farm shop and there is a bakery in nearby Canonmills producing specialities from organic stoneground flour.
Specialities: *stuffed marrow with mushroom sauce; wholemeal pizza; spinach flan.*

MARTIN'S
70 Rose Street North Lane, Edinburgh, Lothian EH2 3DX
Tel: (031) 225 3106
Open: noon to 2 p.m., 7 p.m. to 10 p.m. (to 10.30 p.m. Fri and Sat)
Closed: Sat lunch, Sun, Mon and 2 weeks from Christmas
Martin and Gay Irons' airy French restaurant is tucked away in an alley between Castle Street and Frederick Street. Fish and game dishes are the high points, with anything from warm monkfish salad to venison with whisky and pepper sauce. The kitchen is making increasing use of organic vegetables and free-range poultry.

SUNFLOWER COUNTRY KITCHEN
4-8 South Charlotte Street, Edinburgh, Lothian EH2 4AW
Tel: (031) 220 1700
Open: 8 a.m. to 7 p.m.
Closed: Sun, Christmas
This wholefood cafeteria was launched in 1982 and reflects current ideas about healthy eating. The emphasis is on fresh produce, natural ingredients and low-fat cooking, with nutritional information and calorie counts listed beside each dish on the menu. Organic wholemeal flour and vegetables

appear in many of the salads, quiches and cakes; the owners now have supplies of organic Aberdeen Angus beef reared to Soil Association standards. There are organic wines too.
Specialities: *lasagne; 'nuttie tattie'; nut roast.*

GLASGOW
PETER JACKSON AT THE COLONIAL
25 High Street, Glasgow, Strathclyde G1 1LX
Tel: (041) 552 1923
Open: noon to 2.30 p.m., 6 p.m. to 10.30 p.m.
Closed: Sat lunch, Sun, Mon dinner
Peter Jackson is moving with the times and, like many forward-looking chefs, he pays due attention to ingredients and supplies. Organically grown vegetables are used as a matter of course; there is also good free-range poultry and game as well as a fine selection of cheeses. The cooking is modern, with exotic overtones and a liking for fish.
Specialities: *smoked goose with winter salad leaves; squat lobster ravioli with basil sauce; chicken breast stuffed with exotic fruit and coconut.*

ULLAPOOL
THE CEILIDH PLACE
14 West Argyle Street, Ullapool, Highland IV26 2TY
Tel: Ullapool (0854) 2103
Open: 12.15 p.m. to 2.15 p.m., 7 p.m. to 9.30 p.m.
Closed: 2 weeks mid-Jan.
This converted boat shed opposite the loch now functions as coffee shop, brasserie, hotel and community entertainment centre, with live music, exhibitions and art courses. The food has strong vegetarian leanings, although the menus are topped up with local fish and venison. Jean Urquhart admits that there's a problem in obtaining regular suppliers of organic vegetables in this remote part of the Highlands, but she does her best and always has free-range eggs, organic flour and a dozen or so organic wines shipped in from Edinburgh.
Specialities: *macro rice with stir-fried vegetables; mixed bean moussaka; strawberry and tofu mousse.*

WALLS
BURRASTOW HOUSE
Walls, Shetland ZE2 9PB

Tel: Walls (059571) 307
Open: 12.30 p.m. to 2.30 p.m., 7.30 p.m. to 9 p.m.
Closed: Tue, all Feb., lunch by arrangement Oct. to Apr.
A remote eighteenth-century mansion three miles west of
Walls facing the island of Vaila. New owners Bo Simmons and
Ann Prior run the place in the same style as their predecessors,
building their menus around local and home-grown produce.
Vegetables and herbs are from the garden, while their ewe
provides milk for the cheese. Their main speciality is Shetland
lamb, naturally reared and grazed on the island heather. The
wine list has some organics.
Specialities: *salmon with nettle purée and sheep's milk cheese;
boned leg of lamb stuffed with apricots; apple and boysenberry
flan.*

WALES

ABERAERON
HIVE ON THE QUAY
Cadwgan Place, Aberaeron, Dyfed SA46 0BT
Tel: Aberaeron (0545) 570445
Open: 10.30 p.m. to 5 p.m. (10 p.m. to 9.30 p.m. July and
Aug.)
Closed: end of 3rd week Sept. to Spring bank hol
Aptly named, because this seasonal eating place between the
two harbours of Aberaeron is owned and run by the Holgate
family who are renowned for their honey. Their loyalty to local
and organic produce shows in the classic ploughman's lunch:
organic wholemeal bread with Tyn Grug Farmhouse Cheddar
from Lampeter, salads with organically grown leaves and three
kinds of home-made pickles. Through the day there are soups,
pies, and home-baked cakes as well as buffet lunches: during
high season they also serve dinners. Herb teas and organic
wines to drink.
Specialities: *spinach and cream cheese parcels with mushrooms à
la grecque; Welsh cawl with bread and cheese; gooseberry and
elderflower pie with Guernsey cream.*

BRECHFA
TY MAWR
Brechfa, Dyfed SA32 7RA

Tel: Brechfa (026789) 332
Open: 7 p.m. to 9.30 p.m.; also noon to 2 p.m. Sun
Closed: lunch Mon to Sat
The Flaherty family's converted farmhouse is on the B4310
some ten miles north-east of Carmarthen. It is all beams and
stone walls, with an informal, cheery atmosphere. The menu
has a bias towards local foods, organic produce and vegetarian
dishes. Bread is baked on the premises, and there are some
organic wines on offer.
Specialities: *piperade basquaise; guinea fowl in wine sauce;
meringues.*

CARDIGAN
GRANARY
Teifi Wharf, Cardigan, Dyfed
Tel: Cardigan (0239) 614932
Open: 10 a.m. to 10 p.m. all week
Closed: Nov. to Feb.
A seasonal cafe/restaurant on the riverside, overlooking
Cardigan Bridge and the castle. Dyfed's well-organized
network of organic producers and small-holders provide most
of the ingredients for the kitchen: fruit and vegetables come
from Mike Ray of Pencrugiau, Crymych, and Clean Greens
(the local market stall); Y-Felin Mill, Llandudoch, provides
stoneground flour; cheeses are from Tresaith and there are
supplies of free-range eggs and wholefoods. The short menu
also features fresh fish and Welsh lamb. Main dishes are served
with steamed vegetables or salad. Ten organic wines come
from Haughton Fine Wines.
Specialities: *savoury stuffed pancakes; nut roast with relish;
peach crumble.*

CARMARTHEN
WAVERLEY VEGETARIAN RESTAURANT
23 Lammas Street, Carmarthen, Dyfed
Tel: Carmarthen (0267) 236521
Open: 9 a.m. to 5 p.m. (to 2 p.m. Thur)
Closed: Sun and bank hols
The restaurant is at the back of a popular Victorian-style health
food shop and the food has a healthy bias. Menus change each
day and organic ingredients appear in many dishes, ranging
from lentil and nut burgers and vegetable curry to cheesecake

and fruit crumble.
Specialities: *bean bake; vegetable burger; chocolate and date fudge flan.*

LLANDUDNO
ST TUDNO HOTEL
The Promenade, Llandudno, Gwynedd LL30 2LP
Tel: Llandudno (0492) 74411
Open: 12.30 p.m. to 1.45 p.m., 6.45 p.m. to 9.30 p.m. (to 8.30 p.m. Sun)
Closed: Christmas and New Year
The Garden Room restaurant feels up-market, with an elaborate modern menu to match. Dishes ranging from chicken and crab feuilletés to breast of duck with fig coulis are typical of the style. Some organic herbs, vegetables and free-range poultry boost the supplies of local game and fish, but the big scoring point is the cheese. At least half a dozen Welsh varieties appear, including Pencarreg, and cheese is used as an ingredient of starters and main courses.
Specialities: *deep-fried cubes of Pencarreg cheese on blackberry coulis; Welsh rarebit; warm goat's cheese with mixed salad leaves and walnut dressing.*

MACHYNLLETH
QUARRY SHOP
13 Maengwyn Street, Machynlleth, Powys
Tel: Machynlleth (0654) 2624
Open: 9 a.m. to 5 p.m. Mon to Sat (also 7 p.m. to 9 p.m. Wed to Sat and 10 a.m. to 4 p.m. Sun during July and Aug.)
Closed: Sun
The shop and cafe are linked to the Centre for Alternative Technology, and the philosophy extends to the food. Fresh, local ingredients – especially organic vegetables – are used for soups, pizzas, stuffed jacket potatoes and excellent salads. Unlicensed, but there is barley cup or hibiscus tea to drink.

NEWPORT
CNAPAN
East Street, Newport, Gwent SA42 0WF
Tel: Newport (0239) 820575
Open: 12.30 p.m. to 2.30 p.m., 7.30 p.m. to 9 p.m.
Closed: Tue and all Feb.

This pale pink Georgian house feels like home, with a welcoming, free and easy atmosphere. Eluned Lloyd and her daughter produce wholefood lunches and teas with a Welsh flavour, plus more elaborate evening meals. Fish and local produce feature prominently and salads include organic ingredients; cheeses are from the farmhouse dairies of Dyfed and the wine list features some organics.

Specialities: trout stuffed with apple and fennel; spinach and cottage cheese flan; apricot and ginger cream.

PONTFAEN
TREGYNON COUNTRY FARM HOTEL
Pontfaen, nr. Fishguard, Dyfed SA65 9TU
Tel: Newport (0239) 820531
Open: 7.30 p.m. to 8.45 p.m. all week
Closed: lunch all week
Peter and Sheila Heard's isolated farmhouse is in remote country (from the junction of the B4313 and B4329 take the B4313 towards Fishguard; take the first right, then right again for half a mile). Many ingredients are organically grown on the farm, special diets are catered for, and the concern for health extends to advice about the pollution risks and toxicity of cigarettes. The simple menu has good soups, fresh vegetables and choices for vegetarians.

SWANSEA
ROOTS
2 Woodville Road, Mumbles, Swansea, West Glamorgan SA3 4AD
Tel: Swansea (0792) 366006
Open: 11 a.m. to 9 p.m. (to 5 p.m. Mon and Tue)
Closed: Sun, Christmas Day and New Year's Day
The entrance to this unlicensed vegetarian restaurant is actually on Queens Road. The menu is enterprising and all dishes feature organic ingredients, including fruit, vegetables, herbs, flour and dairy produce.

Specialities: carrot and parsnip timbales with sorrel sauce; garlic, mushroom and broccoli crêpes with Pencarreg cheese; mango cheesecake.

APPENDIX

COURSES AND TRAINING IN ORGANIC AGRICULTURE, HORTICULTURE AND GARDENING

If you want to learn more about the theory and practice of organic growing, the following courses, evening classes, lectures and so on should be helpful. It is worthwhile making enquiries to other colleges, as an increasing number are now thinking about setting up organic courses, or organic options within existing courses. Also, check your local education authority to see if there are any evening classes in organic growing in your area. If you are unemployed you may be able to get funding to go on a course under the Employment Training Scheme that replaced the MSC Community Programme.

The Soil Association has recently introduced a system for approving courses, and this has been noted where relevant. Contact the Association for up-to-date information.

COURSES
Agricultural Training Board (ATB)
National Agricultural Centre, Kenilworth, Warwickshire CV8 2LG
Tel: (0203) 696511
In collaboration with Organic Growers Association/British Organic Farmers, the ATB offers a series of one-day training courses for organic producers held in different parts of the country. Courses approved by The Soil Association. Contact: Richard Collyer.

Cambridgeshire College of Agriculture & Horticulture
Newcommon Bridge, Wisbech, Cambridgeshire PE13 2SJ
Tel: (0945) 581024

Basic introduction to organic gardening run as a short evening class Sept./Oct. May also run summer courses. Contact: Richard Walpole.

Cannington College of Agriculture & Horticulture
Cannington, Bridgwater, Somerset TA5 2LS
Tel: (0278) 652226
Offers occasional evening classes in organic gardening. Also planning a conference on organic growing. Contact: Nick Rigden.

Carmarthen College of Technology & Art
Organic Farming Development Project, CCTA Pibwrlwyd Campus, Carmarthen, Dyfed SA31 2NH
Tel: (0267) 234151
Offers series of one-day courses each covering a specific aspect of organic growing, also week-long 'block courses' on organic growing. Courses approved by The Soil Association. Contact: Roger Hitchings.

Centre for Alternative Technology
The Quarry, Machynlleth, Powys SY20 9AZ
Tel: (0654) 2400
Runs short residential courses (3-4 days). These include: organic gardening, ecological landscaping, holistic gardening. Contact: Lesley Bradnam.

Clashganna Mills Trust
Ballykeelan, Borrin, Co.Carlow, Eire
Offers a non-residential course on organic horticulture aimed at young people/long-term unemployed (who continue to receive FAS allowance while on course). Applicants should have access to one acre of land to develop as part of the course.

Country College
Ashcroft, Rectory Lane, Scrivelsby, Horncastle, Lincolnshire LN9 6JB
Tel: (06582) 4483
Correspondence course on the theory and principles of organic crop production for gardeners, horticulturists and farmers. Provides option to take Royal Horticultural Society's general horticulture examination.

Derbyshire College of Agriculture & Horticulture
Broomfield, Morley, Derbyshire DE7 6DN
Tel: (0332) 831845
Organic farming option as part of the BTEC National Diploma in Agriculture. Also a series of one-day courses in organic farming, run jointly with ATB; short courses on organic growing (City & Guilds

amateur modules) and evening and day courses in organic farming and gardening. Major new organic course being planned for autumn 1990 includes a market gardening option.

Dorset College of Agriculture and Horticulture
Kingston Maurward, Dorchester DT2 8PY
Tel: (0305) 64738
Ten-day introductory course in organic gardening starting March 1990, one day per week (Thur), centred on an organic allotment. Can lead to part of Royal Horticultural Society general horticulture examination.

Dundee College of Further Education
Horticultural Section, Old Glamis Road, Dundee DD3 9LE
Tel: (0382) 819021
Two-part evening class on organic growing starting Spring 1990, for growers and gardeners. Contact: Mr G C Carr.

Dyfed Open Tech Unit
Pibwrlwyd, Carmarthen, Dyfed SA31 2NH
Tel: (0267) 233333
Offers two open learning courses: organic farming and organic gardening. Contact: Max Faulkner.

Eastleigh College of Adult Education
Desborough Centre, Eastleigh, Hampshire SO5 5HT
Tel: (0703) 641251
Six-week organic gardening course starting April 1990.

Elm Farm Research Centre
Hamstead Marshall, nr. Newbury, Berkshire RG15 0HR
Tel: (0488) 58298
Runs courses on organic husbandry for teachers/lecturers considering introducing an organic perspective into their teaching programmes.

Elmwood Agricultural and Technical College
Carslogie Road, Cupar, Fife KY15 4JB
Tel: (0334) 52781
Short course 'Introduction to Organic Farming'. Contact: Mr Alcock.

Emerson College, School of Biodynamic Farming & Gardening
Pixton, Forest Row, Sussex RH18 5JX
Tel: (034282) 2238
International College offering a training course and a one-year

apprenticeship scheme in biodynamic growing (based on the work of Rudolf Steiner). Course approved by The Soil Association.

Knuston Hall
Residential College for Adult Education
Irchester, Wellingborough, Northamptonshire NN9 7EU
Tel: (0933) 312104
Weekend course 'Going Organic' in Sept. 1990.

Lackham College of Agriculture
Lacock, Chippenham, Wiltshire SN15 2NY
Tel: (0249) 443111
Runs short courses on organic gardening (one week). Also a College Certificate in Organic Horticulture by day-release for 30 weeks starting in September each year. Contact: Chris Hall.

Losehill Hall
Peak National Park Study Centre, Castleton, Derbyshire S30 2WB
Tel: (0433) 20373
Short residential courses on wildlife gardening and woodland management/conservation.
Middle Wood Green College
Middle Wood Trust, Roeburndale West, Lancaster, Lancashire LA2 8QX
Runs various short courses, including a practical introduction to organic gardening in 1990.

National Federation of City Farms
The Old Vicarage, 66 Fraser Street, Windmill Hill, Bristol BS3 4LY
Tel: (0272) 660663
Offers organic training in the context of community farms all over Britain on a regular basis. Send sae for latest information in your area. From spring 1990 there will be courses on Basic Animal Husbandry, Economic Organic Production from Polytunnels, and others. Contact: John Bond.

Newton Training
The Old Estate Yard, Loe, Bath BA2 9BR
Tel: (0225) 873805
Offers six-day foundation course on organic horticulture (awaiting approval for City & Guilds, Phase II): one day per week with practical tuition on a working farm. Also planning one-day courses on organic fruit and vegetable production.

Nutshell Training
The Birmingham Settlement, 318 Summer Lane, Birmingham B19 3RL
Tel: (021) 359 3562

A community group running courses for local people; includes 'Grow Your Own' course with a focus on the organic approach.

OATS (Organic Agriculture Training Scheme)
12 Mason Close, Malvern, Hereford & Worcester WR14 2NF
Offers courses/training sessions to groups across the country, particularly community groups, schools and government training schemes. Courses cover the organic approach to community growing and gardening. Contact: Brian Elliott.

Otley College of Agriculture & Horticulture
Otley, Ipswich, Suffolk
Tel: (047385) 350
Runs evening classes on organic gardening and other topics. Also developing an organic advisory centre.

Permaculture Association
8 Hunters Moon, Dartington, Totnes, Devon TQ9 6JT
Tel: (0803) 867546
Runs occasional training courses in permaculture around the country.

Princes Risborough Adult Education Centre
Clifford Road, Princes Risborough, Buckinghamshire
Tel: (024027) 583
Runs daytime and evening classes on Cottage Gardening with an organic emphasis. Contact: Sue Goss.

Pershore College of Horticulture
Pershore, Hereford & Worcester WR10 3JP
Tel: (0386) 552443
Courses on Organic Horticulture run in conjunction with Worcestershire College of Agriculture and their Organic Agriculture course described below. Also holding a series of evening lectures/practical sessions on organic vegetable production during April/May 1990; and several one-day workshops on specific topics (eg. pests and diseases, composting, etc.) in early summer 1990. Contact: Dick Heath.

Plumpton Agricultural College
Plumpton, Lewes, East Sussex BN7 3AE
Tel: (0273) 890454
Series of half-day courses on organic gardening, one per month Sept. – June. Includes talks, discussion and practical work.

Shuttleworth Agricultural College
Old Warden Park, Biggleswade, Bedfordshire SG18 9DX

Tel: (076727) 441
Runs day conferences on organic farming and has organic component in current syllabus of full-time courses.

Sparsholt College of Agriculture
Sparsholt, Winchester, Hampshire SO21 2NF
Tel: (0962) 72441
Runs weekend courses for small-holders and farmers. Also provides specialist evening talks on organic farming.

Welsh Agricultural College
Llanbadarn Fawr, Aberystwyth, Dyfed SY23 3AL
Tel: (0970) 624471
A two-year part-time course in organic farming consisting of 14 one-week blocks, beginning Sept. 1990. Contact: John Bennett.

West Scotland College of Agriculture
Auchincruive, Ayr KA6 5HW
Tel: (0292) 520331
Introductory 20-hour course, 'The Principles of Organic Production' will run over a ten-week period during spring/summer 1990. Also planning specialist courses on particular aspects of organic production to start autumn 1990.

Worcestershire College of Agriculture
Hindlip, Hereford & Worcester WR3 8SS
Tel: (0905) 51310
Runs a five-week block course 'The Principles and Practice of Organic Agriculture'. Has links with Pershore College's courses in organic horticulture (see above). Course approved by The Soil Association.

Yarner Trust
Welcombe Barton Farm, Welcombe, Bideford, Devon
Runs a range of short courses in small-holding skills, including organic growing.

PRACTICAL TRAINING
Ashram Community Service Project
23-25 Grantham Road, Sparkbrook, Birmingham B11 1LU
Tel: (021) 773 7061
Ashram Asian Vegetables Organic Training Project established as an Employment Training Scheme.

National Federation of City Farms
The Old Vicarage, 66 Fraser Street, Windmill Hill, Bristol BS3 4LY
Tel: (0272) 660663

Offers practical organic training in the context of organic farms around Britain.

WWOOF – Working Weekends on Organic Farms
19 Bradford Road, Lewes, East Sussex BN7 1RB
Countrywide exchange scheme whereby bed and board and practical experience are given in return for work on a wide variety of farms, small-holdings and gardens throughout the UK. Weekend, midweek, long-term and overseas stays are available.

Ridgeway Organic Farm Co-op
Kent House Farm, Main Road, Ridgeway, Sheffield S12 3XR
Tel: (0742) 474258
Enquiries welcome from those wishing to learn about organic growing and working co-operatively.

USEFUL ORGANIZATIONS

Many groups and organizations – large and small – are now active within the organic movement. The following (listed in alphabetical order) is a representative selection of the most important. Some are registered charities, others are membership organizations, but all would welcome support, either financial or otherwise. Contact them if you want to find out more about organic food and farming.

Biodynamic Agricultural Association (BDAA)
Woodman Lane, Clent, Stourbridge, West Midlands DY9 9PX
Tel: (05628) 84933
Biodynamic agriculture is based on the teachings of the Austrian philosopher, Rudolf Steiner. Biodynamics aims to work with the formative forces behind nature, both earthly and cosmic. This includes the influence of the sun, planets and stars. Practitioners sow and plant crops according to constellation tables and use special preparations made from natural products applied in homoeopathic proportions. The BDAA has over 600 members and publishes a twice-yearly magazine *Star & Furrow*. Other membership services include books and products, conferences and workshops. The Association also administers the Demeter quality symbol.

British Organic Farmers and The Organic Growers Association (BOF/OGA)
86 Colston Street, Bristol, Avon BS1 5BB
Tel: (0272) 299666/299600
Britain's producer association representing over 1,000 organic producers throughout the British Isles. Membership services include a quarterly journal, *The New Farmer & Grower*, a national

programme of farm walks, an information service, conferences and seminars. It also runs courses in association with the Agricultural Training Board. A regional group network covers most of the UK. An associated company supplies printed bags, boxes and other packaging materials to organic producers.

British Organic Standards Committee (BOSC)
(for contact address see Elm Farm Research Centre below). Chairman: Lawrence Woodward. The co-ordinating body formed in the early 1980s to draw up the standards for organic food production that would act as the basis for all symbol schemes operating in Britain. Representation was drawn from the major organic bodies and other groups with an interest in organic food production. The work of BOSC was largely superseded when the Government set up the UKROFS Committee.

Elm Farm Research Centre (EFRC)
Hamstead Marshall, nr. Newbury, Berkshire RG15 0HR
Tel: (0488) 58298
A charitable organization carrying out independent research into organic agriculture at its 232-acre farm and at other sites around the country. Runs the Organic Advisory Service – a consultancy covering conversion planning, telephone enquiries, visits to established organic farms and soil analysis. Publishes a range of technical books and booklets.

The Farm & Food Society (FAFS)
4 Willifield Way, London NW11 7XT
Tel: (081) 455 0634
Aims to create a social climate which will enable farming to combine the best traditional organic methods with wise use of technology. It promotes the notion of a non-violent system which is in harmony with the environment. FAFS is also an indefatigable campaigner on the issue of more humane treatment of farm livestock. Members of the Society receive a lively quarterly newsletter.

Friends of the Earth (FOE)
26-28 Underwood Street, London N1 7JU
Tel: (071) 490 1555
Not an organic organization as such, but campaigns and provides information on related subjects, such as pesticide and nitrate contamination of food and water, destruction of the countryside etc. A membership organization with around 150,000 supporters.

The Henry Doubleday Research Association (HDRA)
Ryton Gardens, Ryton-on-Dunsmore, Coventry CV8 3LG
Tel: (0203) 303517

Britain's largest organization concerned with organic gardening. As a registered charity its main purpose is to research, demonstrate and promote environmentally safe growing techniques. HDRA now has around 16,000 members who receive a quarterly newsletter and have free access to the 22-acre National Centre for Organic Gardening at Ryton. The Association is involved in many projects, ranging from the conservation of old seed varieties to tree-planting schemes in the Third World. It publishes numerous leaflets and books, provides an advisory service and guided tours, as well as stocking a wide range of tools and equipment for the organic gardener, books, organic foods and wines.

International Federation of Organic Agriculture Movements (IFOAM)
c/o Oekozentrum Imsbach, D6695 Tholey-Theley, West Germany
Tel: (068) 535190 (From the UK, dial 010 49 then omit initial 0)
The global forum for organic organizations with 230 members worldwide. Organizes scientific and other international conferences. Responsible for producing standards for organic agriculture that are the basis for national standards.

The Irish Organic Farmers & Growers Association (IOFGA)
Springmount, Ballyboughal, Co. Dublin
Responsible for admininstering organic standards in the Republic of Ireland. IOFGA has close links with The Soil Association, it administers the independent Irish symbol scheme and has its own logo. Contact: Nicky Kyle

London Food Commission
88 Old Street, London EC1V 9AR
An independent resource for information, research, advice and education on food and public health. Publishes a range of reports, leaflets, books and posters as well as the excellent quarterly, *Food Magazine*.

The McCarrison Society
24 Paddington Street, London W1M 4DR
Tel: (071) 935 3924
Named after the great nutritionist, Sir Robert McCarrison, the Society promotes good health by means of good, whole fresh food. Membership was originally confined to doctors, but is now open to all. Membership services include a quarterly newsletter and conferences. The Society is responsible for the scientific journal *Nutrition & Health*.

National Federation of City Farms (NFCF)
The Old Vicarage, 66 Fraser Street, Windmill Hill, Bedminster, Bristol, Avon BS3 4LY

Tel: (0272) 660663
Co-ordinates the network of over 100 urban farms and community gardens now established in most British cities. Livestock are raised and crops are grown organically. Organic gardeners should note that some will have surplus manure for disposal. Specialist information for the city gardener and small scale livestock producer is available, together with periodicals including the quarterly *City Farmer*.

Organic Food Manufacturers Federation (OFMF)
The Tithe House, Peaseland Green, Elsing, East Dereham, Norfolk NR20 3DY
Tel: (0362) 83314
OFMF is a trade federation acting on behalf of manufacturers, distributors and importers of organic food. Its primary purpose is as a lobbying group representing the organic food industry in negotiations with the British Government and the EC.

Parents for Safe Food
Britannia House, 1–11 Glenthorne Road, London W6 0LF
Formed in 1989 by actress Pamela Stephenson and other celebrities to campaign against the use of Alar in apples. In 1990 plans to widen the debate by looking at other food contaminants.

The Pesticide Trust
20 Compton Terrace, London N1 2UN
Tel: (071) 354 3860
Formed in 1988 to create awareness among decision-makers over the use and regulation of pesticides; to alert workers and consumers to the problems associated with pesticides, and to promote alternatives to present pesticide policies in developed and developing countries. Publishes *Pesticide News* quarterly, and plans to publish other handbooks and newsletters in the future.

The Soil Association (SA)
86 Colston Street, Bristol, Avon BS1 5BB
Tel: (0272) 290661
Our health depends on the quality of our food; the quality of our food depends on the health of the soil. This relationship is vital to the future of life on Earth. The Soil Association is a registered charity, founded in 1946 to further this holistic philosophy. Its symbol scheme licenses commercial food production to the highest organic standards. It conducts campaigns on aspects of agricultural policy and regularly makes representations to the Government. The Soil Association has around 5,000 members, and membership services include a quarterly journal, *The Living Earth*, a network of local groups and an information service.

UK Register of Organic Food Standards (UKROFS)
Food from Britain, 301-304 Market Towers, New Covent Garden Market, London SW8 5NQ
Tel: (071) 720 2144
Set up by Food from Britain at the request of the Government to set production standards for, and establish an approved register of, organic producers and products. The intention is that all producers of organic food should belong to a symbol scheme approved by UKROFS (e.g. the Soil Association scheme) or else register direct with UKROFS.

FURTHER READING

This is a short selection of books covering a range of organic topics and issues, from nitrate pollution to gardening. Many specialist books and leaflets are issued by bodies such as The Henry Doubleday Research Association, The Soil Association and Elm Farm Research Centre.

In addition there are organic journals such as *Living Earth* (from The Soil Association) and *New Farmer & Grower* (published by BOF/OGA) are available to their members. You will also find coverage of organic topics in *Earth Matters* (from The Friends of the Earth) and The London Food Commission's *Food News*. There is also a generally available magazine called *Organic Gardening*, which is sold by most good newsagents or can be ordered direct from PO Box 4, Wiveliscombe, Somerset TA4 2QY

Balfour, Lady Eve, *The Living Soil and the Haughley Experiment* (Faber)
Blake, Francis, *The Handbook of Organic Husbandry* (Crowood Press 1987)
Body, Sir Richard, *Red or Green for Farmers* (Broad Leys Publishing 1987)
Bull, David, *A Growing Problem – Pesticides and the Third World Poor* (Oxfam 1982)
Carson, Rachel, *Silent Spring* (Penguin 1965)
Craig, Frances and Phil, *Britain's Poisoned Water* (Penguin 1989)
Dudley, Nigel, *Nitrates, the Threat to Food and Water* (Green Print 1990)
Erlichman, James, *Gluttons for Punishment* (Penguin 1986)
Gear, Jackie and Mabey, David, *Ryton Recipes* (HDRA 1989)
Hamilton, Geoff, *Successful Organic Gardening* (Dorling Kindersley 1987)
HDRA, *Growing Organically: the work of the Henry Doubleday Research Association* (HDRA 1989)
Hegarty, Patricia, *An English Flavour* (Equation 1988)
Hills, Lawrence D., *Month by Month Organic Gardening* (Thorsons 1988)

Lampkin, Nic, *Organic Farming* (Farming Press 1990)

Lashford, Stephanie, *The Residue Report* (Thorsons 1988)

Lees, Andrew and McVeigh, Karen, *An Investigation of Pesticide Pollution in Drinking Water in England and Wales* (Friends of the Earth 1988)

London Food Commission, *Food Adulteration and How to Beat it* (Unwin 1988)

Mabey, Richard, *The Common Ground* (Hutchinson 1983)

Mansfield, Dr Peter and Monro, Dr Jean, *Chemical Children* (Century 1987)

Mitchell, Charlotte and Wright, Iain, *The Organic Wine Guide* (Mainsteam 1987)

Pye-Smith, Charlie and Hall, C. (eds), *The Countryside We Want: A Manifesto for the year 2000* (Green Books 1987)

Stickland, Sue, *The Organic Garden* (Hamlyn 1987)

——*Planning the Organic Flower Garden* (Thorsons 1986)

Wookey, Barry, *Rushall: the Story of an Organic Farm* (Blackwell 1987)

INDEX

READERS' COMMENTS

To: Thorsons Organic Consumer Guide
    Thorsons Publishing Group
    Denington Estate, Wellingborough, Northamptonshire
    NN8 2RQ

Use this form to comment on any establishment that produces or sells organic food/drink.

Name of establishment _____
_____

Address _____
_____
_____
_____
_____ Postcode _____

Telephone No: (if known) _____

Type of business (e.g. wholefood shop, farm, restaurant)
_____
_____

This establishment **should/should not** be considered for inclusion in the Guide (please delete as appropriate)

Please give a brief description about the business and what it produces or sells.
_____
_____
_____

Name and address of sender (capitals please)
_____
_____
_____
_____